The Best American
Travel Writing 2021

The Best American Travel Writing™ 2021

Edited with an Introduction
by **Padma Lakshmi**

Jason Wilson, Series Editor

MARINER BOOKS
An Imprint of HarperCollins*Publishers*
Boston   New York

marinerbooks.com

ISSN 1530-1516 (print)   ISSN 2537-4830 (e-book)
ISBN 978-0-358-36131-2 (print)   ISBN 978-0-358-36184-8 (e-book)

Printed in the United States of America
1 2021
4500834596

Contents

Contents

Foreword

IN THE BEFORE TIMES, I often composed my travel writing in the present tense. You know how the trick goes, the way the travel writer strains to swiftly bring the reader into a scene: *It's a balmy night in Panama City, and I'm sipping a rum at the bar of the largely empty Ocean Sun Casino . . . I'm lounging on the sunny bow of the expatriate's boat as we shove off from the historic city of Granada, Nicaragua, and into one of the world's largest freshwater lakes . . .* The sleight of hand is to make it seem as though we're jotting off these dispatches on hotel room stationery or poolside or from a tray table in business class. As the days of shutdown dragged on—as we Americans were forbidden to travel to most nations in the world—this approach began to feel as old-fashioned as an epistolary Victorian novel.

What, exactly, is a travel writer who cannot travel? I've thought a lot about this over the past few months. Throughout 2020 I was supposed to have been traveling to Italy, Spain, Austria, and Argentina, among others. That all was canceled when the European Union announced its travel ban, and I've now been grounded at home for more than half a year—the longest I have gone without getting on a plane in at least three decades. Of course, just stating this exposes the travel writer's existential dilemma as one of immense, laughable privilege. Yet here we are. Do not cry for me.

Most days now, I write about travel in the past tense, generally in my old bathrobe at the kitchen table. For instance, I've recently been sifting through notes and snapshots of my last trip, to France in the winter of 2020, only a few weeks before the pandemic hit home. On the evening that Chinese authorities closed down Wuhan, I wandered the ancient streets of Chinon, in the Loire Valley. I'd spent all day with winemakers touring their fifteenth-century limestone caves, then tasting dozens of wines I was supposed to review on assignment for a wine magazine. I had to get up early and do it all over again in the morning, but I was restless.

Even though that was hardly the first winter I'd spent in some European wine region, sipping and spitting and scribbling, I'd begun to question what the point of all this travel had been. My Airbnb rental stood just down the winding cobblestone path to Chinon's eleventh-century castle, about a hundred meters from where a 17-year-old Joan of Arc arrived in 1429, after hearing heavenly voices. She'd traveled there to meet future king Charles VII, who would give her an army to fight the English in the Hundred Years' War; two years later, she'd be captured and burned at the stake in Rouen, then declared a martyr, then canonized. My own visit to Chinon wasn't as noble or epic as Joan's. That night, I ended up at a bar in the town square, where a local guy bet me that I couldn't identify, blind, the very bitter herbal spirit he set before me. He lost that bet, but it was still more like the rake's progress than the hero's journey.

If there are certain moments when I question the value of travel writing, I also know that it's important for the traveler to eventually return to where he or she came from, to write and try to capture the experience of being an outsider in an unfamiliar place. Yes, much of travel writing is soulless and transactional, listicles and charticles and "if you go" tips. Yet at its most ideal, the worth of the genre lies in exploring the tensions of our interior journey vs. our exterior itinerary, in examining our expectations (and hopes and biases) of a destination vs. the reality of what we found, and in measuring the person we are at home vs. the person we become abroad. As I sit working at my kitchen table, I realize I've come a long way from the young man who, 30 years ago, was given the shaggy old bathrobe that I now have cinched around my middle-aged waist. That person could scarcely have dreamed a future of almost ceaseless travel.

That 19-year-old arrived in the northern Italian village of Pieve San Giacomo, at the home of his summer program hosts, wearing Birkenstocks and a UNIVERSITY OF VERMONT BONG TEAM T-shirt. That summer I lived with a family—Anna and Paolo, and their daughter, Daniela—in an aging, rustic, but warm and tidy farmhouse with a stone fountain in the garden, and with dark antique furniture and yapping dogs inside. The chickens in the coop outside my window woke me early in the morning, and I took the train to school in nearby Cremona. In the afternoons, I played soccer with the local boys or rode my bike through the village, and every night I ate homemade salami, hand-stuffed pastas, meat from their animals, and vegetables from the garden, and drank funky, unlabeled wine. I learned some of the local dialect. By summer's end, I had become an adopted part of *la famiglia*.

A vivid meal took place on the Saturday afternoon before I left Pieve San Giacomo. Paolo was working in his fields, and Daniela was in Milan, so Anna and I rode bikes to visit the family's recently widowed aunt Gina, who, as a surprise, had prepared a tremendous feast in my honor, with tables teeming with food in the sunny courtyard. At the end of the hours-long meal, when I could eat no more, Aunt Gina insisted that we tour her house. The three of us entered the cool, dark living room. Aunt Gina fidgeted with a yellowed photograph of a young man in a soldier's uniform and told me it was her husband. There were no other photos of sons or daughters, only a crucifix and an image of Jesus Christ hanging over the sofa.

Aunt Gina motioned for me to stay where I was and shuffled down a long hallway. Anna whispered and crossed herself. We waited for what seemed like 20 minutes and could hear the older woman rummaging through the bedroom, calling *"Un momento, un momento!"* Finally, she emerged from the hallway cradling her dead husband's bathrobe. She thrust it into my hands and urged me to slide it on over my clothes. I hesitated and looked wide-eyed at Anna, who also urged me to try it on, so I wrapped it around my Grateful Dead T-shirt. Silence enveloped the room. I stood with my arms wide, modeling the robe that presumably her husband had worn most mornings while he sipped his caffè corretto. I stood dumbfounded, staring at the sleeves of the heavy, floral-patterned robe—cut too big, less than absorbent, pocket sitting too high for a hand to rest in.

"Molto bello! Elegante!" Aunt Gina exclaimed. She then burst into tears and hugged Anna, whose eyes also welled up. What the heck was I going to do with this? Could this whole presentation possibly

have been all just for me? The one preparing to shove off in a few days with a rail pass and a hostel itinerary? "You'll promise to wear it?" asked Aunt Gina. I knew I had no choice but to smash down what I could in my already stuffed backpack and leave some of my belongings behind. Even as a stupid young American, I knew you didn't refuse gifts from Italian widows who'd just prepared you an afternoon banquet.

That robe was the first of many articles of clothing I've acquired in my travels and carried with me all these years. There are, of course, plenty of souvenir items that I rarely wear. I never find quite the right occasion to show off the brightly colored poncho I found in Peru or the high-collared Sami jacket I got near the Arctic Circle in Finland. The expensive red pants I bought at a boutique in Milan and the Alpine trachten vest I got in Vienna seemed like good ideas at the time. The handmade Majorcan shoes sadly don't fit very well. While I still appreciate the idealism of it, I rarely wear the Portuguese anti-bullfighting T-shirt I received from the two young activists whom I met at a vegetarian restaurant in Lisbon a decade ago. But there are a few cherished items that convey some larger, more essential part of my life as a traveler.

For instance, I own a hand-sewn guayabera, gray with four pockets and two ribbons of intricately stitched designs, that I bought for a few dollars from a woman named Mirna at a craft market in Masaya, Nicaragua, only a few years after my summer abroad in Italy. During my 20s, I spent a lot of time in Nicaragua, which was emerging from more than a decade of civil war, natural disasters, and our own government's attempt to oust the Sandinistas from power. I haven't returned for a dozen years, but every summer when I bring that guayabera out of the closet, the lessons of those journeys come back to me.

On my way from Managua, the capital, to Masaya, to visit the craft market as well as to hike the nearby volcano, I was suddenly stopped and waved over by two police officers standing on the side of the road with automatic rifles. The officers wore buttons with Nicaragua's then official slogan "Brazos Abiertos" (Open Arms) and were smiling but still demanded to see my passport. I handed it over, and they studied it silently. They said they'd have to keep it. I would have to go to the police station the next day and pay a fine to get my passport back. "What can we do here and now?" I said, flashing my wallet. "Can I pay the ticket in cash right now?" They asked for 60 American dollars, which I handed to them, and then I drove on to Masaya.

I spent a couple of hours at the volcano and the market—I was so happy with my new guayabera that I took off my T-shirt and put it on right in the market. Then I drove back to Managua, the capital, the same way I had come. Near where I'd been pulled over, there was an open-air bar with a thatched roof. In the shade, I could see both of the policemen I'd paid, hats off and guns leaning against the bar, lounging and drinking beer. I couldn't help but laugh out loud. I honked my horn and they waved, raising their beer in a toast, still smiling.

Back then I was like many travelers of my post–Cold War generation who lit out for Eastern Europe, Southeast Asia, and Central America, enthralled by destinations that had been off-limits to most Americans for a long time. I had never been anywhere like Nicaragua, and in my sheltered suburban naïveté I marveled at how chaotic and alive it was: how in Managua I could exchange my dollars for córdobas on the side of the road from random men waving money, while hawkers tried to sell me live parrots, monkeys, and armadillos through the car window, and people gave directions such as "turn left at the big statue of the man holding the machine gun and sickle." The reminders of the Sandinista regime were everywhere: Lada taxis, Aeroflot billboards, giant murals, the former soldier camped out in the Plaza de la Revolución guarding the "eternal flame" (which by then was a plastic light) across the square from a cathedral that had been destroyed in the 1972 earthquake. I once stood there with a crowd of 20,000 to watch a huge twilight outdoor Mass that had been called in the name of solidarity, holding a candle and a tiny flag I'd been given by a group of schoolchildren.

Everything in Nicaragua felt so dynamic and immediate, and completely the opposite of the life I lived at home. I would return from my trips with hundreds of pages of callow journal entries in Moleskine notebooks. Soon enough I began to persuade magazines to send me back on assignment. Since travel editors can never resist the allure of The Next Hot Place, pitching always felt ridiculously simple. In those days, the notion that Nicaragua was opening up to vacationing tourists after two decades of strife was irresistible. In buzzy travel-publishing shorthand, Nicaragua was "The New Costa Rica."

In 1996, I was assigned a number of sunny features on the country for mainstream magazines—the kind of articles that would appear between ads for luxury hotels, cruises, and expensive watches. On one occasion I arrived for a breezy assignment with a friend on the day before a heated presidential election, which would result in only the second peaceful transition of power in the country's modern history. All bars and restaurants were closed for three days, as votes for former Sandinista leader Daniel Ortega and right-wing candidate Arnoldo Alemán were counted. One night, when we returned late to our hotel, everything was dark and locked. We banged on the window and were let inside by a shirtless man holding a machete who claimed to be the night manager. It was not exactly the type of vacation the gentle readers of this travel magazine were likely imagining.

On another evening, while staying at a rustic resort at a mountain coffee plantation in a cloud forest full of howler monkeys, my travel companion and I decided to drive down into the city of Matagalpa to find a restaurant we'd seen in our guidebook. When we arrived in Matagalpa, that restaurant was shuttered, along with three others we tried. Meanwhile, hundreds of people were streaming into the streets. Some were shouting and carrying signs. Teens spray-painted storefronts. Pickup trucks crowded with angry-looking men, some carrying baseball bats, circled the center of town. We drove the wrong way down a one-way street, causing the crowd to shout at us. We stopped and tried to read our guidebook by the dashboard light just as a police truck made a sweep of the central square. With guns drawn, they asked us to roll down the window and were flabbergasted to see two gringo tourists looking for a restaurant. "Matagalpa is closed, jefe," they said. The police truck escorted us directly back to the mountain road. I cringe now at how clueless I was to the larger, complex implications of my own cultural voyeurism.

When I returned home to write my assigned pieces, it was nearly impossible to convey the truth of my experience. A consumer travel magazine had to run a long sidebar titled "On Caution's Side" advising readers: "Walking around Managua at night is a bad idea . . . During the day Nicaragua's roads are terrible; at dusk and at night, they're treacherous." A men's magazine insensitively teased my article on its cover as "Guerrilla Vacation in Nicaragua."

I would return to Nicaragua for more assignments, including one about Americans buying up cheap properties for vacation and retirement homes. An American real estate agent took me by boat through an archipelago in Lake Nicaragua called Las Isletas, a collection of more than 350 islets formed from eruptions of the purple-coned volcano Mombacho. The water was placid, and gorgeous palms, mango trees, and giant water lilies surrounded us. A whole indigenous community lived in the tiny coves and channels of Las Isletas: men throwing fishing nets off rocks, women doing laundry, children paddling to school in their canoes. But brand-new homes had sprung up on a number of the islets, as well as huge FOR SALE signs posted next to the indigenous families' shacks on others. A growing number of wealthy North Americans were snatching up Las Isletas. The real estate agent told me he'd sold a half dozen, and there were four islands available to buy that afternoon.

"We're running out of places to go," he told me. "There are very few undiscovered places left in the world." To the younger me, this statement felt like a moment of deep truth, and I included the real estate agent's quote in the article that I eventually wrote, which the magazine teased as "Nicaragua's New Wave," touting the country as "the next new thing under the sun" and explaining, "Americans, it seems, are buying up the place."

When I wear that guayabera now, I can barely recognize the fearless, insufferable thrill seeker I was. But part of the education of travel lies in seeing things with fresh and ignorant eyes—and in being wrong. Which is why it's important to check in with that younger traveler from time to time, to retrace the journeys that remain vivid in my mind, to ask new questions of where I've gone before.

Perhaps no other piece of clothing encapsulates my youthful travel more than a well-worn red hoodie, bearing three yellow dots and the words BEVAR CHRISTIANIA—"Save Christiania." Christiania is the hippie-tastic 80-acre section of downtown Copenhagen that once was an abandoned military fortress and now is home to free-loving squatters who started their own community in 1971 —houses, schools, businesses, sanitation and postal services, newspaper and radio—opposed to the whole idea of government and police. By the late 1980s, the Danish government recognized Christiania as a "social experiment," and it now has several hundred residents. As you leave the area, a sign reads YOU ARE NOW ENTERING THE EU. But what Christiania is most famous for is Pusher Street—one of the city's biggest tourist attractions—where market stalls openly sell cannabis. Fat pre-rolled joints are for sale next to big blocks of hash displayed like baked goods.

Occasionally a right-leaning government threatens to shut down the area, but the citizens of Copenhagen always rally to keep Christiania alive. It was during one of these periods of Pusher Street crackdowns, on a cool summer night about 20 years ago, that I first visited, attending a music festival/political demonstration with hundreds of others, waving Christiania's flag (three yellow dots on a red background) and dancing to electronic music and a few Danish rappers. Our group that night included a bassist for a death metal band, a bossa nova singer, a former circus performer, and my old artist friend Trine, from whom I borrowed the red hoodie that I never gave back.

Oddly, when I wear the sweatshirt now, it signifies for me less Denmark specifically and more a wandering, aimless period of my life—one that, as I reflect today, holds way more meaning than I could have ever imagined. In my late 20s and early 30s, I spent what some might consider to be an eccentric amount of time in Iceland, living there for periods and traveling the island extensively. I would like to tell you that I had a grand purpose. But no, when I wasn't driving around on gravel roads of the most gorgeous, haunting landscapes in the world, I was vaguely writing a travel book about Iceland. That meant most of my time was spent hanging out in the bars and cafés of Reykjavík.

One of those visits, in late summer, was when I met Trine. She was living with a Finnish woman named Eeva-Liisa in a little apartment near the bus station. Trine was shooting photos and waiting to hear if she'd finally be accepted into the Royal Danish Academy of Fine Arts. Eeva-Liisa was an artist, cleaning rooms in a guesthouse, and her ex-boyfriend was a journalist from Helsinki whom I'd met while backpacking in Nicaragua. So, basically, all of us were connected in that beautifully random and serendipitous way that seemed to define Gen X travel life in the late twentieth century, before social media changed everything.

As the summer came to an end, Eeva-Liisa, Trine, and I decided we should leave Reykjavík and see the country. We rented a car and drove the countryside, with the intention of observing the annual sheep roundup, a tradition called *réttir*. In Iceland, there are half a million sheep—nearly twice as many sheep as Icelanders —which roam freely throughout the summer, grazing. *Réttir* is a festive time, full of songs and drinking, as whole farming communities gather to drive one another's sheep to a common pen. It's amazing to watch thousands of sheep driven across the vast empty spaces by people on Icelandic ponies. At one point, we tried to photograph sheep running toward us, but we spooked them so badly that the whole flock veered left and started running in the wrong direction. Angry Icelanders on horseback shouted at us as they tried in vain to get the sheep going back toward their farm.

Soon after, I stopped the car at a field full of wildflowers, underneath a glacier, with the blue sea stretching out from the cliff below us toward the Arctic Circle. Trine got down on her hands and knees and rummaged through the grass, consulting a book titled *Nordens Svampe* (Nordic Mushrooms). Less than 10 minutes later, our car became stuck in several feet of mud. Eeva-Liisa pulled on long rubber boots, and the two of us tried to push the car out of the mud while Trine simply laughed and shot photos. An old Icelandic couple eventually came by in a four-wheel-drive vehicle and pulled the stupid foreigners out with a rope.

Later that evening, we arrived in the northern city of Akureyri to meet up with Janus, a guy from Greenland whom Eeva-Liisa loved but who did not love her back. After dark, we watched the northern lights in the clear sky above the fjord. Janus bragged that he saw the aurora borealis "five or six times a week" at home. He told us that if you whistled, the northern lights would move. I was amazed when he whistled and the yellow streaks shimmered green and wiggled toward us.

Trine and I wanted photos of the northern lights, and so we all drove up to a hill above the town. She set up her camera on a tripod and pointed it at the sky as the car radio played Icelandic pop music. The shot needed a long exposure. Trine left the shutter open, and we stood there waiting, as if we had all the time in the world. We knew we didn't, of course. We knew in the awkward silence of that night that our driftless days would soon come to an end.

It was Eeva-Liisa who eventually sighed and suggested that, just like all the sheep we'd observed at *réttir,* we'd soon enough be rounded up, sorted, and sent back to our homes. It seemed too bleak of a thought at the time: home as our own personal stockade. All three of us would surely face shearings of one kind or another in our immediate futures. Trine would return to Copenhagen and be rejected by the Danish art academy. Eeva-Liisa would return to Helsinki, struggle as a freelance designer, and return home to her family's small village in the north. And I would return to the States and throw yet another false start of a book into the garbage heap.

"Well, we could always come back to Iceland," I said.

"Yeah," Trine said, "but it would never be the same."

As we whistled at the aurora borealis, I wondered aloud if sheep in their winter pens could dream. And if sheep could dream, did they dream of green grass and a glorious summer with no darkness? Of blue fjords and glaciers and mushrooms? We all agreed that they must.

As I sit here now, wearing the musty old BEVAR CHRISTIANIA sweatshirt (its pocket hanging by a thread), typing in the present tense, all this feels like a lifetime ago. We are different people now. When I visit Trine these days, I stay with her family, and we trade stories about our children. We're much more likely to eat at one of Copenhagen's world-class "New Nordic" restaurants than to visit Christiania. I am no longer the sort of naively adventurous person who lights out for politically unstable places with a backpack. In Italy, on my visits to Pieve San Giacomo, I now take time to stop by the grave sites of Paolo and Aunt Gina, who both died years ago.

We aren't the only ones to have changed. The places themselves have, too. So many foreign tourists visit Iceland that, in recent years, it has become a cautionary tale of the consequences of over-tourism. Nicaragua has slid backward, run for the past decade by the authoritarian Daniel Ortega, whose paramilitary forces have killed hundreds. Even the Italy I first encountered is quite different than it was three decades ago, and likely will be transformed even more now that its oldest generation has been hit hard by the pandemic.

What travel has taught me is that the things of the world are only ever temporary—though, once in a while, the temporary can become eternal. I hope that we will be able to travel, to interact with and witness the world again in the near future. When we do, it will certainly seem strange. But when has travel not been strange? We don't need a pandemic to show us that, but the pause we're experiencing can highlight a basic truth: we may or may not walk this way again, and even if we do, we will never be precisely the same people who experienced that journey in the first place. Travel is only ever about a moment in time and space, but it's also about how we choose to hold that moment in our memories. It is always both present and past.

JASON WILSON

Introduction

I BEGAN TO FORGET what day it was after the third or fourth week—something that had happened to me before, on holidays, but never like this. And never for so long.

The sun moved through the living room, slicing different geometric patterns with every hour. Four to five o'clock was the most radiant—I got good at telling what time it was by watching the shadows. Nothing was different from the day before.

We were all locked down, avoiding any contact outside our households with loved ones and strangers alike. We were grounded, huddled under house arrest. A sleepless hibernation. A year of paralyzing fear, disease, exhaustion, and national horror and shame. We saw a plague ripple around the earth, forcing us to shelter from the world. And there was a reckoning in America, a long time coming and hardly over yet.

I write this from my home in New York City on a quiet, snowy February day. The streets outside my window are mostly empty, as they have been for the past year. I usually relish the quiet snow brings. But this past year, the quiet—broken by the screams of ambulance sirens—has been a symptom of fear, not snow. Homebound, many of us have waited and fretted about when this waiting and fretting would end. For others of us, being home has brought danger—home is not always the safest place, just as travel is not always a choice.

Months and months went by last spring, summer, and fall in anxiety, waiting, and unknowing. I felt dead inside and yet alert to every movement in the atmosphere. Jumpy like a cat, but immobilized. Trying to discern information when there was none. Unable to concentrate on anything except the most menial tasks. I obsessed over every minute domestic detail but could see no bigger picture on the horizon.

For the past year, I have found it utterly impossible to write, nary a word. That was the emptiness. In my case, the lack of mobility led to a lack of imagination. I couldn't even read—not one book.

It was easy to avoid thinking about my idleness. We were waiting, after all, for life "to get back to normal." We said things such as "when this is all over" again and again. Only we had no clue what the new normal might be like or when this would all end. (It's still not over as I write.) Life became granular. I busied myself with homeschooling a tween, with wiping down every package and pear that came into the house, and with watching nurses and doctors break down on Instagram, pleading for us all to stay home. I counted the watercooler bottles stockpiled; the unexplainable number of dried apricot packages or granola bags with coconut bought on Amazon. (Who the hell likes coconut in their granola?) I became hyper-focused on the pantry. I could think of nothing but cooking, one meal rolling into another, so that I could feel busy, so that I did not have to think. I moved through the days. And though I spoke often enough, I felt silent, muted. It was like being trapped in a Don DeLillo novel—except my banal life was much less brilliantly written.

We were afraid and told to protect ourselves from a disease we were only beginning to understand. But the barriers we built around ourselves to keep us safe from exposure to the outside world also kept out almost everything I savored about life.

Now life became bland, smaller. I have always wanted to explore new ideas and experiences, to expose myself to as much of the world as I could. Unable to go anywhere, physically isolated from others, I felt in a way that I had ceased to exist as my whole self. I craved wandering and its discoveries like I craved the air.

I cannot imagine a life without travel. I could not do the work I do, or know the things I know about food and people, or understand other cultures and my own, had I not spent a good portion of every year of my life since age four traveling. Going from some place *here* to some place *there* has been the defining constant in my life.

My earliest travel memory is of leaving my grandparents' home in New Delhi, all dressed up in a red coat, with a hood and a bow.

My mother had left two years before to make a life for us both in America, and now I was going to join her. I had a laminated card pinned to the inside of said coat, inscribed with my mother's address and phone number in New York on one side and the same contact details for my grandparents on the other side. A sort of luggage tag, which actually said IF LOST, PLEASE RETURN TO . . .

I have zero memory of being scared—only excitement, and glee. I was always happy to go somewhere. It was staying home that made me sad, perhaps because my mother had made me wait in India for two years while she went abroad. Staying home meant being left out, left back, left behind.

I flew as an unaccompanied minor on Air India. The ticket my mother purchased routed me from New Delhi, to Cairo, to Rome, to London, and finally to my mother's arms in JFK Airport. The whole trip was fun. I remember playing cards with the flight crew, who gave me coloring books with the Air India logo, and I remember feeling like they were my friends. My first choice for several years when anyone asked what I wanted to be when I grew up was an "airline hostess." (That's what we called them back then.) I was obsessed—they seemed to have it all: colorful printed silk saris that fluttered as they walked briskly down the aisle, early-'70s bouffant updos à la Bollywood, and unlimited access to free travel, of course. They were the only examples of female freedom my young eyes saw. They each carried a Samsonite "beauty case," which was the most impractical thing one could lug around during layovers, exponentially heavier than any cosmetics that would fit into it. No matter, I wouldn't realize that fact and so many others until many years later.

That epic journey was the first of many. In an effort to keep me from losing my culture and my mother from losing her mind, I was sent every summer of my childhood, the minute school let out in June, back to Chennai, where my grandfather, a civil servant, had retired from his own peripatetic career. I had become a bit of a fish out of water in India, and I relished being called "the girl who lived in America." This usually followed snickers about my shorts being too short, my stretchy tube tops being too tight and insufficiently concealing, and my general lack of any sense of modesty. It was true, I was oblivious. It was 98 degrees in the shade, but women there walked around—and still do—in six meters of fabric, so, yes, patriarchy.

But the other kids also grilled me about the latest songs and fashions. I brought them Pringles and peanut butter in my suitcase. I showed them my dance moves and all the other kitschy vestiges of American pop culture and became the resident local expert. At the same time, future vice president Kamala Harris was also visiting her grandparents just around the corner—but I have no doubt that she was comparing Indian parliamentary law with the US Constitution, while I was comparing Donna Summer with Diana Ross and knishes with samosas, which explains a lot.

Those trips yoyoing back and forth between two cultures in my formative years helped shape my worldview. They told me there was more than one way of doing things, from what you wore, to what you ate, to what you could think. My bifurcated life showed me as I grew that my beloved grandfather, so learned, brilliant, and kind, was also undoubtedly trapped by his own casteism and racism. He was wrong about people. His views didn't square with what I knew from going to public school in New York City.

Later, when my mother and I moved from New York to Los Angeles, our flights to Chennai passed through Tokyo with a stopover of a day and a half in Singapore. My first time traveling that route alone, I was 15 or 16 years old. In Singapore I was free to roam anywhere and choose my own lodgings based on budget—from the least-sinister-looking man at the airport arrivals lounge. He told me he had a daughter my age, I believed him, and miraculously, it was true.

It was glorious to walk around the muggy streets. It was hot and crowded, but beautiful. Lush and full of palm trees. Not a speck of litter on the ground, this place was so pristine and sanitized, you could eat off the road. It was like someone built a whole modern city in the middle of an island jungle. The smells of foods from different shops and houses hit my nose as I walked the unknown streets. The sounds of sizzling oil in woks piqued my curiosity. I was told that the hawker stands opened only at night, but I was directed to a food court in a mall. In a mall? Singapore is a major crossroads in Asia, and as such it has many malls, where I saw the strangest arrays of people: Well-to-do older ladies dressed to the nines with pearls and big Chanel bags. Young couples holding hands. Big families with several screaming Izod-clad children taking up the whole sidewalk, when there was one to walk on. And then there were the loners like me. I imagined stories for them all.

In Singapore, I felt like I was tasting freedom for the first time, and it ignited a wanderlust that still plagues me.

I don't think I verbalized it to anyone, including myself, but I knew then that I wanted to be a perpetual traveler. I was happiest receiving and experiencing new information about the world, in situ. When I look back now, I can see that while I may never have thought of myself as a travel writer, I have become an accidental one. Every piece of work I have produced, whether cookbook, essay, or television show, has had to do with travel. For me, it has always been more than work. I feel at home in motion and as an outsider.

In June of last year, my new TV series, *Taste the Nation,* premiered. It had taken me so long, with so many trips to Los Angeles and back, to get it made. Seven doors shut before one opened in the spring of 2019. Miraculously, when I had all but given up, the streaming service Hulu green-lighted the show.

By the summer of that year, I was traveling around the country to visit different communities, getting to know people by exploring what they eat. I wanted to show what our country's immigrant cultures are really like. Immigrants are not rapists or murderers, as suggested by the vitriol spewing out of Washington, DC, for years. That propaganda separated families and put children in cages. Having grown up in immigrant communities, I knew that immigrants are strivers, dreamers, adventurers, survivors, people with rich stories. Telling those stories could create a more honest counterpoint to Donald Trump's narrative. I was making a political show disguised as a food show.

As we started shooting, I visited the San Carlos reservation near Globe, Arizona. I went on a walk with Twila Cassadore, an Apache forager who has made it her mission to catalog all of the region's plants. We foraged for wild onions and then made a salsa with barrel cactus. I ate pack rat, or desert wood rat, which terrified me. But it was, in fact, delicious, and I ended up eating more than I needed to for the camera.

That balmy August, I fished crab traps out of a marsh with the Gullah Geechee on St. Helena Island, a sea island off the coast of Charleston, South Carolina. I cooked in the late-afternoon heat with my old friend BJ Dennis. He shared a rice recipe passed down through generations. We cracked crabs with chile-soaked fingers, the sun dipping beneath an indigo sky. Above the din of cicadas, his cousin Dr. Jessica Berry told us about their ancestral language, a patois of West African languages that was almost lost but is now being revived, in no short measure by her work.

In El Paso, Texas, one of our most politically complex border cities, I happily pressed tortillas, grinding heirloom corn that turned from purple to teal as nixtamalization transformed corn into masa.

In Las Vegas, Nevada, I made som tum with Thai women who had married US GIs during the Vietnam War and come to this country as war brides. One of the women spoke with a twinkle in her eye of the love and loyalty of her husband, who was willing to bring her—a divorced woman 11 years his senior and the mother of four children—home to his folks.

In Paterson, New Jersey, I made tamales with a Peruvian dance teacher expert in Quechua traditions, who made it her mission to instill pride and purpose in the children she taught. She showed me how to work with cassava flour for the first time.

It was a spiritual experience to meet all these women, to cook, to laugh, and to learn. This is why I travel.

I undertook an extravagant and impossible 10 trips over six months. The new show's release came three months into the pandemic. Press interviews with food and TV writers kept me occupied. I tried to block out the white noise of anxiety in my head as I spoke of the particulars of each trip.

In this new reality, as we sheltered in place, it was distressing to imagine all of that slipping away. The year before had been a year of hugging strangers and shaking hands, sharing plates of food, peering over people's shoulders at their stoves. I could still see the contours of their smiles.

Now there were only masks. It seemed an eternity ago. Would that kind of roaming ever again be possible?

Talking about the past year made me sad. We had lost a world we would not be able to find again anytime soon. I was thankful I had had the experience of crisscrossing the nation, immersing myself in all those gorgeous communities, but it sank me deeper into a funk. I had the perfect job: to travel, to eat, to discover others, to uncover interesting stories and the people who lived those stories. But even now as vaccines trickle in, new strains of the virus are being discovered. A year in, after empty promises and lies, I wonder when life will resume.

So many of us are stymied by the virus, with varying consequences: the chefs who cannot cook; the teachers who do not
gather with children; the doctors who avoid laying hands on their
patients. I'm a wanderer who cannot wander. COVID, you bastard
thief.

When the email invitation came to edit this anthology, I felt at
once flattered and suspicious. What new travel writing would exist
in this horrendous year? Nearly no one was going anywhere. I was
in stasis like much of the world, gripped by fear, impotence, and
a kind of mental paralysis. On lighter days, which were few, my
state of mind reminded me of a time when I was on an episode of
Star Trek: Enterprise. I played a character called Princess Kaitaama,
who gets kidnapped by a couple of Klingons who whisk her away
to the other end of the galaxy and hold her for ransom. Because
my character refuses to remain docile or compliant, they put her
into a sort of induced coma, a space "stasis," and there I lie in a
glass coffin until Captain Hottie from the starship *Enterprise* comes
to save me, of course. On bleaker days during the pandemic, I was
in that kind of stasis: I had no idea when I'd be able to focus or
form coherent words. The task of editing this collection seemed
daunting.

A few weeks into the new year, I was finally able to pick up a
book and actually finish it. I am indebted to Isabel Wilkerson, the
author of *Caste: The Origins of Our Discontents,* not only for writing
the one book that finally pulled my mind awake, but for giving me
a thorough education on the roots of racism that my American
public school education had failed to do. She shook me out of my
quarantine miasma just in the nick of time.

It was at this point that I began to receive and read the many,
many selections that were prospects for this collection. I read for
hours and hours, deep into the night, unable to stop for breaks.
It was astonishing to read such beautiful prose. And it was a privilege. Turns out, it was an extraordinary year for travel writing—inspiring, actually.

The beauty of good writing is that it transports the reader inside
another person's experience in some other physical place and culture and, at its best, evokes a palpable feeling of being in a specific
moment in time and space.

More than any year in recent memory, 2020 was the year the
world finally, strangely, came together, albeit in collective misery,

dread, and disease. So many world events usually happen "over there" or to "us here," but for the first time in decades, the world —all of it—was threatened, all of us collectively, mortally threatened. We were stopped in our tracks.

We didn't like it. Humans need the freedom to move, to meet with others. Even if we stay put, we need the knowledge that we have the *possibility* of going somewhere. After all the many dead, and all the loss of livelihoods, that, too, was taken away from us this year.

So, what does a collection of travel writing look like in such a year? The pieces I ultimately selected for this anthology give us what we've all missed so badly in this year of isolation. They take us on the journeys we could not take ourselves, both internal and external.

The writers in this collection show us a world that includes the pulsing music of Baaba Maal, Souleymane Faye, Omar Pene, and other phenomenal artists in Jim Benning's "Senegal's Beating Heart." Benning conveys not only the spirit of West African music but also the intoxicating feeling of being in a hot, humid bar with live music vibrating under our feet as we groove and sweat together. How long has it been since we've danced? Ligaya Mishan shares the rich culinary traditions of Muslims in Northwest China, preparing dishes with lamb and wheat, in "Thousand Fields of Grain." How much longer until we can eat crowded elbow to elbow at a beloved local street stall? Jon Lee Anderson reminisces about hunting for musk-ox fur in Alaska at a young age decades ago, when he was innocent enough to come home happily empty-handed but changed forever. They all remind us of why we need to roam.

This volume contains more than one compelling narrative of the devastating, undeniable erosion of our environment in places as far from each other as Louisiana, in "The Losing Coast" by Elizabeth Miller, and the Arctic Circle, in Bathsheba Demuth's incandescent "Reindeer at the End of the World," the first two paragraphs of which are worth the price of this book alone. Or even 36,000 feet under the sea, in "Five Oceans, Five Deeps" by Ben Taub, which reads at times like a suspense thriller.

This is by no means an exhaustive list. The notion of what is "best" is subjective, but this year more than ever, travel writing needed to bear witness, as Paul Theroux states in his salient piece,

"A Fear-Filled Lockdown." He compares our time to Idi Amin's Uganda in 1966.

The discussion of relatability as added value in good writing can be a banal one. I won't bore you here. I read because I enjoy reading. I read to find out about things I know nothing about and perhaps could not ever relate to at all had it not been for the deft stroke of a great writer's pen. I travel for many of the same reasons.

Kiese Makeba Laymon's "Mississippi: A Poem, in Days," is a beautiful slow burn that will stay with you for a long time. It is a heartbreaking and thoroughly relatable piece that captures the anxiety and mounting dread of the first few weeks of the plague. Laymon makes plain what torture the year has been, for so many reasons. The state of carrying multiple traumas at once. Knowing so little while still trying to move forward through life. The misinformation, and the daily non-information, the news gives us, compounding our confusion, our fear. The mendacity of Trump. The quiet panic. The loneliness. Through Laymon's eyes, we see the absurd cruelty of Confederate monuments. It is necessary reading for anyone trying to understand what it is like to stand in the shoes of an African American man in the South.

> In college, my partner, Nzola, and I got into an altercation with two fraternities on Bid Day. Some fraternity members wore confederate capes, Afro wigs, and others blackened their faces. I've written about how they called us "niggers." I've written about how they called Nzola a "nigger b——." I've written about that experience and guns. I've written about that experience and bats. I've written about that experience and how my investment in patriarchy diminished Nzola's suffering.
>
> I have never written about the heartbreak of seeing the future governor of Mississippi [Tate Reeves] in that group of white boys, proudly representing the Kappa Alpha fraternity and its confederate commitment to Black suffering . . .When I saw Tate in that confederate cacophony of drunken white boyhood, doing what they did, I knew he could one day be governor of Mississippi and president of the United States.
>
> That is still the most damning thing I can ever say about a white boy from Mississippi.

Stand, because it is too painful to walk.

How you travel, never mind what for, depends on who you are, the resources you have access to, what you look like, and how the world perceives your very presence in it. There are other pieces

here that illustrate that travel isn't the same for all of us. One is
Latria Graham's "Out There, Nobody Can Hear You Scream," published in *Outside*. This moving letter made me think hard about
the elements of travel many of us take for granted. Graham addresses the unanswered emails from African American travelers
she received after writing an article on loving the outdoors. Her
readers were seeking advice on exploring outdoor spaces while being Black. Remember Amy Cooper, or "Central Park Karen," as
she was affectionately called? She was a white woman who called
911 to report imaginary threats from a Black bird-watcher in New
York's Central Park who asked her to leash her dog. There are
hundreds of thousands of Amy Coopers, and worse. In light of last
summer's reckoning with racism, can anyone doubt that we are all
not afforded the same treatment as we encounter the world? Millions of us knew that already, but if there are those who still don't
see, they will surely be willingly blind forever. The pandemic did
not stop all that, nor did it stop folks from rising up and crying
out. Thank heavens.

It was a frightening, fright-fueled, frightful year. And it bleeds,
as I write, into this one, too.

A few pieces in this book do something else: they hold up a mirror to the past year. No story captures the harrowing experience
of being trapped on a cruise ship, literally stranded by fear and
bureaucracy, better than Doug Bock Clark's "Inside the Nightmare
Voyage of the *Diamond Princess*." We have Glynnis MacNicol's ode
to New York and its die-hard residents, "The New York You Once
Knew Is Gone. The One You Loved Remains," and also the other
side of that coin, Meghan Daum's "I Decided to Leave."

Intan Paramaditha's "On the Complicated Questions Around
Writing About Travel" is a fascinating meditation on what travel
means for different people. The Indonesian author confronts colonialism, the weaponization of racism—or perhaps it is the other
way around—and its likely cousin capitalism, through history and
literature. She examines how other writers have considered gender and class—things some people think nothing about because
they've never had to, while the rest of us have no choice but to
factor it in all the time.

Meg Bernhard searches for the interior life of a young German man by traveling from a small town near Frankfurt, where
she retraces the steps of the youth's life with his bereaved mother,

to Fisterra, off the coast of Galicia, where the nineteen-year-old drowned. It is an attempt to find closure for something deeply personal that has haunted her own interior life. The ache that death leaves is palpable in every sentence.

Leslie Jamison's nuanced piece "The Warmth of a Lost World" is full of another type of mourning. Recounting her recent trip to survey Istanbul's bathhouses just before lockdown, as well as the century-old Russian and Turkish Baths in the East Village of New York City, she longs for a world that contains a certain kind of anonymous intimacy. Jamison captures the ineffable pleasure of letting one's guard down, even among strangers in a state of vulnerable nakedness. When will we again encounter strangers with anything but a visceral defensiveness or suspicion? The brilliance of her story unfolds as she speaks of how pleasure and discomfort can coexist and can often only exist when we push ourselves to bodily extremes in some way.

> When I stood in the room of radiant heat, pouring the ice-cold water over my body, relieving an unbearable heat with a nearly unbearable chill, it made me—briefly, gloriously—a stranger in the habitation of my skin, and then at home more fully than before. I could feel every part of myself in that heat, sweating and alive—an animal among animals, full of all the ordinary aches and hopes. My body wasn't something to be starved or cut or filled with booze until I blacked out; it was something to be taken care of. I found myself newly alive to my own pulse, seized by a pleasure that could hold discomfort in its open palms.

This volume also contains many other pieces that celebrate travel; put right the misconceptions of places we think we know, like Amanda Fortini's "The People of Las Vegas"; and embrace with gusto the pure joy of food eaten in its native land, made with native wheat, by native sons, like Bill Buford's "Good Bread." There is so much here to get us out of our doldrums and help us look forward to rediscovering our ever-spinning and curious world.

I hope you will enjoy reading this collection as much as I have enjoyed putting it together. I hope it will give you the comfort, and also the jolt and illumination it has given me, serving almost as a literary light at the end of a yearlong tunnel.

PADMA LAKSHMI

The Best American
Travel Writing 2021

Inside the Nightmare Voyage of the *Diamond Princess*

FROM *GQ*

1. Cruising

THEY HAD NO idea about the danger. Not as they crowded around the famous champagne waterfall. Hundreds of delighted cruise passengers watched as golden bubbly, poured atop a pyramid of 300 glasses, filled the stemware below. Then the drinks were passed out. Hand to hand to hand. Guests clinked coupes and posed for photos, making the evening feel momentous. It was their fourth night aboard the *Diamond Princess*—a floating city of a ship that had been churning south from Yokohama, Japan—and they were all still unaware of how much their journey would transform them, and even the world.

The Four Amigos, as a pair of American couples called themselves, skipped the champagne waterfall, which happens on almost every Princess Cruises excursion. The sixtysomething traveling companions had seen it before on their annual cruises together. They were happy to turn in early for the evening, thankful for this two-week break from their busy lives. Carl and Jeri Goldman run a mom-and-pop radio station that broadcasts local news and high school sports to a suburb of Los Angeles. Mark and Jerri Jorgensen oversee a rehabilitation center that specializes in pornography addiction in the red rocks of St. George, Utah. This year especially they needed the respite of the cruise. Recently, Jeri Goldman's father had died; Carl had struggled with his health. None of them had been paying much attention to the news as they flew to Japan to board the ship. When they landed in Tokyo, Carl noticed an abnormal number of people wearing face masks, but he thought little of it.

Indeed, for the first four days, there seemed to be nothing amiss as the 18-story ocean liner powered south through the East China Sea. As it did, the ship's 2,666 guests luxuriated in a dozen or so different restaurants, a multitude of bars and nightclubs, four pools, a spa, a casino, and more. All the while, an army of more than a thousand crew members stood ready to gratify their every whim.

Five days into the voyage, the ship docked in Hong Kong, and as the Four Amigos disembarked, health officials scanned their foreheads for fever with thermometer guns. Apparently, a mysterious virus was scything through mainland China. At first the People's Republic had attempted to cover up the flu-like disease, but things had gotten so bad that in the industrial city of Wuhan, nearly 600 miles north, some 11 million people were being quarantined and local hospitals were bursting with casualties. In Hong Kong, so far, the response was modest. Foreigners were being screened at the ports, schools were suspended, and several Lunar New Year events had been canceled. But as the Four Amigos toured the city and watched a light show dazzle the city's skyline, the throngs weren't noticeably diminished. After all, you couldn't halt life.

For a week more, the *Diamond Princess* cruised on. The Amigos took a memorable kayak excursion in Vietnam, among the karst monoliths of Ha Long Bay. They enjoyed street food in Taiwan. But while there, panicky headlines and more temperature guns made the virus impossible to ignore. Still, they considered themselves safe, unaware that an 80-year-old passenger—a man who had coughed through the first third of the cruise before disembarking in Hong Kong—had been admitted to a hospital, where it was discovered that he was infected with COVID-19.

When the ship was two days away from returning home to Yokohama, a typo-riddled email from a Hong Kong port agent arrived in the inboxes of cruise line personnel, alerting them to the danger that had been found: "Would kindly inform the ship related parties and do the necessary disinfection in needed. Many thanks!"

Officials at Princess Cruises say the company had learned of the infected passenger hours earlier, when they were tipped off by a news report. Before long, they received another, clearer warning, this one sent by an epidemiologist from the government of Hong Kong. But seemingly nothing was done aboard the ship that aroused the concern of most passengers, including the Four Amigos. Cruise line officials maintain that the day after the ship received the first warning, its crew began sanitizing public areas more frequently, put out extra hand sanitizer, and switched buffet utensils more often.

Of course, such measures couldn't be expected to do much against a virus that was currently crippling China—especially on a cruise ship, an environment designed to pack people in and then entertain them with communal activities. And the virus had already had ample time to attack people's lung cells until they coughed it into the air, where it might linger in a mist for three hours. Then, if the virions weren't inhaled, they could still settle on an elevator button or a roulette wheel and survive up to three days, waiting to hitchhike on an unsuspecting hand to an itchy nose. At this point in the cruise, the coronavirus could be anywhere and in anyone.

On what was supposed to be the cruise's final night, February 3, while the Four Amigos were enjoying a multicourse meal in the mirrored Savoy Dining Room, they all agreed that they hoped the trip would never end. Suddenly the ocean liner's intercom came to life. In his Italian-inflected English, the ship's captain told all on board about the infected passenger. Accordingly, he said, when the *Diamond Princess* reached Yokohama, everyone would need to stay on the vessel for an extra day while Japanese health officials screened them. The Jorgensens gave each other a look that said: *What does that mean for us?* But soon enough, guests went back to their surf and turf. Before long, the baked Alaska was paraded out, accompanied by marching band music and diners festively waving their napkins.

The Four Amigos soon retired, but many of the other passengers continued their evening at the Skywalkers Nightclub or took in a show at the 740-seat theater. They were still on vacation, after all. Dealing with the real world could wait.

2. *Security*

Growing up in claustrophobic Mumbai, India, Sonali Thakkar had been desperate to see the world. When a friend encouraged her to interview for a job with Princess Cruises, she hesitated. What Thakkar knew of cruises consisted of what she'd seen in *Titanic*—hardly an endorsement for a career at sea. But she ended up getting the job and loving it, spending her early 20s pinging between continents as a security patrolwoman aboard several Princess ships. The long hours she spent managing the gangway—monitoring those who boarded and disembarked—could be taxing, but after her shifts, she'd visit the top deck to take in the panoramic view of the ocean or a glamorous port city, and the stress would melt away. Besides, she'd happily put up with a lot for the chance to earn about twice what she'd make at home.

Not long after the captain's announcement, the 24-year-old Thakkar received an urgent call ordering her to the gangway. She had been off duty, but the ship had sped up to reach Yokohama early and now the city was in view. Soon she was standing at the weakly illuminated gangway, squinting into the liquid dark of the harbor while the ship anchored slightly offshore.

It was freezing outside, and down here by the waterline, Thakkar could hear none of the cheer of the parties going on hundreds of feet above. Her radio crackled, announcing the approach of several small Japanese boats, which drew alongside the hulking ocean liner. Even before the captain's announcement, the crew had heard rumors of an infection, but Thakkar claimed that management told them not to worry. Now, as she counted roughly two dozen Japanese health care workers in protective gowns and masks being helped aboard by deckhands, she began to get an inkling of how bad things might actually be.

The Japanese officials were marched directly to the captain's office. Not long before midnight, the captain reportedly returned to the intercom, finally ending the night's revelry, ordering everyone back to their rooms.

In the morning, the *Diamond Princess* was subdued. The ship idled close to shore but never touched the pier, as if landing might infect Japan. Some of the guests still circulated between the restaurants, but many stayed close to their rooms as the Japanese health care workers fanned out across the ship to assess the virus's spread. Passengers, including the Four Amigos, expected to disembark the following day. But when the next morning came, the captain's voice again rang out from the speakers barnacled to the walls and the ceilings. Nine passengers and one crew member had tested positive for COVID-19. All passengers were to return to their cabins, where they would remain quarantined for two weeks by order of the Japanese government. Rather than release 3,700 potential vectors—who could infect Japan or their farther-flung homes—public health officials were transforming the *Diamond Princess* into a floating quarantine center.

Thakkar was given a mask and a new set of duties: patrolling the hallways in her naval-looking uniform. Guests would open their doors and, from their thresholds, ask what was going on. But all she could tell them was to go back inside and remain calm—she didn't know anything more herself. Of course, Thakkar was concerned about contracting the illness. But she also told herself that she was no longer the timid girl who had never left India: she was a Princess Cruises security person, and she was going to do her duty —even if that had unexpectedly changed. Once she had guarded the passengers from the outside world; now she was protecting it from them.

3. Inside

As Hong Kongers, Yardley Wong and her husband had been aware of the outbreak before many others on the ship—and the loss of a close friend to SARS, a similar virus, 17 years earlier, primed them to take this outbreak seriously. The fortysomething couple had worn masks and practiced some social distancing measures since the start of the cruise; after the captain's announcement, they locked themselves away in their cabin, even as many guests still roamed the ship.

While they waited anxiously for the Japanese health care workers to reach them, they ordered room service, and when it arrived, they sanitized the utensils before eating. Sometimes Wong heard the crinkle of plasticky protective gear in the hallway, and through the peephole in the door, she glimpsed blurry figures in surgical masks and gowns—though they always passed by.

Finally, around 11:30 p.m., officials arrived to take their temperature—and found no sign of fever, though it was hard to tell because the couple and the health workers barely spoke a common language. Wong and her husband went to bed thinking they were okay, but were woken by a knock at 4:30 a.m. This time the figures at the door had upgraded to hazmat gear: face shields, goggles, and shoe coverings. They swabbed the Wongs' mouths. Wong then watched as her sample was inserted into a tray alongside what seemed like a hundred other vials—and she wondered what these tests meant about the virus's spread. The pair managed a few more hours of restless sleep, until they were roused by another announcement from the captain. Everyone, he told the ship, would need to remain inside their cabins for the whole two-week quarantine.

For the Wongs, the world shrank to a room of about 150 square feet, much of that taken up by a queen-size bed. The cabin's primary decoration was a big TV and two large mirrors hung facing each other to create the illusion of spaciousness. There were no windows, and this relatively cheap room was about as far from fresh air as possible: on an interior hall of a middle deck, near the laundromat. This wasn't the sort of cabin highlighted in advertisements.

Wong and her husband might have endured this confinement easier if they hadn't been traveling with their then six-year-old son, who was sharing their bed. To occupy him, they had the TV and an iPad, on which he played *Fortnite.* At first they used in-room exercise routines to burn off his energy, before passengers were eventually granted an hour each day on deck, during which time they tried to run him ragged while carefully staying six feet away from others.

But they couldn't divert their boy's attention from the fact that the situation was quickly worsening. On the second day of the quarantine, the captain announced that the number of cases had doubled to 20. The following morning, February 7, there were 61. Fear stuffed the cramped room. The family still hadn't heard back about the results of their tests and had to hope that no news was good news. Infected passengers, they had grasped, were being taken off the ship. Through their peephole, Yardley Wong and her husband had watched neighbors be escorted down the hall with hastily packed bags by men in hazmat suits, presumably en route to Japanese hospitals.

The couple was terrified about what would happen if one of them tested positive. They were caring not only for their son but also Yardley Wong's elderly parents in the cabin next door. The family worried about whether her frail father could survive an infection. A single vent supplied the Wongs' room with air, which was so dry, Wong said, "you could make Italian cured ham with it." The desiccated oxygen was giving her family raspy coughs—or was that the coronavirus?

Wong distracted herself by helping others. Using her fluency in English, Mandarin, and Cantonese, she acted as a one-woman switchboard for older passengers who didn't know how to use the internet, taking messages from family and friends via social media and then relaying them through the ship's telephone lines. She appreciated that Princess Cruises was trying to ease the situation, making the ship's usually expensive Wi-Fi available for free and offering psychological counseling over the phone. The company had already promised to refund the trip and pay for guests' journeys home. Still, passengers were growing restive, blaming the cruise line for everything from a lack of clean bedsheets to lost medications, including essentials like insulin.

Meanwhile, Japanese officials were struggling with their response. Lacking enough kits to test everyone on board, they reportedly left feverish Americans in their cabins for multiple days before finally sending them to hospitals where they tested positive. Passengers were given N95 masks and alcohol wipes, but this seemed risibly inadequate, given the rapidly growing number of infections. Day 5: 69. Day 6: 135. Many passengers felt underinformed, left to glean details from news reports based on leaks from the Japanese health ministry. Some hung banners off the side of the ship—one apparent bedsheet was painted with the plea for help: "Serious lack of medicine, lack of information."

Eventually, Wong's son asked her, "Am I going to get it?"

Normally, Wong would have tried to ease his worry, but she couldn't deny reality. "If either of us gets it, we may not be able to see each other for a while," she said. Her son started crying.

Later he said, "Mama, I don't want to be here anymore. I just want to go home."

Now she wanted to weep. "Just a few more days," she promised him. "Just a few more days."

4. *"The Passenger Is King"*

From the glass-walled bridge of the *Diamond Princess,* Captain Gennaro Arma endeavored to protect the souls entrusted to him.

He had brought them to harbor but not yet to safety. Arma had been with the cruise line for more than 20 years and looked like the movie-star version of a gracefully aged captain. He'd grown up on the Italian coast, enchanted by his seafaring family's stories, and landed a job as a Princess Cruises cadet not long after graduating from maritime school. He rose rapidly through the ranks, and when the *Diamond Princess* made its maiden voyage, in 2004, Arma was its senior second officer. By 2018, he was the captain, steering the vessel through typhoons by pointing the bow into the oncoming storm.

Arma was undaunted by high-stakes challenges—in fact, he relished them. But this was unlike anything he'd faced before. And now, rather than having the absolute authority that he typically had at the helm, he was following orders from both the Japanese government and his corporate command chain. He was working, he later told me, with "no playbook, no dedicated training, no dedicated protocol." With the aid of Japanese officials and his crew, Arma was essentially trying to convert his ship into a colossal luxury hospital and oversee the logistics of food delivery, sanitization, and health care for a small city. In his daily PA announcements, he exhorted guests and crew alike to rise to the challenge, repeating the motto that it was only through pressure that coal became a *Diamond Princess.*

Most of the 1,045 crew members responded with enthusiasm to Arma's leadership—at least at the beginning. Kitchen staffers pivoted from restaurant service to delivering three meals a day to 1,337 cabins. Dede Samsul Fuad, a gee-whiz 28-year-old Indonesian dishwasher, worked 15-hour shifts, scraping food off plates and steaming them in an industrial dishwasher. He had heard of doctors in Wuhan falling sick after working too hard, but the motto drummed into him by supervisors had always been "The passenger is king." Fuad, Thakkar, and other members of the crew I spoke with took sincere pride in working hard during such a time of need. But it was also true that being a dishwasher or security guard on the *Diamond Princess* was a dream job that they couldn't afford to lose—as it was for the other Indians, Indonesians, Filipinos, Ukrainians, Hondurans, Venezuelans, and other citizens of 48 mostly developing nations who made up the majority of the ship's frontline staff.

Though masks and gloves were handed out, the crew had little training in dealing with a disease of this virulence. "Anybody would be scared for their life, because day by day more and more people were getting infected," said an Indian crew member who asked for anonymity, as did other staff, afraid of retaliation from Princess Cruises. "And we knew people were dying." The Indian man described colleagues delivering food and then running back to their cabins to jump into scalding showers or wash their hands in hot water until they hurt. As the days dragged on, the service workers began to question if their sacrifices were worth it.

Another Indonesian dishwasher described watching the virus tear through the large kitchen where he worked shoulder to shoulder with some 150 people—a number that declined as fewer showed up for work. A little less than a week into the quarantine, he started feeling ill. He wasn't sure it was coronavirus, but he decided to quarantine himself in his tiny room for 15 straight days, reasoning that if Princess Cruises couldn't protect him, he'd protect himself.

Most of the crew were housed in quarters beneath the passenger decks. There were no giant windows with sweeping ocean views, no scintillating chandeliers. Hallways with exposed piping led to small rooms packed with bunk beds. The crew could quickly tell that their home was becoming a hot spot, especially the mess hall, where more than a hundred people at a time might visit the buffet. Later, a report released by the Centers for Disease Control and Prevention validated this fear, noting that in the early stages of the outbreak three-fourths of all the infected crew members were food-service workers—employees who could easily spread the disease to other crew and passengers.

Some staffers tried to take whatever precautions they could. An Indian man told me that he ate only packaged foods—and boiled all his own drinking water in his room with an electric kettle—and avoided getting sick. But he was lucky, and some of the employees accepted getting infected as inevitable. As the CDC report would later show, not long into the quarantine the disease was infecting more crew than passengers, who were hidden away in their cabins while the staff kept working.

For government officials and corporate leaders, the question of whether it was fair—or even safe—to quarantine the passengers but not the crew was obscured by the priority to keep the ship operational. And so the poor took care of the rich, and the citizens of less powerful nations served those from more powerful nations, and the *Diamond Princess* remained a miniaturized version of the global order—because what other way could things go?

Once all the passengers had been trained to stay in their rooms, Thakkar returned to her normal post at the gangway, where her main activity was now counting the infected passengers as they were escorted off the ship. Most of the infected walked to waiting ambulances, but some left on stretchers. On the eighth day of the quarantine, she counted 39, bringing the total to 174. A native of the tropics, Thakkar had bundled up for the northern winter, but by the end of that shift, she was shivering—and coughing. She called the ship's doctor, who ordered Thakkar to isolate herself in her windowless cabin.

Eventually, she tested negative, but her roommate was found to be positive and was taken away. Thakkar was left to worry what her own symptoms meant. She dreamed of home and the aloo paratha her mother made. On her phone, she scrolled through headlines about the virus's dangers. Quarantines, it was becoming clear, are designed to protect only those on the outside—those on the inside have to fend for themselves.

Thakkar decided to take the situation into her own hands. She video-called an Indian news station. "We are requesting for help from Indian government," she said in accented English, her face hidden by a surgical mask, her eyes bright with fear. She and other staff "do not want to stay in the same environment that we are, since we have found out there are coronavirus-infected people."

Thakkar wasn't the only one desperate enough to launch this kind of modern SOS, as a fellow Indian, a cook, had already been issuing video appeals via Facebook to the prime minister of India. Fuad, the Indonesian dishwasher, who was so resolute at the start, would also later beg his government to rescue him.

In making her plea, Thakkar joined hundreds of others broadcasting from the *Diamond Princess,* some with serious messages, others using their moment in the historical spotlight to write reviews of their every meal. Indeed, many passengers essentially streamed life on the inside with their smartphones. And what wasn't being FaceTimed up close was being captured from afar by TV cameras set up onshore. Helicopters buzzed the ship and literal boatloads of journalists pulled alongside as international interest in the ordeal intensified. The world couldn't look away because the corona-virus was now surfacing in scores of nations, and it was becoming clear that what Thakkar and the rest were suffering might provide a glimpse of what everyone would soon endure. Indeed, the num-ber of *Diamond Princess* cases was exploding to such an extent that by day 9, when it reached 218, the ship had more cases than every nation in the world except China.

5. *The Suite View*

Six decks above where Thakkar was entombed, the Goldmans and the Jorgensens watched the drama unfold from their neighboring mini-suites. On their combined balcony, they had a view of men in hazmat suits marching passengers to ambulances, but it didn't seem likely to them that they'd get sick. They were the kind of se-niors who hit the gym rather than putting on pounds by the pool during cruises, who always took the stairs, and who still seemed to have more vigor than many people half their age.

Certainly the quarantine was an inconvenience: they had to frantically shuffle schedules and delegate business tasks back home. But they were able to work remotely, even if they had to wake up at 2 a.m. to account for the time difference. Otherwise, the quarantine had its bright spots: Fancy meals were dropped at their door, the balcony provided ample fresh air, and thanks to being in connected quarters, their best friends could come over whenever. Both couples' suites contained two areas, each with its own TV, an essential convenience for the Goldmans, who could never agree on whether to watch sports (Carl Goldman) or the Hallmark Channel (Jeri Goldman) and would otherwise have (somewhat) jokingly bickered over the remote. Ultimately, the Americans recognized they were lucky, and they were determined to look on the bright side of things.

This mindful optimism was actually the origin of their friend-ship. The Goldmans and the Jorgensens had met about a decade before at a motivational life-coaching training. Together, all four now subscribed to a set of teachings that boiled down to "the law of nonresistance," as they described it—fundamentally, making the best of the current moment. They had all used it to overcome the doldrums of middle age, and the Jorgensens taught a bit of it in their rehab center. Now, as Jerri Jorgensen said, "this is a chance for me to see if I'm ready to live what I'm teaching."

To stay fit, they made an obstacle course and raced through their joined rooms, and they washed their laundry in the bathtub to reduce the workload on the crew. The four shared a similar, zany humor, and the husbands played goofballs to their deadpan wives to relieve everyone's anxiety with laughter. Carl even began blogging his upbeat perspective of life on the ship: "My wife's reaction to the toilet paper" being delivered "was like giving her a diamond ring."

Unlike Thakkar, they never feared for their lives or livelihoods. They were healthy and had American passports and successful businesses, and a senator's aide had personally assured them that their situation was being monitored. But as the four watched a movie on the evening of Valentine's Day, not long before the quarantine was scheduled to end, Jerri Jorgensen became feverish. They didn't call the ship's medical center, figuring they'd see how she felt the next morning—and by then she was better.

Coincidentally, a knock rattled the door that morning. Several days earlier, the Jorgensens had been swabbed because Mark was taking immunosuppressants for a kidney transplant, putting him at increased risk for the coronavirus. Now the test results were being delivered by Japanese health workers in hazmat gear. They didn't speak English, so they thrust a piece of paper toward Mark, showing a positive result. "Wow, okay, when do you need me?" Mark said. But the masked head shook no. It was Jerri Jorgensen who was being summoned. Jerri: a mountain biking and workout fanatic who had her white hair done up in a fauxhawk, the Amigo who had always been the healthiest. On day 12, she became one of the 285 positives from the *Diamond Princess*.

Jerri wasn't given long to load a backpack. She chose not to take anything sentimental—just her passport, wallet, some toiletries, and a book called *The God Who Weeps*. It taught an appropriate lesson for the time, she said, that "God is not this ruler with a magnifying glass, waiting for us to screw up so he can zap us, but sympathizes."

It wasn't an option for Mark to join her, and when the time came, Jerri told him, "See ya when I see ya," trying to lighten the moment. Then, following the law of nonresistance, she let an ambulance bear her away, telling herself: *Next adventure!* She watched out the window as they drove four hours beyond Tokyo's conurbation. The day darkened. Streetlights sharpened. She had no idea where she was being taken.

Not long after she left, the remaining Amigos found out that all of the 428 Americans aboard the "floating petri dish," as Carl called it, were going to be evacuated by the United States government. Mark considered rejecting the offer, but eventually he and the Goldmans decided that there was no point in him waiting; he wouldn't be able to see his wife in the hospital, anyway—and he could always fly back if she took a turn for the worse. For the first time, Carl's lighthearted blog took on a dark tone. "We are shaken and devastated that we have been removed from our friend," he wrote. "The next league of our journey may take days. I am uncertain when I will be able to post again."

6. The Hot Zone

Even before the world's attention fixated on the *Diamond Princess,* Dr. James Lawler knew what was coming. Lawler, a director at the Global Center for Health Security, had previously worked on pandemic preparedness in the White Houses of both George W. Bush and Barack Obama. As disturbing data had begun emerging from Wuhan, Lawler and numerous other infectious-disease experts and senior government officials had kept up a worried discussion on a private email chain titled "Red Dawn." On January 28, while most of the world was oblivious to the exploding pandemic, Lawler had written darkly: "Great Understatements in History . . . Pompeii—'a bit of a dust storm[,]' Hiroshima—'a bad summer heat wave[,]' AND Wuhan—'just a bad flu season.'"

But what, exactly, the federal government should do about the emerging pandemic, as well as the Americans trapped in increasingly dire straits on the *Diamond Princess,* was unclear. By early February, the Trump administration's Coronavirus Task Force was debating responses to the spiraling catastrophe. The CDC recommended not bringing the American passengers home—the thinking being that they might carry the disease with them to the United States, which still had very few confirmed cases, and Japan could capably handle the quarantine.

But as the number of infected ship guests exploded, one American passenger, Arnold Hopland, called his friend, Republican congressman Phil Roe of Tennessee. Hopland is a doctor, and his detailed testimony of the unfolding disaster convinced Roe that action needed to be taken. At a congressional briefing about the coronavirus, Roe managed to catch the attention of Robert Kadlec, a senior official in the Department of Health and Human Services, with promises of an "ace in the hole on this ship" who could offer "on-the-ground" intel.

An international conference call was arranged in which Roe and Hopland spoke with senior officials from the Trump administration, the CDC, and the State Department. From his room on the ship, Hopland made the case that he and other Americans could be safely repatriated and then quarantined in the United States. If they weren't evacuated soon, he argued, they would be in danger. Congressman Roe backed Hopland up. "I'm an old country doctor," said Roe, who once practiced as an ob-gyn, "and I was like, 'Let's get them off, or they'll be infected.'" Kadlec and the others were convinced.

When the government decided to act, officials knew exactly whom to call: James Lawler, who combined years of scientific expertise with field experience in the world's most dangerous hot zones. Along with a Harvard physician, Lawler took the reins of a squad of 15 professionals from federal Disaster Medical Assistance Teams. Officials from the United States and Japan had already been discussing disaster-evacuation scenarios in preparation for the scheduled Summer Olympics in Tokyo. Now they activated those protocols to smooth the American medical team's arrival. On Friday, February 14—around the same time Jerri Jorgensen was developing her fever—Lawler and his team assembled in the lobby of a Yokohama hotel.

Their plan was to test all the Americans aboard the *Diamond Princess* for the coronavirus—and then, 72 hours later, fly at least the uninfected ones out on chartered cargo jets. Those who tested positive would presumably be transferred to Japanese hospitals.

On Saturday morning, Lawler and three other American physicians followed a Japanese doctor onto the *Diamond Princess*. They were wearing special helmets and breathing oxygen fed from hoses via their hip-mounted respirators—high-end machines called

PAPRs that Lawler considered so important that he had made a stopover in Los Angeles to acquire them on his way to Japan. But through his face shield, he watched their street-clothed guide "screwing around with" his surgical mask, surprised that another medical professional could be so cavalier.

As they marched through the cruise ship galleries—eerie as a circus turned into a crime scene—he noted that some of the Japanese health workers were not observing quarantine protocols. While a portion were outfitted in hazmat gear, others were simply wearing blue bonnets and surgical masks. He spotted passengers moving freely around some parts of the ship, and regularly clothed crew, wearing only masks, swabbing down the hallways. No wonder the disease had continued its wildfire spread. He began to worry about the Japanese health workers who were shuttling between the ship and the pier where the rest of his team waited. As soon as he disembarked, he warned the Americans to isolate themselves as best they could and to keep six feet away from the Japanese health care workers at all times.

Lawler wasn't the only one who considered what he was seeing dangerous. Kentaro Iwata, an experienced Japanese virologist who visited the ship, later broadcast a video in which he described the quarantine as "completely inadequate in terms of infection controls." Ultimately, at least six Japanese bureaucrats came down with the virus from the *Diamond Princess,* as did a Japanese health worker. And Japanese officials eventually acknowledged the quarantine was flawed.

On Saturday afternoon, Lawler learned that the evacuation planes previously scheduled to arrive Monday night were now going to be on the ground the next day—Sunday. His team's ambitions to test everyone were reduced to making sure that all the passengers were healthy enough to endure long, uncomfortable flights home on cargo jets.

The next day, Sunday morning, Lawler's response team divided into three units and spread out across the ship, checking the American passengers. Lawler estimated that he walked 10 miles that day in his heavy gear. It was around 10 p.m. when Lawler tracked down the last American, in the crew quarters. When Lawler exited the *Diamond Princess,* his countrymen were filing off the ship in a cold rain, their luggage hauled toward a line of buses by Japanese in hazmat suits. Dozens of Americans decided to stay behind for various reasons, but those consenting to be evacuated were now headed to the airport.

As they left, Lawler rushed back to the hotel, packed, and then, together with the Harvard doctor, frantically searched the deserted streets for a taxi, worried they were delaying the evacuation flights. It was around 1 a.m. when they finally found a ride, and the cabbie earned a big tip by racing the wrong direction up one-way streets to the airport. But rather than missing their planes, the doctors found them empty, except for crew. Something was very, very wrong.

7. The Goat Rodeo

The Amigos, reduced now to three, along with the 325 other American evacuees, were still waiting on the buses. They had spent three hours idling on the pier and then, once they drove to the airport, sat on the tarmac for two more hours. Now, as the delay extended into a sixth hour, the passengers were nearing revolt. They were exhausted. And more problematically for the largely elderly passengers: the buses had no bathrooms.

Meanwhile, in Washington, DC, where it was still Sunday afternoon, the fate of the waylaid evacuees was being decided. Around the time the passengers were exiting the *Diamond Princess,* Japanese officials had blindsided their American counterparts with the news that some of the passengers boarding the buses had actually tested positive several days before. Soon many of the highest-level members of the Trump administration's coronavirus response team, including Dr. Anthony Fauci, were arguing about what to do. Representatives from the CDC continued to fear spreading the virus. William Walters, the deputy chief medical officer for the State Department, wanted to bring everyone home anyway. Those urging the evacuation noted that the planes had been prepared with isolation units to contain the sick.

As the debate raged, the evacuees were demanding to be let off the buses, quarantine be damned, to find a bathroom. Carl was breathing so hard his masked breath fogged his glasses as he strained to control his bladder. Some seniors were crying. Finally, a few were allowed to relieve themselves in bottles beside the bus or were brought to a nearby terminal.

In the end, Walters and the State Department won the argument. Kadlec, the official from Health and Human Services, supported Walters and said later that "the notion of leaving Americans behind at that stage of the operation was not acceptable." But the CDC, still worried about airlifting the virus to America, disagreed with the decision so vehemently that it refused to be named in the news release announcing it. (Officials from the CDC did not respond to multiple requests for comment.)

Finally, after the lengthy and complicated process of being cleared remotely by Japanese immigration, which contributed to the delay, the passengers rushed off the buses and made for the jets. From his vantage, waiting on one of the two planes, Lawler saw the incoming stampede of seniors. He had hoped for an orderly boarding, but instead the scene resembled "a goat rodeo," he said, using a military term from his 20 years as a navy doctor. "There was just chaos."

As the crowd pressed onto the cargo plane, Lawler watched as sleep-deprived nonagenarians stumbled through rows of ancient airline seats, bolted into place across trip-hazard tracks that normally held pallets of supplies. Few people heeded his directions to sit. Instead, they fought toward four portable toilets that had been secured to the rear of each plane.

The holds of the toilets quickly filled; two soon reached capacity and were taped off. "The back of the plane just reeked," said Mark. "People were throwing up back there. It was so disgusting." Once in the air, Carl estimated, the line for the toilets on his plane ran about 50 people long and took 30 minutes to get through. Jeri Goldman said the "smell was unreal. We had to put ourselves under a blanket, it was so bad." Jeri eventually escaped by knocking herself out with Benadryl, and Carl was so exhausted he fell asleep without aid.

But a few hours later, Carl woke, feverish. A temperature check, and then he was marched to the back of the plane, which had been cordoned off by a large plastic sheet, duct-taped to the fuselage. There he tried to ignore the coughs of the other passengers and the stench now emanating from right beside him.

Lawler was on the second plane, separate from the Three Amigos. During the 16 hours of flying, Lawler ministered to evacuees —continuing his two-day, nearly sleepless marathon of doctoring —and was not surprised when some started showing symptoms in the air. He had already guessed that many were still incubating, but once he had his orders that everyone was coming home, he thought this was for the best, given that America would have the capacity to quarantine and treat everyone effectively.

When the flights landed in America, CDC officials took over the care of the asymptomatic passengers, such as Mark, who de-planed and would be quarantined for two weeks on military in-stallations. Meanwhile, the patients who'd tested positive at the last minute and mid-flight, as well as their spouses—including the Goldmans—continued on to Omaha, Lawler's home base. When they arrived, Carl felt strong enough to deplane on foot, but he was instructed to get into a stretcher—which made for dramatic TV footage as he was wheeled across a tarmac packed with ambu-lances. Emergency vehicles convoyed the sick to the University of Nebraska Medical Center, where Carl was transferred into Amer-ica's only federal quarantine unit. Finally the goat rodeo could end, and Lawler and his team took command of every detail of his patients' treatments. Still, he was forgiving of the improvised repatriation. "Overall, that's a remarkable feat," he said. "It was the best anyone could do, given the circumstances."

8. Homecoming

Carl Goldman was sealed away in an isolation room on a special floor of a medical building in downtown Omaha. The unit had last been used during the Ebola outbreak of 2014 and soon housed more than a dozen of the most serious American cases from the *Diamond Princess*—approximately as many confirmed cases as there were in the rest of the country at the time. To access the negative-pressure ward, Lawler and other medical officials donned top-level protective gear—PAPRs, Tyvek jumpsuits, and double gloves—all the while being monitored by another staff member to ensure each step was properly performed. When they exited, they show-ered in a specialized room.

Most of the time Carl communicated with his doctors through a double-paned window or a computer monitor and microphone. It was by video that he was informed that he had been officially quarantined by a second government, his own. Carl's experience of the disease was relatively mild—mostly a low fever and a cough—so he sweated and drank voluminous quantities of Gatorade while also trying to keep his life as normal as possible, keying away on his iPhone, calling in to work, and resolutely updating his blog.

As Carl's quarantine extended, the number of infections worldwide boomed exponentially—into the tens of thousands, then hundreds of thousands, and then, with the undiagnosed included, most likely into the millions.

Soon it was announced that two elderly passengers from the *Diamond Princess* had perished from the virus. Then a third. Then a sixth. "Our vacation," Carl blogged, "has now turned beyond tragic."

A month blurred past. Carl's fever faded, though it took longer for him to dislodge his cough. He paced, trying to regain his strength. As he improved, he was moved to a new room, which took him 14 steps to cross; eventually he was counting out 10,000 steps a day. He celebrated his 67th birthday with a cake slice topped by an unlit candle—no fire was allowed in the ward—and his doctors and nurses sang "Happy Birthday" over the camera feed. Lonely and homesick as Carl was, he considered himself fortunate, writing, "The blessing that tops the list is having total control of the television remote. That's a first in my marriage." As March progressed, he watched the coronavirus news constantly, trying to keep up with where the world was careening while he was in stasis.

Carl had long ago lost what the Four Amigos jokingly called "the Great Quarantine Race." His wife, Jeri, had finished her quarantine nearby, but never tested positive, displaying a hardiness she attributed to a mushroom powder and four-times-a-week cryotherapy sessions. Before long, she was back in California, overseeing their radio station again, though feeling something like a leper, as her return sparked panic in their community.

The Jorgensens were also home. Jerri Jorgensen's coronavirus infection had been luckily anticlimactic, and her greatest trial at the Japanese hospital occurred when Google mistranslated "constipation" while she was trying to communicate with her doctors. Once her 14 days were up, she flew home and was soon back to slickrock mountain biking. Not long after being quarantined on the military base, Mark Jorgensen had tested positive. He was airlifted to a hospital in Utah and then, as he had no adverse symptoms, eventually released to spend the rest of his quarantine at home, where he and Jerri cohabitated while wearing masks and staying six feet apart.

By the time Carl was released, in mid-March, the World Health Organization had declared the coronavirus a global pandemic. America's longest-serving quarantinee was a different man from the one who'd left for his cruise—his hair grown shaggy as that of a prophet returning from the wilderness. When he arrived home, his dogs licked him and his wife hugged him, and the physical contact alone felt like winning the lottery. That night, Jeri handed Carl the TV remote, for the first time, he claims, in their entire marriage. He selected the nightly news, filled with predictions of economic depression, and of a death toll worse than any war. It wasn't just that he'd changed; the world had changed, too.

9. *The Locked Church*

By the time Carl left quarantine, Jan Swartz, the president of Princess Cruises, had spent weeks sleeping with her phone at hand. Her days of crisis management began early and ended late. From 6 a.m. to 11 p.m., she commanded the company's response from a situation room in its California headquarters. Twice she flew to Japan to keep closer tabs on the operation and greet disembarking passengers. But even when the *Diamond Princess* was finally emptied in Yokohama, her trials continued.

In early March, an outbreak discovered aboard the *Grand Princess* required 2,000 passengers to be quarantined. Later that month, some 2,700 passengers who'd disembarked from another ship, the *Ruby Princess,* were asked by the Australian government to self-quarantine—at least 22 deaths would be connected to this outbreak, and a homicide detective would later be tasked with investigating whether the crew had misled authorities. (In a statement, Swartz said that Princess Cruises would cooperate, calling the inquiry "an opportunity for all to learn from this tragic event.")

Reporters for *Bloomberg Businessweek* found that executives at Princess and Holland America Line—which are run by the same parent company, Carnival Corporation—kept ships sailing despite being aware of the coronavirus danger. Roger Frizzell, the chief communications officer for Carnival Corporation, said it was "utterly absurd to believe a cruise vacation company had any foresight that COVID-19 would become a global pandemic when . . . governments and experts around the world had no such insight at the time." Cruise ships operated by other companies were similarly caught up in the crisis. Eventually, the CDC would find evidence of at least 25 ships incubating the coronavirus, and an investigation by the *Miami Herald* would link 2,592 infections and 65 deaths to cruise ship outbreaks, while emphasizing that the true number was probably higher.

In mid-March, the day after the World Health Organization declared the coronavirus a worldwide pandemic, Swartz finally called a stop to all her cruises. Critics said the decision was long overdue. "We were making the decision as quickly as we could," Swartz told me, "based on the information that we had." Within a day, all other major cruise lines also called a halt. The cruise ship era had ground to a stop, and possibly ended forever, as the industry faces unprecedented legal and financial challenges.

Before long, Yardley Wong and her husband and son were settling back into a semi-normal version of life in Hong Kong—the whole family having dodged infection after their preemptive self-imposed quarantine. Hong Kong was successfully stamping out minor flare-ups of the virus, for after discovering its first case just three days after America found its own, it had quickly introduced many of the regulations that the United States would adopt only months later—social distancing, travel restrictions, and closing public institutions and schools. The decisive actions of Hong Kong and other places—such as Taiwan, South Korea, and New Zealand—meant they had just a tiny fraction of the cases in America. Their quick efforts had actually been informed by insights drawn from the *Diamond Princess:* as the ship became a self-contained floating experiment, it provided the world's best data set on the virus, confirming crucial facts about how the disease spread, especially through asymptomatic carriers.

In late March, the CDC reported that out of the *Diamond Princess*'s 3,711 passengers and crew, 712 had tested positive. Eleven Americans were still hospitalized in Japan. Nine people had died. These numbers were infinitesimal compared with the vast casualties steadily accumulating across the globe, but these were a few of the original germs from which a huge tragedy would grow.

Most regions were not dealing with their outbreaks as successfully as Hong Kong, especially America. "We're prepared, and
we're doing a great job with it," President Trump declared on
March 10. "Just stay calm. It will go away." Two days later, Lawler
wrote to numerous senior government officials on the "Red Dawn"
email chain and desperately urged implementation of stronger vi-
rus-control measures, similar to what "has worked in Hong Kong."
The 80-page email chain, first quoted in the *New York Times,* docu-
ments in extraordinary detail the White House's failure to heed
numerous warnings in time to stop the virus. "We are making every
misstep leaders initially made . . . at the outset of pandemic planning in 2006," Lawler declared. "We have thrown 15 years of insti-
tutional learning out the window and are making decisions based
on intuition," he wrote, predicting catastrophe. During his time
working for Bush and Obama, Lawler had participated in simula-
tions of similar pandemic scenarios, and what he was seeing now,
he told me, was "kind of like watching a movie that you've watched
before."

When the time came for Captain Arma to leave the ship, the
Diamond Princess was empty. Thakkar, Fuad, and many other crew
members had been airlifted home by their governments—though
long after the American evacuation, and only after they issued
more pleas on social media.

Before bidding goodbye to the ship, Arma had stood alone on
the glass-walled bridge. The normally stoic captain was emotional.
He had been with the boat since it was built and had guided it
safely through every storm, until this one. He felt like he understood what he called her "beautiful soul."

One last time, he switched on the PA, in order to speak to the
ship itself. It wasn't her fault, he told her. He promised that they
would see each other again, and he wished her a good night, his
words echoing in the vacant galleries and cabins. They had done
their best, he and his ship—and like all good captains, he was the
last person to leave. As he strode off the gangway in his crisp uniform, he was the very image of debonair fortitude. Except his true
expression was hidden behind a protective mask.

It was a mid-March night when he returned to his seaside Italian hometown. Everything was locked down; the streets were deserted. At Italy's overwhelmed hospitals, hundreds of patients were
perishing every day. Arma asked his driver to stop at an ancient

basilica, which held an icon that had succored seafarers for millennia, through medieval and modern plagues. In times like this, what more could a man do? The Catholic captain bowed his head, and outside the locked church, he prayed. For himself and his family. For the souls of his former passengers. For the dead, and for those still living.

Mississippi: A Poem, in Days

FROM *Vanity Fair*

Day *1*

22 AMERICANS ARE dead from coronavirus, and Donald Trump tweets, "We have a perfectly coordinated and fine tuned plan at the White House for our attack on CoronaVirus."

I hear from Joe Osmundson, writer, friend, and scientist, that I should not attend the Association of Writers Programs, a conference I say I am too tired to attend, a conference where I will not be paid for attending. "The government is way behind on this," Joe writes. "Experts in our community are the best we have. I've been talking to a lot of friends working on this, and I trust them a lot."

"Should I fly, fam?" I ask him.

"It's not 'US' we're doing this for," he texts back. "The risk for you is still low, but it's kinda like what do we owe our elders and the folks with compromised immune systems."

"Thanks for this," I write back. "I'ma sit my ass at home and not go to these other events on my schedule."

These other events are paid readings I'm supposed to do in Ohio and West Virginia. These events are where I make most of my money. The first event in Ohio is sold out, but I tell myself that I'm sure they'll postpone before the 10th. I assume the same thing about West Virginia.

I am lonely. I am afraid.

I drive to the casino in Tunica, Mississippi, one of the poorest counties in the United States, and lather my hands in sanitizer.

It could all be so much worse, I tell myself, not accounting for how bad I will make it.

Day 2

31 Americans are dead from coronavirus, and after meeting with Republican leaders, Donald Trump says, "It's about 26 deaths, within our country. And had we not acted quickly, that number would have been substantially more."

These paid events I am booked to attend have yet to be canceled. It took Grandmama, the person who will get most of the money I make for these trips, a year working in the chicken plant to make the kind of money that awaits me for these two events.

Grandmama is one of the elders Joe talked about. She is a 90-year-old Black woman from Mississippi, and her immune system is severely compromised. She believes she is still alive because of hard work and Jesus Christ.

I have my agency tell the folks in Cincinnati that I will not under any circumstance be signing books or shaking hands at the event.

We all have to be safe.

Later that night, I sign books. I shake hands. I hug people. I feel love. I lather my hands in sanitizer. A monied man at the event gives me a ticket to see Lauryn Hill, who is also in Cincinnati. I tell organizers of the event that I'd rather go to the Lauryn Hill show than go to dinner.

I skip Lauryn Hill.

I skip dinner.

I congratulate myself on skipping both, on looking out for elders, and people like my grandmama with compromised immune systems.

It could all be so much worse, I tell myself.

Day 3

38 Americans are dead from coronavirus, and Donald Trump says, in his address to the nation, "The virus will not have a chance against us. No nation is more prepared or more resilient than the United States."

I am outside of my hotel in Cincinnati, waiting for a car service to drive me to Marshall, West Virginia. When the lanky old white man with large knuckles pulls up, I place my bags in his trunk. I do not shake his hand. Neither he nor I have on a mask or gloves. I am headed to West Virginia to get this money in the back seat of a new black car driven by an old white man.

I lather my hands in sanitizer.

Barely out of Cincinnati, the driver tells me he is a preacher. We talk about his church, his calling, his time living in the Bronx, his wife's abusive upbringing, all the powerful men he's driven place to place. He stops talking for a bit, and I look at the land we're zooming by. I am a writer. I should be writing about land I've never seen. I lather my hand in sanitizer, open my phone to type a sentence.

"It could all be so much worse," I write.

I get to West Virginia two hours before I'm supposed to have dinner with the organizers of tonight's event. Kristen walks me from the hotel around the corner to the restaurant. There is a long table of around 10 folks already sitting down.

"How y'all doing?" I ask, faking a laugh. "I guess we're not doing handshakes, huh?"

I am forever a fat Black boy from Jackson, Mississippi. I hate to be trapped in white places where I do not know anyone Black. My mama and grandmama rarely sit with their backs to doors. I choose the seat at the end of the table, next to a young brother whose hairline makes me remember Mississippi.

Under the table, I lather my hands in sanitizer.

I am sitting across from two powerful white people whose rhythms I cannot pick up. I cannot tell when they will laugh, when they will fidget. I cannot tell if they actually laughed or fidgeted. The white woman in front of me does not want to be there. I find out that the university is preparing to suspend in-person classes and begin distance learning.

No one is coming to this reading tonight, I tell myself. That's definitely for the better, as long as I can still get my check.

I order a Thai cauliflower wrap and fries. There is no way I'm eating that wrap. Or the fries.

I eat all but one of the fries when the brilliant brother with the familiar hairline offers me some sanitizer.

"You think we could shake hands now?" he asks.

"Oh absolutely," I say, and shake the hands of all the incredible students, thanking everyone for wanting to come out in such a scary time.

I ask for a to-go box for my wrap and say that I hope to see y'all at the reading. On the way to the reading, I stop back by the hotel because I don't need my backpack smelling like old cauliflower. White people treat Black people who smell like old cauliflower like Black people.

I'm scared. I'm tired. I'm lonely. I need my check. I don't want to be treated like a Black person by white people while trying to dodge coronavirus.

It's hot in my room. I'm sweating way too much. I take off the shirt beneath my meager hoodie. It's drenched. I place the cauliflower wrap on the counter.

I think I have coronavirus.

Or I'm just fat. Or I'm just nervous.

I think I have coronavirus.

I get to the venue. The white woman who greets me walks with a limp. I walk with a limp. She kindly takes me to the greenroom. A gentle tall white man knocks on the greenroom door and pulls out a huge bottle of sanitizer.

"Your agency told us you needed this."

"Oh wow," I say, trying to act like I had no idea. "That's weird. Thanks."

After the reading, some of the astounding students whom I had dinner with come onstage and ask me to sign their books, take pictures, shake hands. I sign their books, take pictures, shake hands. I walk out to the foyer, sit at a table, and sign more books. After all the books are signed, I walk out and meet the gentle tall white man who gave me the sanitizer. He is going to be taking me back to my hotel in his truck.

We talk about coronavirus. We talk about Randy Moss. We talk about Jason Williams. We talk about coronavirus.

As we get to my hotel, I'm wondering whether I'm supposed to shake his hand since I'm convinced both of us have coronavirus.

The tall gentle white man keeps both hands on the steering wheel and tells me bye.

"Thanks," I say out loud.

My room smells like old cauliflower. I take two showers, lather my hands in sanitizer, and I try to dream.

Day 4

40 Americans are dead from coronavirus, and Mississippi governor Tate Reeves is cutting short his European vacation because of Donald Trump's European travel restrictions.

At five in the morning, another white man picks me up to drive me to the airport. He does not speak. I give him a big tip when he drops me off. He holds the money like I'd hold a boogery Kleenex given to me by a white man driving me to an airport.

"Thanks," I say out loud.

I am wearing a black hoodie, a black hat, a black Bane mask, black headphones. Hanging around my neck are two dog tags. One, a quote from James Baldwin, says, "The very time I thought I was lost my dungeon shook and my chains fell off." The other, a quote from Lucille Clifton, says, "they ask me to remember but they want me to remember their memories and i keep on remembering mine."

I take a selfie on the plane and place it on Instagram with the caption: "Strange times when you have to be on the road to make money to help care for a miraculous 90 year old woman who you won't be able to touch for 14 days . . . Kindness. Tenderness. Generosity. We can do this."

Fourteen days, I tell myself. *It could all be so much worse.*

"The virus will not have a chance against us," Donald Trump says, later that afternoon.

Day 5

413 Americans are dead from coronavirus, and Donald Trump will not say, "I am sorry."

Governor Tate Reeves decides that the one abortion clinic in Mississippi is not an essential business that should remain open, but gun stores are. I've written around Tate without saying Tate's name for eight years.

In college, my partner, Nzola, and I got into an altercation with two fraternities on Bid Day. Some fraternity members wore confederate capes, Afro wigs, and others blackened their faces. I've written about how they called us "niggers." I've written about how they

called Nzola a "nigger b——." I've written about that experience
and guns. I've written about that experience and bats. I've written about that experience and how my investment in patriarchy
diminished Nzola's suffering.

I have never written about the heartbreak of seeing the future
governor of Mississippi in that group of white boys, proudly representing the Kappa Alpha fraternity and its confederate commitment to Black suffering. I have never admitted that after playing
basketball against Tate all through high school, and knowing that
he went to a public school called Florence, not a segregation academy, like so many other white boys we knew, it hurt my feelings to
see Tate doing what white boys who pledged their identities to the
Old South ideologies were supposed to do.

When I saw Tate in that confederate cacophony of drunken
white boyhood, doing what they did, I knew he could one day be
governor of Mississippi and president of the United States.

That is still the most damning thing I can ever say about a white
boy from Mississippi.

Day 6

9,400 Americans are dead from coronavirus, and Donald Trump
will not say, "I was wrong."

Mama is scared because the nurse we pay to take care of Grandmama will not wear her mask for fear that it could hurt my grandmama's feelings.

I am scared because Mama will not stop going to work. She
sends me a eulogy she wants me to read if she dies. The eulogy
confuses me. There is so much left out. She wants people to know
her dream was to be of use to the world, and particularly Mississippi. But the eulogy is more about the places Mama has been than
the justice work she's done. I do not argue with Mama. I tell her
that if she dies before I die, I will read the eulogy as it is written.

It could all be so much worse.

I get an email from the writer Cherry Lou Sy, saying that one
of those dead 9,400 Americans is my former student Kimarlee
Nguyen. Kimarlee and I shared a classroom at Vassar College.
Long before she was my student, Kimarlee would greet me with
this raspy offering:

"Yo, Kiese!"

When we finally shared a classroom, I was unable to adequately protect Kimarlee from the phantoms haunting most American classrooms. Phantoms need hosts. Many white hosts need phantoms. These phantoms encouraged Kimarlee to write her Cambodian self out of her writing. They disciplined her for not erasing her family's rememories of the Khmer Rouge.

Kimarlee accepted her sadness, her fatigue, her anger, and then along with James and Charmaine, she willed herself to write more deeply into the historic imagination of ancestral spirits.

I always assumed coronavirus would take my grandmama, my mama, my aunties, my friends, me, possibly in reverse order.

I never ever assumed it would take my students.

Day 7

104,051 Americans are dead from coronavirus, and Donald Trump will not say, "I am sorry." After Darnella Frazier, a 17-year-old Black girl from South Minneapolis, courageously films police executing a survivor of coronavirus named George Floyd, and Breonna Taylor, an EMT tasked with aiding those with coronavirus, is shot by police five times in her own house, incredibly effective protests begin out in the United States.

The week before savvy young folks longing to breathe and break fill Jackson, Mississippi, streets, a lone white Jewish teacher in Oxford, Mississippi, cuts his hands and places bloody handprints all over the biggest confederate monument on the campus of "Ole Miss." The Jewish brother spray-paints "spiritual genocide" on all four sides of the monument before being arrested.

Instead of covering the monument, workers are told to cover "spiritual genocide" with what looks like swaddling cloth.

I help bail the Jewish brother out. I help bail out folks in Mississippi, in Minneapolis, in Louisville.

I go home alone.

I am 45 years old, the exact age Grandmama was when I was born. Just like Grandmama at 45, I live alone in Mississippi. Yet unlike Grandmama, I have no children, no grandchildren. I own no land, no garden, no property, and I am afraid of walking in my neighborhood under the light of a moon or sun.

This should not haunt me. But phantoms move at their own speed.

I sit in this house, once the site of a confederate mansion, alone, afraid to go outside, afraid to let anyone outside see me.

I am more successful than I've ever imagined. Yet, I am terrified of sleeping because my body no longer knows how to dream. I know that people die in their dreams. I am not afraid of death. I am afraid of being killed while dreaming. Driving while Black. Jogging while Black. Dreaming while Black. Fighting while Black. Loving while Black. I wonder if movement, mobility, love are the features of Black life the worst of white Americans most despise.

Day 8

108,278 Americans are dead from coronavirus, and Donald Trump will not say, "I am sorry," or "I was wrong."

It is my mama's birthday. I planned to be with her today but I cannot. She is up north. I am down south. It is also Governor Tate Reeves's birthday. I wonder how he celebrates with the phantoms that hover around the Mississippi state flag I assume he keeps somewhere in his house.

Day 9

113,774 Americans are dead from coronavirus. I wonder why so many white folks are contacting me today. Half are asking me if I'm okay. Half are telling me that they are ready to learn.

Fuck. Fuck.

I drive by the two massive confederate monuments in Oxford. Black officers are guarding them both. I want to ask the brothers if they are humiliated guarding monuments that commemorate our destruction. When they start answering, or radioing for backup, I want to say, "Oh, one sec, bruh."

Then I want to blast the first verse of "Fuck tha Police."

I imagine the brothers, parked in the shadows of the armed monuments, banging a beat on top of their cruisers, and all of us rapping "Fuck tha Police" until backup arrives.

When the white officer arrives, I imagine getting all bougie

Black professor on them, explaining that white Mississippians cling to the confederacy not because they lost the Civil War, but because they cheated in a rigged battle against Black Mississippians. Their monuments are memorials of our suffering at the hands of folk who never had to pay, play, live, or fight fair.

But they already know that. Every Mississippian, whether they admit it or not, knows that.

What they don't know is that "Fuck tha Police" was one of our memorials, one of our most evocative monuments. And every member of N.W.A. had roots in the south. I wanted to play it so badly as I watched that police precinct in Minneapolis burn and when Trump sicced his National Guard on peaceful protesters so he could get a photo Beelzebub would be jealous of.

I want to bump "Fuck tha Police" right now.

The existence of the song is proof that even if we could not bring as much material suffering to white folk as they did to us, we could memorialize and channel the spirits of those beaten and killed by nasty-ass cheaters. Mama's greatest worry is that I will be shot out of the sky by these cheaters. She is right. One day, I will not get up off the ground. Mama knows that in my dreams, we soar, bulletproof. And often, we crash. In my actual dreams, I run like Ahmaud. I shoot midrange jumpers like George. I heal like Breonna. I rap every lyric to "Fuck tha Police" in a Monte Carlo packed to the brim with them and Mingion and Tim and Henry and David fiending for new ways to love each other.

I fantasize about doing to white folks and their police what they do to us. And more than fantasize, I remember and relish publicly rapping words Grandmama could never whisper outside of her house.

But there is a way to commemorate our losses and our wins without humiliating queer folks, and subsequently morally debasing those of us who are not queer. Those who we seek to humiliate, we eventually seek to destroy.

And that first verse of "Fuck tha Police" does not fairly memorialize or commemorate the lives of queer folks. I had to stop rapping to it over two decades ago. I had to stop listening to it in 2015. As absurd as it sounds, the only thing harder than giving up "Fuck tha Police" was giving up lying to people I purported to love, giving up disordered eating, and giving up gambling.

Queer antagonism, like trans-antagonism, like anti-Blackness, is an addiction broken only by honest reckoning, consistent practice, and the welcoming of radical spirits.

Like most Mississippians, I am an addict. Like most Americans, I am a coward.

I wave at the Black officers guarding the confederate monuments. They wave back. Adia Victoria's "And Then You Die" churns in the background, and I drive myself home.

Fuck. Fuck.

Day 10

125,039 Americans are dead from coronavirus, and Donald Trump has not publicly worn a mask. The tender nurse we pay to take care of my grandmama has contracted coronavirus, and the Mississippi legislature—pressured by young people's power and the threat of losing money—has finally agreed to take down the Mississippi flag. Though it would have been politically devastating, Governor Tate Reeves could have stopped or slowed the flag from coming down.

I want to believe Tate did right for Mississippi because he remembers how wrong Black Mississippians have been done by white folks in Mississippi.

I cannot substantiate my belief.

Day 11

126,929 Americans are dead from coronavirus. While the virus is surging in Mississippi, Governor Tate Reeves vetoes a bill passed unanimously by the legislature that grants relief and forgiveness to residents in Jackson who cannot pay their water bill.

I tell myself it could all be so much worse.

Day 12

128,761 Americans are dead from coronavirus, and according to civil rights icon Frankye Adams-Johnson, it doesn't matter if Governor Reeves or President Trump makes masks mandatory, says "I'm sorry" or "I was wrong."

The Awakening, she says, has begun.

The Mississippi flag no longer exists, and Ms. Frankye Adams-Johnson says that these times are biblical. Growing up in Jackson, Ms. Adams-Johnson was one of our civil rights superheroes. She grew up the child of sharecroppers right outside Jackson. Frankye marched with students from Brinkley high school to support protesters doing the lunch counter sit-ins downtown. Before they could get downtown, the high school students were arrested. Since there were too many students to fit in the paddy wagons, the police put the Black children in garbage trucks and took them to jail. An officer hit Frankye in her back with one of his rifles, then cocked the rifle and aimed it at her head. Frankye was 17 years old the week Fannie Lou Hamer was nearly beaten to death in Winona and her youth leader, NAACP field secretary Medgar Evers, was assassinated in his Jackson driveway. Not soon after that, Frankye left Mississippi for New York.

I lather my hands in sanitizer before asking Frankye what she thinks of the young people who are risking it all for freedom during a pandemic, what the fall of the Mississippi flag means to her, and if it could all be so much worse.

"That rag sheet coming down won't erase history but, let me tell you something, Kiese, it sure helps release some of the pain I carried.

"When we sang we shall overcome out in front of the Black Masonic temple, those crackers would be out there with that rag sheet talking about, 'We shall keep the niggas down.'

"Mississippi sent me running for freedom in New York in 1967. My son was born there. Thirty-three years later, New York sent me running back to Mississippi to breathe. The young folks are experiencing what we experienced. They are awakening to the smells of freedom.

"It's an awakening. Call it what it is.

"They know this thing is rotten. They see that America, as we know it, is crumbling. You know who the hippies were? They were the master's children who'd turned on their parents. I don't care who you are, once you get that awakening, you will risk it all for freedom.

"The coronavirus is just terrible, but it has a Biblicalness to it, you know? It's a rich time for writers to write. It's a rich time for awakenings. It's forced me to sit still and consider my own memories.

"The young people are working their way to the eye of the storm so we can all be free.

"They have given me so much joy. I worry though, about the battle scars, the trauma, the crumbs they will be given. You have to know yourself better than you know your enemy.

"That is what we didn't do.

"This is an awakening. But there are prices to be paid for awakening in this country. That's really all I can say."

I wipe the sweat from my neck, the tears from my eyes, and I lather my hands in sanitizer.

It could all be so much worse.

Day 13

130,646 Americans are dead from coronavirus. Mississippi is surging, and President Donald Trump and Governor Tate Reeves have failed to make masks mandatory, or say, "I was wrong. I am sorry."

Here's what I want to believe:

Tate Reeves and all these white Mississippians who, just like us, immediately smell the difference between a collard and a turnip, who come from sharecroppers, who hear that bended brilliance in the blues, who hate the way northerners use the south as a convenient shield against their trespasses, who feel the daily grace Black folks from the deep south have offered white folks from the deep south in the face of unrelenting humiliation, are being played by a devilish, desperate northerner who has allowed his daddy issues to ruin and eventually run his marriages, businesses, friendships, soul, and now his nation further into hell. There is a part of these white southerners—like Tate Reeves, our white cousin by blood and culture, who refuses to heed the spirits of awakening—that is not evil or irrecoverable, but just easily seduced by power, inferiority complexes, and a longing to be accepted by a manipulative maniac who glided into the presidency with the cowardly winds of white American resentment at his back.

Here's what I know to be true:

Tate Reeves and most of these white Mississippians are no more regionalists, or lovers of Mississippi and the deep south, than Donald Trump is a patriot and lover of the United States of America. They are not haunted by phantoms. They are dedicated ghouls, spirit-repellent patriarchs who use each other and a muddled understanding of Jesus Christ to ensure the suffering of the most vulnerable. Abusive power tastes, touches, smells, sounds, and feels really good to gobblers of grace. They are not 19-year-old boys trying to decide between right and wrong; they are grown men who have chosen to model meanness for their posterity. They will torture and humiliate everyone close to them to maintain the power to abuse. They will never ever say or mean, I am sorry for making living harder than it needs to be. I am sorry for feeding off your humiliation. I am sorry for never confessing my actual sins to the world. I am sorry that your life means less to me than my ego. They will never say, I am sorry. They will only remind Americans and southerners foolish enough to listen that it all could be so much worse.

The truth is, were it not for this awakening led by our young people and old spirits, they would be absolutely right.

Day 14

131,870 Americans are dead from coronavirus, and I am turning in my piece to the editors at *Vanity Fair*. I know there is no incentive, credential, or subsidy for the spirits that guide us. Every dime of the money I make from this assignment will go to help residents of Jackson who cannot pay their water bills.

We are awakened, I want to believe.

75 miles from the armed confederate statue in Oxford, Emmett Till's childish body was destroyed. 70 miles from that armed confederate statue, Fannie Lou Hamer was nearly beaten to death. 160 miles from that armed confederate statue, Medgar Evers was murdered as he entered his home. 80 miles from that armed confederate statue, Martin Luther King was murdered in Memphis.

It took way too much Black death to get here.

I am wandering around the spiritual consequences of materially progressing at the expense of Black death. I want to be courageous. I wonder, though, when courage becomes contagious—

when courage is credentialized, subsidized, and incentivized—if it is still courage at all.

Today, as I prepare to push send, and I lather my hands in sanitizer, it feels a bit too much like cowardice.

Maybe I'll wait to send tomorrow. Maybe I won't send at all.

The Lafayette County Board of Supervisors, a group of white men, unanimously vote to keep the armed confederate monument in the middle of Oxford, the town where I live, teach, and write.

Humiliation, agony, and death are what I feel.

"It could all be so much worse" is what the worst of white folks want us to recite.

The worst of white folk will not be persuaded; they can only be beaten. And when they are beaten, they fight more ferociously. They bruise us. They buy us. That is why we are so tired. That is why we are awakened. We are fighting an enemy we've shown exquisite grace, an enemy we've tried to educate, coddle, and outrun, an enemy that never tires of killing itself, just so it can watch us die.

Titillation.

I lather my hands in sanitizer and google gun shops in Lafayette County on my phone. I do not believe in guns. I do not believe in prisons. Yet I know I need one if I am to continue living alone in this Mississippi, American town.

I look at the grizzled cotton fields outside my truck window on Highway 6. I want to ask, Where am I?

But I know.

This is not home.

If this is home, it is not healthy.

I do not want to humiliate. I do not want to be humiliated. I do not want to kill. I do not want to be killed. I want us to be free. I know what I feel. I know what I've felt. I must buy a gun if I continue to live in Oxford, Mississippi, so I cannot continue to live in Oxford, Mississippi, no more. It took way too much Black death to get here, and here is where I'd love to live without guns, without prisons, without monuments of humiliation, without the undervalued expected sacrifice of essential workers, without the worst of white folks. Here is where I'd like to tenderly, honestly, radically live and love with you.

And here, one day, will be Mississippi.

LESLIE JAMISON

The Warmth of a Lost World

FROM *The New York Times Magazine*

THE LAST TIME I went to the Russian and Turkish Baths, tucked into the basement of an old tenement in the East Village, it was early March—right before the end of the world as we knew it. In retrospect, I'm sure the virus was down there with us, in that warren of saunas and steam rooms; in that blue-tiled plunge pool of icy water and that primeval nerve center called the room of radiant heat, a dark cave with a huge oven seething behind its rough walls, lined with wooden benches which had absorbed the sweat of thousands of strangers for more than a hundred years. This was no small part of the holiness of the baths for me, the way they brought together strangers, past and present: the tattooed hipster with a handlebar mustache who dunked his head under the icy water of the cold plunge with performative nonchalance; the impossibly thin old woman who looked like a once-ballerina or a once-junkie, her skin steaming in the darkness; and the swarthy Russian man with salt-and-pepper hair who moaned under the sway and crack of oak branches slapped across his back.

That winter evening I was a year into my separation—poised at the cusp of divorce, at the cusp of pandemic, at the cusp of my city's shuttering—but that night my body was close to the bodies of these strangers, whose stories I would never know. We didn't need to speak; we were sharing the heat and the darkness, tucked away from the chill. We were sharing our very bodies, sweating and exhaling into the same thick air we were all breathing. A few weeks later—once the virus filled our hospital wards and the city plunged into quarantine—everything about that night would come to seem not only impossible but unthinkable: that closeness and casual touch, all that mingled breath and sweat. That night would eventually seem like the distillation of what we lost. But back then, it still belonged to us, our bodies shrugging and sighing, our toes curled and our foreheads beaded, our bodies leaking tears of ache and release. We were part of something together, something big and silent and many-headed. It held us all.

Just a week before that final trip to the East Village baths, at the end of February, I flew to Istanbul to visit its legendary hammams. Turkey is home to some of the most stunning bathhouses in the world, and I was hoping that visiting these Old World ancestors of the East 10th Street baths might help me understand why I loved their descendants as deeply as I did.

Late February was the last moment when it still seemed possible that everything might not change; that for Americans, COVID-19 could remain a problem on the other side of the world. Coronavirus cases had recently peaked in China, and epidemics were blooming elsewhere—South Korea, Italy, Iran. The Istanbul Airport was decorated with now-ominous tourist banners that read GATEWAY TO ASIA, with immigration officers checking all our passports for stamps from China. Passengers in blue masks kept their distance from one another and warily eyed anyone who coughed or sneezed. But Turkey hadn't yet been hit by the pandemic, and in the hammams of Istanbul, I spent time in a world where it was still possible—still natural, still untroubled—to get close to the bodies of strangers. In those marble dens scattered across the city—Cemberlitas, Cagaloglu, Kilic Ali Pasa—there was no social distancing, only the humidity of collective exposure, naked skin on marble. Other people weren't yet seen primarily as potential disease vectors, but as subjects of pleasure, tender animals, hungry for care and touch, all of us lying side by side in the radiant heat.

The first hammam I visited was Cemberlitas—one of the oldest baths in the city, commissioned in 1584 by the head of the imperial harem—near the labyrinthine alleys of the Grand Bazaar and the old Ottoman arcades of the Misir Carsisi spice market, its crowded aisles lined with cases full of sugar-dusted Turkish delight and amber perfume bottles. Often built near mosques to allow for ablutions before prayer, hammams have deep roots in holy traditions, and the central chamber at Cemberlitas itself felt like a place of worship: an octagonal marble slab under a stone dome that showed the sky through round portals. Lying across that marble slab, my skin striped by the wavering shafts of sunlight, I felt less like a worshipping supplicant and more like an offering laid across an altar.

A woman named Gamze rubbed down my body with the *kessa*, a rough glove made from woven goat hair, and then draped my raw skin in the cascading bubbles of the swinging *torba*, a fine mesh towel dipped in copper tubs of olive-oil soap to heap shimmering white hills along the knobs of my spine, feathery and fizzy against my scrubbed skin, silken and gentle where the *kessa* had been vigorous and bracing. It was an experience of sublime submission, yielding to the kneading hands of a stranger, that was close to the opposite of the ceaseless bodily vigilance that would follow during quarantine and its containments: measuring my body's distance from other bodies, trapping my breath with a mask, caring for other people by staying away from them.

When the hammam arrived in the Western imagination, largely by way of eighteenth-century European travel narratives, it was a breathlessly described, Orientalist fantasy—a seductive, elusive cloister, a sexualized sanctum of intimacy and indulgence. In a letter dated April 1, 1717, the aristocrat and epistolary scribe Lady Mary Wortley Montagu describes visiting in the city of Sofia a set of baths "that are resorted to both for diversion and health," where "sofas of marble" are full of women reclining totally exposed: "all being in the state of nature, that is, in plain English, stark naked, without any beauty or defect concealed." More than a century later, *Le Bain Turc* (The Turkish Bath), a now-famous oil painting completed by Jean-Auguste-Dominique Ingres between 1852 and 1859, brought Montagu's portrait to visual life in its crowd of nude women reclining beside a tiled bath. They are curvy and bejeweled, naked save their golden bracelets, ruby-studded necklaces, and pearl-drop earrings. The world of the painting is at once sensuous and coy, simultaneously yielding to the gaze of a viewer —by proffering these naked bodies—and refusing it, by offering a glimpse into an ultimately inaccessible world beyond the viewer's reach and understanding.

Of course the Western fantasy of Turkish baths was always underwritten by racism disguised as veneration. David Urquhart, who became one of the most influential architects of the Victorian "Turkish bath movement" after returning from his service in the British Embassy in Constantinople at the end of the 1830s, described the ancient Turks as the "filthiest of mortals," who initially discovered public baths as a "practice of their enemies" before adopting and perfecting them. Eventually, Turkish baths came to represent a space of loosened bodily inhibition that was always largely a projection of desires that Victorians had trouble claiming for themselves. Part of the fantasy of the baths has always been about the grace of purgation—this urge to slough away the lesser parts of ourselves and let our better selves emerge instead: rarefied, whittled, purified. As the surgeon Erasmus Wilson wrote, "I hardly know a more curious or more beautiful sight than that of the healthy skin of a practiced bather, spangled over with limpid drops of perspiration like dewdrops on the petals of a rose."

The zealotry of these Victorian Turkish bath enthusiasts often reads like an investment in pleasure—the pleasures of proximity, thrilling contact, physical extremity—trying to cloak itself in the more serious clothing of medical necessity. During their surge of popularity across Britain and America in the mid- to late 1800s, Turkish baths were attributed with nearly mystical powers. They were not only purported to treat the symptoms of an impressive array of conditions—including rheumatism, leprosy, eczema, acne, gout, insomnia, constipation, opium craving, barrenness, night sweats, dropsy, dyspepsia, diabetes, St. Vitus's dance, herpes, bronchitis, paralysis, and insanity—but capable of elevating our souls. "As the sun benefits the whole animal and vegetable creation, so does the Bath greatly renovate our whole physical nature, and, thus purified, renders us more capable of appreciating our higher or spiritual nature," wrote Charles Shepard, the Brooklyn physician who built the first Turkish baths in America in 1863.

When Shepard opened his Turkish baths on Columbia Street, in Brooklyn Heights, however, business was slow. On the first day, "but one bather came," he wrote. "After four days there came four more, though one of them had been brought in by dint of persuasion." But Shepard advocated tirelessly his so-called "Improved Turkish bath," including an inspired pamphlet telling the story of how a depressed Cupid—drawn as a gnomelike man with wings protruding from his tunic and spurs on his boots—had been "persuaded to try a Turkish bath" and ultimately "was both cured and converted, and is now one of the heartiest champions of the hammam." By their fifth year, the Columbia Street baths were giving over 15,000 baths annually, and were soon joined by other baths across the city. "'Open the pores of the skin and let out the impurities,' is written by the very finger of God upon every human body," wrote the American doctor—and savvy entrepreneur—E. P. Miller in an 1870 pamphlet titled *The Improved Turkish Bath: What Is It, Who Should Take It, Why, When, How, and Where.* (On the last question, he was happy to suggest his own newly opened baths on West 26th Street.)

My favorite baths have always been the ones on East 10th Street, built in 1892 and housed for decades beneath three dormitory floors full of boarders. By the time I became a regular, more than a hundred years later, they were still tucked into the same basement, though it was no longer the same 10th Street; now there was a kava bar and a crystal store across the way. Downstairs, however, the primal intensities remained unchanged: the room of radiant heat still nearly 200 degrees, like a calloused body barely containing an incredible fever. (In 1993, one resident of a neighboring building complained that the heat from the saunas was so intense he could fry an egg in his own bathtub.)

It was during my early years of sobriety, a decade ago, that I first found solace in communal baths. In the absence of other forms of extremity, I was drawn to the quiet thrill of pushing my body to the edges of what it could stand. In the baths, I got so hot I couldn't think about anything but the heat, and in truth, I found relief in the discontinuity between the tangled abstractions of my own interior afflictions—a faltering relationship, a new life without booze—and the brute physicality of the baths, their steamy mists and icy plunge.

"The skin is what you live in; it is your habitation," Urquhart wrote in his 1865 *Manual of the Turkish Bath.* "There is an intoxication or dream that lifts you out of the flesh, and yet a sense of life and consciousness that spreads through every member." A century and a half later, when I stood in the room of radiant heat, pouring the ice-cold water over my body, relieving an unbearable heat with a nearly unbearable chill, it made me—briefly, gloriously—a stranger in the habitation of my skin, and then at home more fully than before. I could feel every part of myself in that heat, sweating and alive—an animal among animals, full of all the ordinary aches and hopes. My body wasn't something to be starved or cut or filled with booze until I blacked out; it was something to be taken care of. I found myself newly alive to my own pulse, seized by a pleasure that could hold discomfort in its open palms.

One winter night a year ago, I went to the baths with my friend Anna. I was just a few months into my separation and still struggling with the two nights a week I spent apart from my daughter. Anna and I both had babies who were somewhere else; at every moment they were not drinking from us, our breasts were filling up for the next time they would. We put on our plastic slippers and went underground, sat in the room of radiant heat, with a trough full of cold water and the skeletal ex-ballerina, who looked as if maybe she lived underground, as if she needed that hot room like God needed a holy book to live inside of. The heat was nearly unendurable, but that wasn't the problem so much as the point. I thought of something my friend Harriet had said: that we were always trying to call experiences either bearable or unbearable, as if they had to be one or the other, when they were often both at once. Which is one way to describe letting myself get impossibly hot, and then standing to dump the cold water over my head: how good it felt to need something so badly, then reach for it.

In Istanbul, I visited six hammams in 36 hours. The vaulted stone atrium, trickling fountain, and low couches full of lounging pillows at the Kilic Ali Pasa hammam, originally built by the sixteenth-century Ottoman architect Mimar Sinan, felt far removed—in their poshness—from the building's origins as a bathhouse for the royal navy. At the Ayasofya Hurrem Sultan, constructed in the shadow of the Hagia Sofia by the same architect for the emperor Sultan Suleiman's wife, Roxelana, there were partially excavated fragments of the original plumbing system visible under transparent floors. (Roxelana was enslaved early in life but ended up becoming a woman of unprecedented political power in the Ottoman Empire, and her bathhouse was the first in which the men's and women's areas were constructed as mirror images of each other.) At Cagaloglu, the most luxurious of all the hammams I visited, an elegant man greeted me at the door and asked if it was my first time at a hammam; when I told him the ones I had already visited, he looked at me as if I'd just said something utterly irrelevant and said, "This is your first time at a hammam."

The pleasure at Cagaloglu came at me from every direction: glass lanterns illuminating the sauna walls in jeweled shades of tangerine and cobalt; the clouds of bubbles from the *torba* touching me like something from another realm; my body, scrubbed and tingling and laid out on a warm towel, served strong black tea and fed dried apricots and almonds, sugared squares of Turkish delight presented on a silver-lidded platter. It felt less like a Turkish experience than the perfected version of a Western fantasy of a Turkish experience, as if Ingres's nineteenth-century painting had been brought to life.

My attendant, Ayten, smiled at me with a care that felt genuine as we transitioned from one pleasure to another, gently holding my elbow to move me between them, clasping my hand as we walked across the slippery marble floor of the central chamber. Our dynamic felt simultaneously absurd and strangely, unplaceably familiar, until I eventually realized it reminded me of caring for my toddler daughter back at home, except I had become the child. For an hour, Ayten was my mother, making sure my feet were carefully tucked beneath the striped maroon robe before she fed me tea and cherries, just like I always made sure my daughter's little legs were covered by our fuzzy blanket when we snuggled together on our couch at home to read books. "Get cozy!" she would say, less request than command.

It can be easy to believe pain has a monopoly on profundity, that we access truth or salvation through suffering, from the story of Christ's crucifixion to the mundane ravages of our own daily lives. But perhaps the Western obsession with Turkish baths, in all its fantasizing and fetishizing, has been in part an attempt to claim pleasure as something more than indulgence, more like a mode of survival. Pain claims so much of us; why not give pleasure its due when we can?

Visiting the hammams of Istanbul was like taking a rigorous course in pleasure itself, a syllabus committed to exploring the granular texture of bodily enjoyment, and to proving that pleasure holds its own pathways to meaning, that it might matter most at precisely those moments when it seems most out of place. Life finds unexpected ways to make this argument. In line at the grocery store a few weeks after I returned from Istanbul, just a few days before lockdown, with my own cart full of diapers and Pedialyte, I admired the cart of the elderly woman standing in front of me. It held nothing but cookies and beer. Her cart seemed to be telling me, *You'll need those diapers, but that's not all you'll need.* She had so many years of living under her belt. I bet she knew a fair amount about pleasure, and also about endurance—how each permits the other, and how impossible they are to separate.

Pleasure demands presence. It invites you to inhabit your body more fully; no part of you is held at remove. For centuries, the Turkish bath has embodied the seductive prospect of seeing other people's bodies not simply physically exposed but also psychically exposed, caught inside the particular vulnerability of enjoyment. There can be a radical honesty to pleasure, a profound nakedness in surrendering fully to unguarded, unselfconscious states of enjoyment. It's harder to hide or dissimulate when you're enjoying yourself.

Describing the baths in her eighteenth-century Turkish Embassy letters, Montagu was not only struck by them as spaces of exposure but by the fact that they functioned as a protected social space for women: "In short, it is the women's coffeehouse, where all the news of the town is told, scandal invented, etc." She was a foreigner describing intimacies she had no access to—spoken in a language she could not speak, fitted into narratives of her own design. What she was describing in her letters wasn't so much the culture itself but her own fantasy of a certain kind of intimacy and female society.

But beyond the screen of those projections, a robust culture of public bathing has been thriving for centuries. Over lunch one day in Istanbul, Sabiha Çimen, the Turkish photographer who took the photographs that accompany this article, told me about the Mihrimah Sultan, a hammam she used to visit. It always felt like a retreat from the city's frenetic bustle, she told me, another world within the ordinary world of the streets and crowds. A few hours later, I found its nondescript entrance above a staircase tucked beside a gas station on Fevzi Pasa, a busy road that took me past an evening-gown shopping district and a bridal-gown shopping district and a special micro shopping district that seemed to specialize exclusively in silken bathrobes.

The Mihrimah Sultan hammam had a different aesthetic than

the tourist hammams in the old city: less elegance, more comfort. The lounge had a big-screen TV and three drooping purple balloons tied to the plume of a potted fern; a big plastic column full of multicolored drugstore luffas stood like a sentinel in the corner. Two attendants smoked at the top of the staircase; another emerged from the office with a tub of hummus in one hand and a plastic bag of simit in the other. Inside the hammam itself, most of us wore only the plain black underwear we had rented for 5 liras apiece. Instead of fairy-tale mounds of shimmering white bubbles from the *torba*, we squirted drugstore shower gel across our backs. The staggering grandeur of the old-city hammams had been replaced by something humbler, the dusky sky visible through portals cut into the stucco dome, its curves streaked with rust-red trails of dripping water.

The pageantry of luxury had been replaced by genuine sociability, and the women gathered all around me with their friends and sisters and cousins and daughters, perhaps talking about some of the same things I spoke about with my friends back at the 10th Street baths: the hourly exhaustion of taking care of children; the guilt and weariness and gratitude of showing up for work and motherhood; and never having enough of ourselves to do justice to either one. In that heat, it was always harder to hide anything. We were wrung-out and woozy, blissfully depleted; there wasn't much energy left for dissimulation or sugarcoating. We were "stark naked, without any beauty or defect concealed." At the Mihrimah Sultan, the women conspired and consoled all around me, chatting about the smallest minutiae of their lives and resting their tired thighs and exposing their C-section scars, testifying with their very presence to our collective faith that taking care of our physical bodies could help alleviate their psychic burdens.

Gazing at the ghostly Brooklyn streets from my apartment window three weeks later, in the early days of quarantine—watching my toddler daughter try to feed my mother strawberries through a cell phone screen—the memory of those baths ached like a ghost limb, the memory of that way of being with strangers, brushing against their skin, sweat mingled with their sweat. During these past six months of isolation, as we have learned to keep our bodies at a distance—six feet away from one another, or homebound—I have found myself thinking frequently of the hammams of Istanbul, across an ocean, and the 10th Street baths, just across the East River, their crowded, humid rooms so much the opposite of our sparse streets. Communal baths offer a microcosm of the promises of urban living: How does sharing spaces of pleasure help bind people together? What do we lose when we lose the ability to live among the bodies of strangers? The baths distill the dream at the core of inhabiting a city: to feel connected to something larger than yourself.

The baths ask us to recognize in brute, visceral, undeniable terms the truth that every stranger's face conceals hidden layers of wariness and fragility: bad days at work, fights at home, kids who won't go to bed; and sudden pockets of joy: the weekend paper in bed on a lazy morning, a burger grilled in the park with a friend of many years, a child's glee at crafting a sandwich from two wooden slabs of bread and a wooden tomato. We can know intellectually that everyone we see contains multitudes, but it's easier to feel it in the baths, where everyone's impassivity is cracked open—at least in brief glimpses—by physical extremity and pleasure.

On the sidewalks these days, I've grown familiar with furtive, apologetic moments of eye contact with strangers, measuring the distance between our bodies and then apologizing to each other— with resignation, without language—for transgressing the margin. Whenever I see someone instinctively recoiling at unintentional contact, I find myself hoping that even as we keep our bodies far apart, we still find ways to tell one another, *You deserve to be touched.*

During the early stages of reopening New York City—when curbside retail returned in Phase 1, or outdoor dining in Phase 2 —I would sometimes joke with friends that the 10th Street baths would only reopen once we reached Phase 300. Though Istanbul's hammams reopened in June—many with temperature checks and attendants wearing face shields—it still seems far from a possibility here in New York. This way of being with strangers seems like the last one we'll get back.

But the question of whether we will ever return to the baths is more than simply logistical. Wondering whether we can ever truly return to them is a way of wondering whether we'll ever return to a state of bodily ease with strangers. How long will this muscle memory endure—the part of us that's wary of any kind of bodily proximity, that's wary of our own bodies and the bodies of others as vectors?

In the way that absence illuminates desire, and breakage illuminates function—you don't notice the doorknob until it twists off in your hand—quarantine has made it plain to me how much I miss the daily, unspoken, casual company of strangers, the people whose names and lives I'll never know, who populate my ordinary urban days with their bodies on the subway, their glances on the sidewalk, their stray comments at the ATM, their hands holding whole milk and gummy bears in front of me in the bodega line.

It was in the early months of my separation that I started to become acutely aware of this gratitude for the peculiar anonymous company that urban living offers—for the café just downstairs from my new apartment, where many of the same regular customers gathered each morning: the amiable elderly man chain-smoking and mansplaining transatlantic politics; the mom-friends with their parked bassinets; the twentysomething boys reading Bakhtin and Heidegger who never offered to help me carry my stroller up the stoop stairs. In the aftermath of my household unraveling, it was an acute and unexpected comfort to find this daily ragtag cohort just downstairs—a looser household, but a household nonetheless.

Walking late at night on Flatbush Avenue, I appreciated all the anonymous strangers I passed for the ways they suggested, even if I didn't know their stories, how many different ways it was possible to craft a life. The man buying mangoes at the bodega just before midnight? Maybe he was a father of five. Maybe he was a single father of five. Maybe he and his husband were trying to adopt. Maybe he and his wife had been trying to have a child for years. Maybe he and his wife knew they didn't want a child; maybe they were saving up to travel the world instead. Maybe he lived alone with his aging mother. Who could know his story? I never would. But I didn't need to. I only needed to know, through his presence on that sidewalk, that so many plotlines for a life were possible.

When we lose the ability to live among the bodies of strangers, we don't just lose the tribal solace of company, but the relief from solipsism—the elbow brush of other lives unfurling just beside our own, the reminder of other people's daily survival, the reminder that there are literally 7 billion other ways to be alive besides the particular way I am alive; that there are countless other ways to be lonely besides the particular ways I am lonely; other ways to hope, other ways to seek joy.

During the first five months of quarantine, the café below my apartment stayed shuttered. The sidewalk beneath its awning was littered with cigarette butts and the occasional empty beer bottle. Rats scuttled across the pavement at night, as desperate and confused as the rest of us. At one point someone propped a plastic wreath against the locked café door. It looked like a grave site. But at the end of August, nearly six months after quarantine began, the café reopened. My pleasure at its return was acute and bodily, like chugging ice water on a hot day. The people were once again gathered on the sidewalk—enjoying their coffee, the sunlight, the voices of their friends and the voices of strangers.

When we finally return to the baths, our ease won't be the same. It will always hold the memory of this virus and the collective isolation it has plunged us into. But perhaps the intimacy of our reunion won't be compromised but sharpened by deprivation, and it will be with deepened hunger that we find our way back into one another's company again.

To the Swimmer in the Borneo Rainforest

FROM *Off Assignment*

IT WAS THE end of July in the Borneo jungle, a place without clocks, days still guided by the sun's movements. You were leaning against your rusted silver truck, wringing calloused hands together, a brimmer hat pulled down low. I'd traveled by bus over the mountains from the town where I had been teaching English for the last eight months. We were the first ones to arrive at the volunteer base, a stilted wooden house burrowed amidst lush plants. We had little in common, you with your indigenous Dusun tongue, me with my American Midwest twang. But we were both young and bold and had seen a local NGO's Facebook plea for volunteers; the project in question used waterfalls to create electricity in rural villages. We both wanted to bring light.

The mission director was an elderly Malaysian man who spent his free time voyaging on foot into the jungle, collecting seeds of rare flora and preserving them in his backyard. Dotting his land were miniature palm trees, otherworldly orchids, and carnivorous pitcher plants. We sat beneath the shade of big green elephant ears, watching the other volunteers trickle in, a mix of peninsular Malaysians, Sabahans, Italians, and an Englishman. I realized I was the only woman on the team. "You'll go with him," the director said, motioning toward you. I nodded, making an internal pact to keep my hair up, hat down, and pull equal weight as the men; I would not be seen as a weak link.

You drove the truck while I rode shotgun. We ventured five

hours down that uneven dirt road, deep into the jungle that hadn't yet been destroyed by palm. I was annoyed you'd been assigned as my caretaker, but this amused you, judging by the glimmer in your eye on an otherwise stoic face. While we didn't speak much, you occasionally whispered phrases in Dusun, which I tried to recount in English. *Alawa*, you'd say, pointing at flowers out the window. *Beautiful.* Once we discovered we both knew all the words to Biz Markie's "Just a Friend," we played it on repeat from your cassette player.

We spent five days together, carrying heavy pipes into the forest, binding them with acrid glue that made my head spin. You were quietly strong, muscled from days tapping rubber trees on your father's land. We both loved the water, and instead of taking lunch breaks with the group, we swam at the falls, careful not to catch each other's eye. I knew Syariah [Shariah] law mandated strict boundaries between women and men, so for the last months I'd been careful to avert my eyes when spoken to and never shake hands with a man. Even during the grueling labor of lugging tubes and water turbines side by side with the male volunteers under the equatorial sun, I wore an oversized T-shirt and baggy pants. I never stayed long in the water, self-conscious that my shape might be visible through the wet cloth. After the cool respite of each swim, I'd return to the house to change and help the village women peel garlic cloves, clumsily trying to mirror their expert motions.

You were always the last to quit work for the day. At night, you cleaned yourself for prayer, then sat on the wooden porch of the main house smoking joints. I sat across the planks and wrote. You looked so pensive that I longed to touch your arm and ask what you were thinking; but even here, in the remoteness of the jungle, I knew that was forbidden. Gradually, I stopped being annoyed by your guardianship, and instead grew grateful for your company. I noticed how you stayed near me during the day, close enough to help me lift pipes when they grew laden; in return, I'd scamper up ladders to help you run wire.

It happened on the last night of the trip. The villagers and volunteers crowded anxiously around a wooden door frame, our breaths drawn as you put your hand on the final light switch installation. When the light flickered on, we whooped and hollered, and the best tapai was brought out to drink. We danced for hours, chewing betel under the single bulb while the Ranau brothers played guitar, and I believed then in pure good, the power of common cause. I let myself laugh uninhibitedly. You and I sang "Original Sabahan" together, a Dusun song my students had taught me. *Mantap!* you laughed. *Amazing,* I smiled back.

I stayed up late that night helping the village women clean. After sweeping the floors, I began the short walk to the girls' sleeping quarters, feeling my way through the thick, humid air, my eyes adjusting back to the black night. Deep in the jungle, the night grows so dark it's impossible to see one's own outstretched hand. It was the first time I'd been completely alone.

A male figure broke the darkness. It was another volunteer, but a shell of the man I'd worked with all those days. The sweet rice wine had gone bitter on his breath. He made a sound like a snarl and grabbed my arm. Up close, his eyes were blank, but his grip was strong. I fought until I couldn't and instinctively screamed your name. At that moment, you emerged, taking him to the ground. You still spoke softly when you instructed me to lock myself in the girls' quarters. I scrambled inside and curled up on the damp ground, listening to you struggle with him as his fists still managed to knock on the wooden door. I held my breath until he stopped, the last drop of strength seeping from my body. I learned later you sat on his chest until he passed out.

In the morning, you woke me and we quietly left. As you started the truck, you asked in hesitant English if I'd felt scared. I said no and I meant it: more than fear I felt defeat. I'd proven what so many people believe to be true: that it *is* dangerous for a woman to travel alone, to participate in roles thought to be "man's work," to assert space in this world. I was weak; I'd needed you. The home, community, and new life I'd opened myself up to in Borneo had been lost in minutes. As we drove away from the village, I rolled down the window to watch the endless expanse of banana trees, some now strung with thick power lines. I always loved looking for the leaves with purple hearts. This time, I let them pass unnoticed.

You offered to drive me straight to my house so that I wouldn't have to risk seeing the man again. I gratefully accepted. We had already traveled nine hours when you asked if we could stop by your village; you had something to show me. It was just about the last thing I wanted to do. I was exhausted and nauseous, my skin caked with red soil. But I grudgingly agreed, and you blazed right off the road through grass as tall as I was. We emerged at a riverbank.

It was sunset, the hazy orange hues streaming through the forest canopy. We were alone. We stepped out of the truck and stood for a while in silence, because you're someone whose silence is peaceful and warm and we didn't need to fill the gaps. You looked at me, because you knew what I would do and I did it, and when my body hit the water, it was freeing and pure, and the night before dissolved away. In the fierce current that flowed toward the vast South China Sea, I fought vigorously under the surface toward the other bank. When I came up for air, I believed again in the jungle's magic, the rush of resurgence pulsing through its trees and waters. You stood watching from the edge of the bank, and then you said, as if you knew: *Strong swim.*

I Decided to Leave

FROM *GEN*

THREE WEEKS AGO, I fled New York City for the countryside. I know there are arguments against this, some expressed more thoughtfully than others. I ran through them one by one as I was sitting in my Manhattan apartment, wondering whether my limited options were even worth contemplating. The shaming campaigns against defectors hadn't quite begun yet, but I knew they would soon enough. I also knew that guilt awaited me no matter what I did, and not just because guilt is the organizing principle of my existence. I had a new guilt source in my life: a puppy.

Nearly a year after losing my St. Bernard, Phoebe, I had, somewhat unexpectedly, acquired a 10-week-old Newfoundland. At first, I thought the timing would be perfect. Due to coronavirus, my upcoming trips and engagements were being canceled one by one. Not yet grasping the seriousness of the situation, I thought, *This is great!* So much uninterrupted time with the puppy and no need to pay dog sitters or lean on neighbors for favors. But then it wasn't just events being canceled but life itself. The outdoors was being rationed. The air itself was deemed unsafe.

I decided to leave. It didn't feel great, but it didn't feel wrong. It was one of those least-worst choice kinds of choices. It helped that I would travel with a close friend, a neighbor with whom I have a strange sort of platonic partnership, but he probably wasn't going to stay long. This was my gig, my choice. Not to mention my puppy (per our agreement, my friend would do all the cooking but assume no puppy duties other than playing with him, a deal I was happy to make). I chose our destination after an evening of

Airbnb research, deciding on a place far in the corner of south-west Virginia because it was seemingly in the middle of nowhere yet within an hour of a hospital that wasn't yet pegged to be over-run. (Moreover, it was within two hours of two decent-sized cit-ies with their own larger hospitals.) I packed up a few changes of clothes, a lot of books, and every medication I had sitting around even if I couldn't remember what it was for. I brought a copy of my health care proxy in case, God forbid, I ended up on a ventilator in that hopefully-not-overrun hospital. I dropped my rent check in the mailbox on the way out of the building, holding the envelope with the Clorox wipe I'd used to lock my door and push the eleva-tor buttons. Then I met my friend in front of the building, put the puppy in the car, and made a 10-hour drive.

We emerged from the car into the kind of place you should be with a new puppy even when there's not a pandemic going on. There are pastures in three directions and a forest grove in the other direction. There are cows roaming in the distant pastures and the occasional wild turkey strutting through the grass. There's a deck right off my bedroom so I can grab a flashlight and trundle the puppy out in the middle of the night to relieve himself. When I think about trying to care for a new puppy in my apartment building in Manhattan, all I can think is I don't know what I was thinking. When I think about trying to do so while sharing eleva-tors and lobby space with neighbors who were already getting sick (before I left one called me, febrile, early in the morning asking me to take his dog out; he released the dog into the hallway, closed his apartment door behind him, and I walked the dog wearing latex gloves), I think about the potential hospital bed I freed up in New York City and pray that, despite being healthy after a 14-day self-quarantine, I don't somehow end up occupying one here.

I've had puppies before, though I guess it's like they say about childbirth: you forget the pain every time. The reason babies of any species are so ridiculously cute is that otherwise you'd kill them. Puppies have the cognitive function of infants but the physi-cal capabilities of ransacking burglars—incontinent burglars that are happy to relieve themselves on the floor even as they steal your jewelry (swallow it, actually) and rip apart your sofa. This puppy (for the sake of his privacy I'll withhold his name for now; also I kept changing his name up until recently) is actually remarkably well mannered, at least so far. But the thing is we're in a rented house, an Airbnb owned by astonishingly kind people who live across the road. Times must be hard in Airbnb land, because when I first got in touch and asked if they'd consider two New Yorkers who would self-quarantine for 14 days and a Newfoundland puppy who "would never be unsupervised," they said sure. *Are you crazy?* I thought. I'm still not sure whom I meant by "you."

We made good on the quarantine promise and then some. Nearly a month in, there's nowhere to go anyway, so other than a lone trip to Walmart for groceries and supplies after those initial 14 days, I've stayed mostly on the property (my friend goes for hikes and bike rides while I tend to the canine baby). And herein lies the essence of my quarantine. While the rest of the world withers under the weight of existential horror, my world has been reduced to an endlessly repeating cycle of eating, defecating, romping, gnawing, and sleeping. (The puppy's cycle, that is; mine is even more banal because it doesn't contain gnawing.) Indiscriminate peeing happens at all times during this cycle; any time the puppy rises from a lying-down position, he will immediately urinate with the nonchalance of a yawn. This means that even while he's sleeping I am on alert for the telltale leg shuffle that precedes his rousing onto four legs, at which time I must scoop him up, kick open the nearest door, and deposit him onto the lawn to do his business.

The property isn't fenced. That's part of what makes it so idyllic. It also means the puppy can't go out without my chaperoning him. He's outdoors at least 60 percent of the time. This is a good thing. I want him to be on that grass every possible second. I have taken dozens of nearly identical photos of him on the grass in various states of silliness or repose. But it also means that at least 60 percent of my time is spent ambling after him—occasionally playing fetch or trying to leash-train him, but mostly trying to wear him out by dragging around a giant tree branch that he chases as though it were a mechanical rabbit at a greyhound race.

The more recently he's eaten, the longer it takes to wear him out; on average every meal is followed by an hour of commotion. Because he eats three times a day, this means there are at least three hours a day in which I am doing some version of dragging around the tree branch. I know we're approaching the finish line when he becomes so demonical that he's biting my pant legs and squirming like a toddler when I pick him up to keep him from running toward the forest, a source of forbidden fascination. If the grass is wet, which it frequently is, I'll have to towel him off and leave him in the mudroom to dry, at which time he'll hurl himself against the door trying to come into the kitchen. After several minutes of that, he'll pass out for an hour or sometimes more. This is my time to do everything in my life that isn't puppy-related. Unless the grass is wet, in which case I have to change into dry clothes, clean the mud off the floor, and *then* do everything in my life that isn't puppy-related. By which I mean doomscroll on Twitter or watch the news.

Since arriving here I have done next to nothing that isn't puppy- or news-related. Eighty percent of my emails remain unanswered. Friends send texts and I take days to reply. Someone straight out asked me if I was ill, since I hadn't replied to his emails. I haven't done a single thing on Zoom. I've read maybe a total of seven pages from the books I brought. I did manage to fill out a series of online forms to change my health insurance and it took an entire day. A month ago, I had what felt like a million projects in the works. I had so many balls in the air I was dizzy from looking up. Now I've dropped them all. Ideas that as recently as February I thought about nonstop haven't crossed my mind in weeks. Instead I think about the last time the puppy pooped in relation to the last time he ate. I think about what time I next need to feed him and then run him around outside in order to tire him out so I can eat my own next meal in peace. I have these series of thoughts three times a day. I wish I could say there was something Zen-like about this state. Instead, I feel physically exhausted, professionally irresponsible, and, of course, guilty—not just about leaving New York but about having to eventually take the puppy away from all this grass and go back there.

If the puppy is indoors and not napping, I leap up roughly every five minutes to make sure he's not peeing on the floor, chewing a rug, or, in his latest discovery, licking the sides of the toilet. The paragraph you are now reading took two hours to write because I got up four times, two of which required prolonged trips outside to pee and then root around in the bushes. Sometimes I try to bring my laptop outside, the idea being that I'll work as the puppy plays on the grass. But natural light is no friend of the computer screen. I can't see what I'm doing, and before I know it I can't see the puppy. He's wandered to the other side of the house, or crawled to his favorite hangout space underneath the porch, or started making his way toward the forest. And so I'm off again.

There are coyotes and even black bears around here. The coyotes would gladly grab a little pup if they could. The bears might hurt one if they got startled. Overhead, hawks with nearly five-foot wingspans glide low enough to incite worry as well as thrill. When I first arrived, the puppy was 21 pounds. Google tells me that's right around the cutoff weight for a raptor to grab a creature in its talons and carry it to its demise. What are the chances? Minuscule, but not worth taking. So I sit on the porch steps and stare into space as the puppy rolls on the grass. When I grow bored with the porch steps, I sit on the grass as the puppy rolls on me. Hours pass. Days pass. Weeks pass. Soon, a month will have passed.

This is no way to live. Except right now it's the only way to live. What's happening in the world is too vast and strange and horrifying to make sense of yet. The pandemic is a painting on a canvas so big you can't step back far enough to even see what's been rendered. One evening around twilight I took the puppy out for his fortieth bathroom break of the day. I walked about 10 yards into the pasture and turned my head toward the house. It was lit up from the inside, a tableau of Americana perfection against the rolling fields and streaks of indigo clouds that hung over the mountains. Through the living room window, the television was in direct view, the channel turned to CNN, where a three-way split screen between Anderson Cooper, Sanjay Gupta, and Anthony Fauci radiated through the glass like a laser beam. It encapsulated everything about the moment, at least this particular moment of this particular night. I thought that if I could take a picture it might help me make sense of the moment. I thought about how someday I'd look back at the photograph and say, "Boy, that was a scary time." I thought about how someday when the puppy is a big grown-up dog I might tell people about our earliest days together and how strange it all was.

I reached into my pocket for my phone, but before I knew it there was a MyPillow commercial on. As of this week, the puppy weighs 30 pounds. I'm not sure we're going home anytime soon.

The New York You Once Knew Is Gone. The One You Loved Remains.

FROM *GEN*

NEW YORK CITY is not as deserted as the pictures will lead you to believe.

After recently undergoing two weeks of isolation for COVID-19–like symptoms, I emerged from my apartment expecting to find, like the man in the famous *Twilight Zone* episode who accidentally survives an atomic blast in the bank vault where he works, that New York had disappeared while I'd been waiting things out upstairs.

But it was still there. Indeed, as I climbed onto my bike to run errands for myself and some others—arguably the most socially distant form of travel possible these days—the streets felt immediately familiar. To know New York City by bike is to know it intimately in a way not possible by foot or car. It's like being thrust into the bloodstream of a great beast, privy to its every pulse. You need only go a few blocks before the rhythm of the lights and motion of the traffic reveal themselves; you learn the beats and melody of the streets the way you learn any song.

Despite its muted movements and darkened storefronts, the city I pedaled into was not new to me. Anyone who's held a job that puts them at odds with the 9–5 world—or rather the 7–midnight world, as New York schedules so often run—knows this particular city. It's the "my shift ended at 4 a.m." New York. Or "my shift starts at 5 a.m." It's early Sunday morning in August New York. It's

Audrey Hepburn emerging from a lone cab on a deserted Fifth
Avenue to stare longingly into a Tiffany's window New York. It's
Thanksgiving night or Christmas Day New York. It's the New York
of for better or for worse.

And now it's something else, too. E. B. White said there were
three New Yorks: the city of those who were born here, the city of
those who commute in daily, and the city of those who come here
"in quest of something."

To this list, we may now add a fourth: the New York of those
who stayed.

It is, of course, not a holiday, nor is the city nearing the end of
a long night. The witchy New York hour between yesterday and
today is now the New York of all day, every day. A nightmarish
bizarro world set to the soundtrack of sirens. Everything is still
here, but off. Even as I thrilled to the empty streets—rounding
Columbus Circle in an uninterrupted sweep that made me think
of the red-tailed hawks I now enviously watch gracefully circling
the skies over my neighborhood—I couldn't escape the ominous
sense that the city had slipped its axis. It was the wrong time of
year for this empty, the wrong time of day. The sun itself felt in the
wrong place, and the light hit at odd angles. The beat of the city
was now the beat of an unhealthy heart, lurching unevenly from
one pulse to the next.

Music evokes memories, and the refrain of the city's stillness
reminded me of past moments when I've had its streets to myself. Sailing down a now-vacant Fifth Avenue, I recalled biking
the same stretch during the 2004 GOP convention, when Bloomberg had shut it down to cars. I vividly remember reaching 34th
Street, and seeing a young man on a delivery bike thrown to the
ground by NYPD officers because he had stopped a few inches
past some security cones that had been set up. Now food-deliv-
ery people are on the front lines, risking their health to keep us
fed, and the restaurant sector that has long been the lifeblood of
New York alive.

There are other reminders of past traumas, too. After 9/11,
the streets were plastered with photos of loved ones who had gone
missing. Now they are plastered with CLOSED BY COVID notices.
In 2012, after Hurricane Sandy, portable generators and gasoline
became the most valued resources in the hardest-hit areas. Now

it's yeast and pulse oximeters and toilet paper. This time everyone is newly in love with the bully in Albany instead of a bully in Gracie Mansion. So many firefighters lost their lives after running into the burning towers on 9/11 that for a long time people would stand back and clap when the red engines went by. Now we throw open our windows at 7 p.m. and cheer, issuing our own barbaric yawps across the rooftops, as much for the extraordinary health care workers risking their lives as to assure one another we're still here.

And yet all past comparisons are faulty ones. Yes, New York City has been sucker punched before, to use the term Anthony Fauci employed on *The Daily Show* recently to describe how COVID-19 has hit the city. We have been abandoned by past presidents, too. And we most definitely have a history of inept mayors. We've lived through plagues, more than once. But we've never been hit in a way that has turned the very things that make us great into what will kill us.

We are a city of congregators. We are so used to being jammed up against one another, so thrilled and challenged and comforted by it that maintaining social distancing requires the mental vigilance of giving up an addiction. For years, New Yorkers have been advised by those who've left the city that bigger houses and more land can be found elsewhere for a fraction of the price—as if everyone here doesn't know exactly the demands of the deal they struck in staying. Exchanging ease for the possibility of magic. It's not recklessness that finds us edging past the six-foot demarcation zone in the lineup at Fairway, it's habit. Empty space here is an invitation. In a city of people used to rallying in an emergency, be it large or small, we have been forbidden from using our greatest strength. This virus is perverting everything: it's Gotham's kryptonite.

Even so, you can detect a thrill in those who remain at the fact that we have the parks, exploding with spring colors and smells, to ourselves. That once you've survived the blocks-long lineup of people waiting to get into Zabar's—reminiscent of the old Depression soup kitchen photos, except for the fact everyone is a responsible distance apart—it's so blissfully empty inside it feels like strolling through the Met after dark. That one can now drive from Brooklyn into the city for an errand and back in an hour, instead of blocking out an entire morning for a simple task.

In New York, distance has always been best measured in time: What's the use in knowing something is three miles away when those three miles are so congested by traffic, or involve so convoluted a subway route, that it will take you an hour to traverse it? Now seven miles in New York is nearly the same as seven miles in Wyoming. This collapsing of time is thrilling until you feel the way it has shrunk the city, normalized it. Third Avenue on an August afternoon, Central Park under a full moon, the Brooklyn Bridge after midnight: biking the empty city roads has been one of my greatest joys. But what is an open road without a destination on the other end? What is New York without anywhere to go? And with no one that you can meet?

New York is unique in that it's the only city that seems to require from its residents a declaration of departure. There is a copper plaque behind the bar at Knickerbocker, a long-standing tavern in Greenwich Village, that reads WHEN YOU LEAVE NEW YORK YOU AIN'T GOING NOWHERE. A deep-seated fear that this may be true seems to have driven generations of writers to itemize the reasons they are leaving. Or perhaps because moving to New York requires a particular resolve and desire for reimaging oneself, leaving it demands the same.

The reasons people have left the city in this moment are myriad: what sane person would stay in a small apartment with children if there were more spacious pastures available elsewhere; why risk infecting an elevator in a building full of old people if you don't have to; perhaps relatives need caretaking elsewhere; perhaps you do. But it's notable that for the most part those slipping away have done so silently, lest their departures define them in some way. They are especially slipping away in Manhattan, quiet hallways and a new absence of garbage the only evidence of their flight.

This time, too, the dynamic has shifted. For a while now a stable life in the city has been accessible only to the super wealthy, the cost of living pushing out long-standing residents with fewer resources and making life nearly impossible for those who long to start the quest but lack the connections to fund it. But to leave now, however practical or painful that decision may have been, is a measure of resources. You have other options.

The ones who remain also do so for many reasons: because

they're needed here, on the front lines or in their homes; because, as is the case in so many of the city's hardest-hit neighborhoods, they have no other options; because they are not being allowed out; because so much of their identity is wrapped up in the city that to leave would simply be worse than whatever they risk by staying. Or maybe it's simply that it's home. But now the challenge is how to be a New Yorker without New York.

In truth, the city has been vanishing for a while and at an astonishing rate; to be a New Yorker of the last decade is to have developed an awareness that the storefront, restaurant, building you are passing by—many empty long before the pandemic arrived thanks to vertiginous rents and insatiable landlords holding out for tenants with deep corporate pockets—may very well not be there tomorrow. For years, as the pace of development and gentrification picked up, it has felt like living one very long goodbye. Even so, it was impossible for any of us to prepare for the disappearing act of the last two weeks of March.

In the original "Goodbye to All That" essay—which was as much a farewell to youth as anything else; its writer returned, after all, and has resided on the Upper East Side for many years now—Joan Didion wrote, "It is easy to see the beginning of things, and harder to see the ends." But in the case of this pandemic, the beginning was the end. In many ways, the abrupt closures of the last month have mimicked the sudden loss of a loved one: the immediate disorienting grief when everything is upside down and your brain, stretched between what was and what is now, does acrobatic maneuvers trying to exist in both places at once.

And yet, as I wound through the Village past blocks of dark storefronts and favorite restaurants that have again and again marked my nearly 25 years in the city, wondering if I'd ever feel their embrace of familiarity again, I was reminded less of death than my mother's long decline into dementia. The person I knew and loved and needed very much, the person who had in ways good and bad defined who I was, was disappearing before my eyes, but the body of my mother remained. In Alzheimer communities, it's known as anticipatory grief: The confusing and extraordinarily painful process of understanding that what you see before you is not actually there. And may never be there again. Of caring for the body and grieving for the soul. Of not looking away.

New York is still here, but it is also not. For those of us who have remained, the task seems to fall somewhere between caretaking—we *will* order pickup and takeout from the places that have served us so well, we *will* do our shopping for our neighbors—and refusing to let go. We ain't going nowhere. New York in this moment may be saying goodbye to us, but we refuse to say goodbye to New York.

Good Bread

FROM *The New Yorker*

IN LYON, AN ancient but benevolent law compels bakers to take one day off a week, and so most don't work Sundays. An exception was the one in the quartier where I lived with my family for five years, until 2013. On Sundays, the baker, Bob, worked without sleep. Late-night carousers started appearing at three in the morning to ask for a hot baguette, swaying on tiptoe at a high ventilation window by the oven room, a hand outstretched with a euro coin. By nine, a line extended down the street, and the shop, when you finally got inside, was loud from people and from music being played at high volume. Everyone shouted to be heard—the cacophonous hustle, oven doors banging, people waving and trying to get noticed, too-hot-to-touch baguettes arriving in baskets, money changing hands. Everyone left with an armful and with the same look, suspended between appetite and the prospect of an appetite satisfied. It was a lesson in the appeal of good bread— handmade, aromatically yeasty, with a just-out-of-the-oven texture of crunchy air. This was their breakfast. It completed the week. This was Sunday in Lyon.

For most of my adult life, I had secretly wanted to find myself in France: in a French kitchen, somehow holding my own, having been "French trained" (the enduring magic of that phrase). I thought of Lyon, rather than Paris or Provence, because it was said to be the most Frenchly authentic and was known historically as the world's gastronomic capital. Daniel Boulud, the most successful serious French chef in the United States, was from there, as was Paul Bocuse, the most celebrated chef in the world. The restaurateur Jean-Georges Vongerichten had trained in Bocuse's kitchen, as his sauce-maker. "Lyon is a wonderful city," he told me. "It is where it all started. You really should go."

Why not? My wife, Jessica Green, a wine educator and lecturer, lived for the next chance to pack her bags. (She also spoke fluent French, which I did not.) And our twin boys, George and Frederick, were three years old—possibly the perfect age to move to a new country. Our landing, though, was surprisingly rough. Lyon seemed unwelcoming, suspicious of outsiders, and indifferently itself. "Our town is not easy to love," a Lyonnais novelist had written in the '30s (the fascist Henri Béraud, who was also not so easy to love). "It is an acquired taste. Almost a vice."

We got an apartment by the river Saône, situated auspiciously on the Quai Saint-Vincent. (Vincent was the patron saint of winemakers.) A gnarly first-century aqueduct column by a post office reminded us that the Romans had been here. In entryways, I found stone stairs rendered concave by boot traffic. Farther up the quai was a former monastery courtyard, overgrown but graceful. In our quartier, there were workshops, not shops: a bookbinder, a violin repair person, a seamstress, a guitar-maker, a one-room pastry "factory." The next street over, Arabic was the principal language, and women, their heads covered, fetched water by bucket from an archaic faucet.

There was also—on the nearby Place Sathonay—a porn shop, park benches occupied by drunks, drug deals, graffiti on most surfaces, dog shit everywhere. At a playground, sparkly with bits of broken glass, we watched small children hitting one another. And yet the quartier, for all its in-your-face grittiness, also had energy and integrity and an abundance of small eateries. The food wasn't grand, but it was always honest, characterized by *bon rapport qualité-prix*—good quality for the price, an essential feature of the Lyonnais meal. Our apartment was opposite a mural called *La Fresque des Lyonnais*, two millennia of the city's famous citizens painted onto a six-story windowless wall. The same building housed Bob's boulangerie, where, friends told us, you could find the best bread in the city.

The boulangerie was where the boys discovered the word *goûter* (from *goût*, meaning "flavor," and probably the single most important word in the entire language). A *goûter* is an afternoon snack—eaten universally at 4 p.m., when children get out of school—and an exception to two of the city's implicit rules about food: you do not eat standing up, and you never eat between meals. A *goûter* is devoured instantly. The boys discovered Bob's *pain au chocolat* and didn't understand why they should eat anything else.

They also discovered Bob's baguettes, which Frederick developed a practice of assaulting each morning before eating: breaking one open with his hands, sticking his nose inside, inhaling, and then smiling. On Wednesdays, when Bob was closed and we bought baguettes elsewhere, Frederick subjected them to his test and, without fail, found them inedible. (Bob was thrilled by Frederick's findings.) Bob's bread had aromatic complexity and was long in flavor in ways that we'd never known before. We were at his boulangerie every day. Some days, we went three times, which concerned him: "You've had enough bread today. Go home!"

We had been in Lyon a month when the evidence was inescapable: I couldn't find a restaurant to take me on. I had cooking experience, but it was mainly Italian, and Italian, I was discovering, didn't count. I was at home pacing (panicking, frankly), when I declared to Jessica, "I'm going to work for Bob. In fact, I'm going to walk over there now and present myself."

It was eight in the evening, but I was pretty sure he'd be there. Bob was known for his extreme hours, his light on in the back when the rest of the quartier was dark. And he *was* there, but he was heading home for a nap.

Bob knew why I was in Lyon. He also knew that I hadn't found a kitchen to work in. So, when I made my proposal, straight out —"Bob, I've decided, on reflection, that I should start with you, in your boulangerie"—he knew that he was my backup: that, in effect, I was lying.

"No," he said.

"No?" I pressed. "Bob, you make the best bread in the city. I want to learn why."

His gaze drifted above my head. He seemed to be imagining what it might be like for me to work there.

Bob was 44. He was jowly and wide of girth and, when unshaven, looked something like a genetic intermarriage of Fred Flintstone and Jackie Gleason. His hair was brownish and shaggy and usually matted with flour. There was flour in his beard and on his clogs, his sweater, and his trousers. (He wore an apron, but it didn't help.) Bathing was not a priority. He slept when he could, and seemed to live by an internal clock set to an alarm that was always going off—yeast, dough-making, the unforgiving speed of a hot oven. He knew that his bread was exceptionally good, but he did not see himself as a genius. In a city of food fanatics, he was just a baker. He was, in fact, just Bob. And he wasn't even that. His real name was Yves. (No one knew why he went by Bob. I once asked him, and he was vague: "Somebody, a long time ago . . .")

"Yes," he said slowly: *Oui-i-i-i.* He actually seemed to be getting excited. I could see excitement in his fingers. They were drumming a counter. "Come. Work here. You will be welcome."

"I will see you tomorrow." I thanked him. We shook hands. I made to leave.

"You live across the street, right? You can stop by anytime. If you can't sleep, come over. At three in the morning, I'll be here."

I thought, *If I can't sleep at three in the morning, I don't go for walks.* But I understood the message. Bob was making himself available. *I'll be your friend,* he was saying.

At three on a weekday morning, when I set out for my first training, the city was lonely. The river was cold-making to look at and thick like motor oil when a barge appeared (suddenly, unexpectedly) a few feet away. From Thursday to Sunday, Lyon was all-night drinking, loud music, car burnings, vandalism, vomiting. Now there were no vehicles, no people, not a light on in any apartment.

Bob was clearly waiting for me. He ripped open a 50-kilo sack of flour, lifted it without a sign of strain, and emptied it into a large steel basin. He grabbed a milk carton with the top cut off and told me to follow him to a sink—a startling sight, filled with coffee paraphernalia, grounds everywhere, a sandwich floating in something black, a wet roll of toilet paper. He negotiated the carton to a position under the faucet and ran it hot.

"You arrive at the correct temperature by a formula involving two other factors," Bob explained. "One is the temperature of the air. This morning, it is cold—it is probably two degrees. The other is the flour—"

"How do you know that?"

"It's the temperature of the air."

"Of course."

"These two factors added together, plus the water, should equal fifty-four degrees Celsius." So if the air was two degrees, and the flour was two degrees, the water would have to be 50.

"Hot," I said.

"Exactly."

The water from the tap was steaming. Bob filled the carton.

I asked, "Bob, you don't use a thermometer?"

"No."

"Do you own a thermometer?"

"No." He considered. "You know, I might."

Bob poured the water into the basin and started an apparatus attached at the top, a kneader. It appeared to have originally been operated by turning a crank, and at some point had been upgraded with a washing-machine motor. Two hooks, looking like prosthetic hands, scooped up the dough very slowly. "It is no faster than if you did this with your own hands," he said.

"Then we take some of last night's dough." *La vieille pâte.* It was brown and cakey, wrapped in plastic film. He pinched a bit between his thumb and forefinger and tossed it into the basin. He took a second pinch, scrutinized it, thought better of the quantity, and tossed in half. This, in effect, was his "starter," yeasts still alive from last night that would be woken up in the new batch. It wasn't the only source. I knew enough about yeasts to know that, here, they were everywhere. You could peel them off the walls. You could scrape all you needed from underneath Bob's fingernails.

I looked around. On every available surface, there was an unwashed coffee mug. Fabric *couches,* used for shaping baguettes, were draped across wooden poles, like beach towels still damp from last summer. A light bulb dangled from the ceiling. There were the flickering blue lights of the ovens. The darkness put you on your guard. You could trip here and die.

He stopped the kneader and tore off a piece of dough. It was thin and elastic. "You can see through it," he said, laughing as he stretched it across my face like a mask.

Tonight's dough would be ready the next afternoon. The morning's baguettes would be made, therefore, from last night's.

"Let's get breakfast," Bob said.

An off-track-betting bar opened at six. The coffee was filthy, the bread was stale, and the clientele might be flatteringly described as "rough" (phlegmatic one-lunged hackers knocking back sunrise brandies, while studying the racing odds), but, for Bob, they represented companionship. He was at ease among them. He introduced me as the guy he was training to make bread, his way.

Bob had not set out to be a baker. In his 20s, he worked in a law library in Paris, a job that he loved. His father had been a baker. His older brother Philippe was a great one, who had already opened three bakeries, as well as doing stints at ski resorts in the winter and in the Caribbean during the spring.

It was Jacques, another brother, who discovered, by accident, the boulangerie on the Saône. He had come upon a space for rent, situated in front of a footbridge, but it was filthy and filled with trash. He investigated: two floors, thick stone walls, a worn stone staircase, and, in the back, an old wood-burning oven. He wiped off the soot. It said 1802. He became excited—the river, the history (*La Fresque des Lyonnais* was then being painted on the back wall)—and summoned his father, Philippe, and Bob. "My father looked at the property from the outside and said, 'Yes, this is a good boulangerie,'" Bob told me. "'Bread has been made here for a long time.'" The family bought the boulangerie, for what was then about $11,000, and got it ready. (It was probably—I couldn't keep myself from thinking—the last time the floors were cleaned.)

Bob returned to Paris, and a sign went up: PHILIPPE RICHARD ARTISAN BOULANGER. But it seems unlikely that Philippe intended to remain. He had a family and a business in Nantes, eight hours away. He called Bob: quit your job, he said, and come run the boulangerie with me. In effect, he was beginning Bob's training (what in French is called a *formation*), helping him find his calling. "Without Philippe," Bob said, "I would be nothing." After a time—six months? a year? Bob couldn't remember—Philippe announced that he needed to return to Nantes. He'd be back, he said. It had been 15 years. Bob hadn't changed the sign. "I will never take it down," he said.

From our balcony, with a mountain breeze coming off the Saône, the smells of the boulangerie were inescapable. When you live here, you have no choice: Bob's bread enters your living space. The boulangerie was the village equivalent of a campfire. It held the restaurants together. It united chefs and diners. It made the quartier a gastronomic destination.

Once, I asked Bob for his secret: "Is it the yeasts? Are they what make your bread so good?"

"*Oui,*" he said very, very slowly, meaning, "Well, no."

I pondered. "Is it the leavening?" Bob always insisted that a slow first rise—called *le pointage*—was essential to good bread. Factory bread-makers use high-speed mixers to whip a dough into readiness in minutes. Bob's took all night.

"*Oui-i-i-i.*"

"The final resting?" Bread gets its deeper flavor in its last stages, people say.

"*Oui-i-i-i.* But no. These are the ABCs. Mainly, they are what you do *not* do to make bad bread. There is a lot of bad bread in France. Good bread comes from good flour. It's the flour."

"The flour?"

"*Oui,*" he said, definitively.

I thought, *Flour is flour is flour.* "The flour?"

"*Oui.* The flour."

Bob bought a lot of flours, but a farm in the Auvergne provided his favorite. The Auvergne, west of Lyon, is rarely mentioned without an epithet invoking its otherness. It is *sauvage*—wild—with cliffs and forests and boars. Its mountains were formed by volcanoes, like so many chimneys. In the boulangerie, there was a picture of a goat on a steep hill. It was kept by a farmer friend, who grew the wheat that was milled locally into a flour that Bob used to make his bread. The picture was the only information that Bob's customers required. Who needs a label when you have a goat?

For Bob, farms were the "heart of Frenchness." His grandfather had been a farmer. Every one of the friends he would eventually introduce me to were also the grandchildren of farmers. They felt connected to the rhythm of plows and seasons, and were beneficiaries of a knowledge that had been in their families for generations. When Bob described it, he used the word *transmettre,* with its sense of "to hand over"—something passed between eras.

George and Frederick, enrolled in a neighborhood school, were learning their new language, hesitantly at first and then with sudden fluency. Jessica, with a mimic's gift for languages, spoke with authority and ease.

Was my French improving? No.

Did my French even exist? *Meh.*

I had a bad episode with *four*—the word in French for "oven" (pronounced as if someone has just hit you hard on the back). It sounds the same if the ovens referred to are in the plural (*fours*). And *fours* were, of course, what Bob baked his bread in, the blue-lit, glass-door contraptions on the ground floor.

One afternoon, there were two people in the back of the boulangerie: Denis, Bob's sole full-time employee, and me. Denis—30, with cropped blond hair and dressed in white, like a proper baker—was upstairs. I was below, making dough. When I bounded up to retrieve a sack of flour, Denis asked: The bread—was it still in the oven (*au four*)? At least, I think that this was what he said. He repeated the question, and this time it was more like "Don't tell me that the fucking bread is still in the oven?" What I heard was strong emotion and *"four."*

Four, I said to myself. *Four.* I know that word.

"Four?" I said, aloud this time, which was provoking, probably because it wasn't "yes" or "no."

"Au four? C'est au four? Le pain!"

Denis bolted down the stairs in what seemed to me like histrionic distress. I heard an oven door being slammed open and a bread tray yanked out on its rollers.

"Oh, putain!"

For me, the door was the prompt. Of course. *Four!* It's "oven"!

The bread was ruined. (*Putain* means "whore." *Pute* is also "whore," but *"Putain!"* is what you say when you've burned a full tray of baguettes.)

One evening, Bob announced, "Tomorrow, we do deliveries. It is time to meet the real Lyon."

Bob delivered bread via an ancient dinky Citroën that he hadn't washed—ever. On the passenger seat were plastic sandwich wrappers, a half-eaten quiche, a nearly empty family-size bottle of Coca-Cola, and editions of the local paper, *Le Progrès,* that lay open at such specific spots as to suggest that this is what Bob did while driving: he caught up on the news. He pushed it all to the floor and invited me to sit. Inside was a fine white cloud, as though the air had reached a point of molecular flour saturation and none of it would quite settle. The car explained why Bob so seldom bathed. Really, what would be the point? (In the wintertime, Bob had the appearance of an old mattress.)

Bob drove fast, he talked fast, he parked badly. The first stop was L'Harmonie des Vins, on the Presqu'île, a wine bar with food

("But good food," Bob said). Two owners were in the back, busy preparing for the lunch service but delighted by the sight of their bread guy, even though he came by every day at exactly this time. I was introduced, Bob's new student, quick-quick, bag drop, kisses, out. Next: La Quintessence, a new restaurant ("Really good food," Bob said, pumping his fist), husband and wife, one prep cook, frantic, but spontaneous smiles, the introduction, the bag drop, kisses, out. We crossed the Rhône, rolled up onto a sidewalk, and rushed out, Bob with one sack of bread, me with another, trying to keep up: Les Oliviers ("Exceptional food"—a double pump —"Michelin-listed but not pretentious"), young chef, tough-guy shoulders, an affectionate face, bag drop, high fives, out.

One eating establishment after another: in, then out. Many seemed less like businesses than like improvisations that resulted, somehow, in dinner. Chez Albert, created on a dare by friends. Le Saint-Vincent, with a kitchen no larger than a coat closet. In the Seventh Arrondissement—industrial, two-up–two-down housing, gray stucco fronts—we arrived at Le Fleurie, a bistro named after a Beaujolais *cru,* as accessible as the wine. "I love this place," Bob said: a daily chalkboard menu on the sidewalk, 12 euros for a three-course meal (lake fish with shellfish sauce, filet of pork with pepper sauce), polemically T-shirt–and–jeans informal, the food uncompromisingly seasonal (i.e., if it's winter, you eat roots). Bob walked straight to the back, a sack on his shoulder, the familiar routine. Then, the day's last delivery completed, he asked after Olivier, the chef, and was directed to the bar.

Olivier Paget, Bob's age, was born in Beaujolais, father a plumber, grandfather a vigneron, cooking since age 16; normal chef stuff, including stints making fancy food with *grands chefs,* like Georges Blanc, with whom Boulud had trained. But Paget, his training complete, situated himself in a remote working-class district, made good food at a fair price, and filled every seat, every lunch and dinner: tight.

"This," Bob said, "is my idea of a restaurant."

As Paget poured glasses of Beaujolais, Bob confessed to liking the idea of *grande cuisine*—cooking of the highest order. He still hoped that one day he would experience it properly. "I tried once" —a meal at Paul Bocuse's three-star Auberge, with Jacqueline, his wife. No one could have arrived with higher expectations. Few could have been more disappointed.

It wasn't the food, which Bob doesn't remember. "We were condescended to," he said. Waiters sneered at them for not knowing which glass was for which wine, and served them with manifest reluctance. (Jacqueline is Cuban and Black. That evening, there was one other Black person at the restaurant: the footman, dressed up in a costume reminiscent of southern plantation livery.) The bill was more than Bob earned in a month. It had been a mugging.

Bob knocked back his Beaujolais, and Paget poured him another, and, as I watched the easy intimacy between them, I believed that I was starting to understand what I had been seeing all morning: a fraternity, recognized by a coat of arms visible only to other members.

Through Bob, I learned about the city's eating societies, a proliferation of them: one for the *bouchon* owners; another for the *bouchon* eaters. One for the true bistros, and another for the modern ones. There was the Gueules de Lyon, which, by the designation of its members, included the city's eight coolest, philosophically unfussy, kick-ass restaurants. At least three societies were committed to hosting a real *mâchon*. (This is the all-day Lyonnais "breakfast" practice, featuring every edible morsel of a pig, limitless-seeming quantities of Beaujolais, and loud, sloppy parades of singing men who, by then, are trying to remember how to get home. I feared it.) And there were serious grown-up societies, like Les Toques Blanches, whose members were the grandest of the region's *grands chefs*.

When I crossed the city, I met people I knew through Bob. I was starting to feel at home.

And then I quit.

I stepped into the boulangerie to tell him.

"*Bonjour,* Bill."

"*Bonjour,* Bob. Bob, I have decided to go to cooking school."

I could have hit him in the nose with my fist. He took a step back, as if he had lost his balance. "Oh," he whispered.

What had I done? I tried to explain, how I needed to learn kitchen skills first.

"Of course."

And that I would be back soon. If he would have me. That there was so much more to learn.

The air seemed to be leaving him. His shoulders sloped. He was just a baker, his posture said. He was Bob. Just Bob.

"You're going to L'Institut Paul Bocuse," he said—the most prestigious school in France. It was a statement, not a question.

"I am."

He whistled.

"But I will be back."

He didn't believe me.

We stood like that. He seemed to be thinking.

"At L'Institut Bocuse, you will learn *la grande cuisine*," he said forthrightly, with energy.

"I don't know."

"Of course you will." He seemed excited. "For the first time in my life, I will eat a grand meal and enjoy it. You will make me something from the repertoire of *la grande cuisine*. It will be like Bocuse but without all the Bocuse."

"Of course I will," I said.

He smiled.

I tried working for Bob on Saturdays, but it was too much. Then, after L'Institut, I found work in a restaurant kitchen. ("Good food there," Bob said, "but bad bread.") Bob continued to be in our life. He made a bread, combining American and French flours, that expressed our friendship. We called it a Lafayette.

More than a year later, we asked if we could take him out to dinner. It was an indirect apology. I hadn't cooked for him yet.

He picked the day: a Tuesday—i.e., not a school night. (Bob closed on Wednesdays, like the schools, so he could be with his young daughter.) He had both bathed and shaved, a radical sight. He had also determined the itinerary, which began with his friends at L'Harmonie des Vins, because they had just taken delivery of *the* new Saint-Péray, a small-production white wine made by Alain Voge. Bob taught us that, where we lived, a wine sometimes has a release date, like a play's opening night.

Bob talked and talked and talked. He knew plenty about us. He wanted us to know about him. He talked about his father, a farmer's son ("My grandfather, my great-grandfather, my great-great-grandfather, all of them, for generations, were *paysans*"), who became the renowned town baker, a patriarch whom his many children sought advice from before making major decisions, and who, for no reason that anyone understood, no longer spoke to Bob's mother. ("It was strange. He spoke to the rest of us.")

About his mother, 85, who pretended not to be distressed that her husband of 59 years and the father of her seven children no longer spoke to her.

About his wife, Jacqueline, who was a single mother when he met her, on a vacation to Cuba, and who agreed to marry him only if the proposal was blessed by her priest, a disciple of Santería, the Caribbean religion.

About returning to Cuba to attend a ceremony, people dancing and chanting, until the priest stopped the proceedings: "He held my face between his hands, and looked into my eyes, and declared, 'Your family traded in the flesh of our ancestors. You cannot marry Jacqueline. Leave my sight.'"

About his returning to France, heartbroken, and being told by his mother that there was merit in the priest's declaration, that there had been a terrible rupture in the family, because one branch traded in slaves and the other found the practice unacceptable. About how Bob returned to Havana and explained his history to the priest, who then blessed his marriage.

About his six siblings (by then we were at Les Oliviers, Bob talking faster and faster to say it all): Marc, an archivist in Paris; Jacques, between Paris and Lyon, doing this and that; a couple of sisters; another brother; and *then* Philippe, dear Philippe, four years older than Bob, and the one he talked to the least because he thought about him the most. "Philippe," Bob said, "is my greatest friend. He is half of my soul."

When Bob was growing up, every member of the family worked in his father's boulangerie at Christmas and Easter. Bob had emerged with a refrain: "Everyone deserves good bread." It was like a calling or a social imperative. A *boulanger* can be counted on by the people he feeds.

Once, I asked Bob, "Which of your breads makes you the proudest?"

No hesitation. "My baguette."

"Really? The French eat ten billion baguettes a year. Yours are so different?"

"No. But mine, sometimes, are what a baguette should be."

Bob took one and brought it up to the side of my head and snapped it. The crack was thunderous.

The word *baguette* means "stick" or "baton," the kind that an orchestra conductor keeps time with, and wasn't used to describe bread until the Second World War, probably—and I say "probably" because there is invariably debate. (There is even more about how to define a baguette: Should it weigh 250 grams? Two seventy-five? Do you care?) Tellingly, the word appears nowhere in my 1938 *Larousse Gastronomique,* a thousand-page codex of French cuisine. Until *baguette* became standard, there were plenty of other big-stick bakery words, like *ficelle* (string), and *flûte* (flute), and *bâtard* (the fat one, the bastard). It doesn't matter: it is not the name that is French but the shape. A long bread has a higher proportion of crust to crumb than a round one. The shape means: crunch.

When I made baguettes, I was astonished at both the labor and the unforgiving economy—you pull off a small piece of dough and weigh it on an old metal scale, roll it out, grab one of the *couches* from a pole to let it rest, let it rise again, slash it, bake it, and then collect 90 centimes for your efforts. The slash is effected by a light slice with an angled razor blade, *une scarification,* done so weight-lessly that you don't crush the loaf. But I had trouble with the slash —I couldn't do it without exerting pressure, just as I couldn't roll out the dough without squishing it. Bob had a touch that seemed to be lighter than air; he left no fingerprints.

The result was irresistible. Once, when we were having lunch at Le Fleurie, Bob directed my attention to a woman on the far side of the room: well dressed, gray hair in a bun, eating by herself. She was removing a sliced baguette from the basket and meticulously putting it, piece by piece, into her purse, where there appeared to be a napkin to fold it into. She closed her purse and put her hand up for a waiter's attention: *"Plus de pain, s'il vous plaît."* More bread, please.

I popped into the boulangerie late one morning. Bob was in the back. No one else was there. I waited several minutes before he walked out.

"I was on the phone with my mother. My brother Philippe. He had an aneurysm this morning. He is dead."

Il est mort.

Bob was pale, flat eyes, no affect, able to relay the news but seemingly unable to understand what he was saying. "He is fifty. He *was* fifty. An aneurysm. This morning."

Bob left to attend the funeral. When he returned, he was ponderous, in manner and movement. One morning, he didn't show up at the boulangerie. Another time, I watched him standing by a street light, seeming to stare at nothing. The light changed, then changed back. He didn't cross. His thoughts were like a black tide moving back and forth inside his head. I feared for him.

"I have to change my life," he told Jessica. "I must make Lucas a partner." Lucas was the first baker Bob employed who had his lightness of touch. "I have to share the workload."

He seemed to have instantly gained weight. He wasn't sleeping. The nights, he said, were the hardest: "That's when I think of him. I have never been closer to a human being, those nights, making bread."

One Saturday night, as Bob mourned, a kid threw a rock at the back-room window, shattering it. On Saturday nights, everyone comes into Lyon. It is noisy and drunken, and stuff happens. On this particular Saturday, Bob was in the back, thinking of his brother. The broken window was an affront. Bob, apparently, gave chase down the Quai Saint-Vincent.

Is it possible that Bob thought he could catch the vandal? By what impulsive leap of the imagination did he regard himself as a sprinter?

The quai there was badly lit, the curb stacked with boards left over from a construction project. Bob tripped and fell and broke his leg. He had to pull himself back onto the sidewalk to avoid being run over. Bob, whose work means standing on his feet, had to give up the boulangerie for an inconceivably long time.

Roberto Bonomo, the quartier's Italian chef, was in touch with Bob and provided updates. After a month, he was still supine, Roberto told us, but the break seemed to be healing. Bob had attempted walking with crutches.

I began preparing a dinner for his return, a *grande cuisine* dish that I had been practicing, *tourte de canard* (duck pie). Bob needed some love and affection. He would, I was sure, really like a piece of pie.

The boulangerie continued—Lucas's bread was flawless—with one persistent problem: the flour kept running out. Lucas didn't know how often Bob ordered it. In most bakeries, you buy flour in bulk; it is always there, you don't think about it. But Bob got his flour from small farmers who valued its freshness. It was, in effect, milled to order. He might get some at the beginning of the week. On Friday, he would ask for more. Or on Wednesday. The deliveries would be stacked by the staircase: 40 big, dusty sacks, 50. Lucas, suddenly without flour, had to close until the next delivery.

One Sunday, Roberto threw a party, only his regulars, his best food, the best wine. Bob promised to come, Roberto said: "He'll be on crutches, but he'll be there." When we turned up, Bob hadn't arrived yet. Babysitter issues, Roberto said.

Bob died while we were drinking wine and eating bruschetta. A clot developed in the leg, came loose, rushed up an artery, and lodged in his lungs. He knew at once that he was in fatal trouble. Jacqueline called an ambulance. He was unconscious before it arrived.

I learned this in the morning. I rushed down to the boulangerie. I didn't know what else to do. I opened the door, and the bell jingled, and Ailene, one of Bob's helpers, came out from the back, because it was the routine to come out at the sound of the bell. She saw me and stopped, lower lip trembling, holding herself still. I thought, *If she carries on as though nothing has changed, if Lucas makes the bread at three a.m. and she sells it, can we all pretend that Bob is still at home recuperating?*

The bell jingled, and one of the quartier's restaurant people appeared, a waiter. He was bald, quiet, thin, one of the five people who ran Chez Albert, a purple-painted place, decorated with chicken images, that served good, unradical food. The waiter was bearing a large bread sack that needed filling. He handed it to Ailene and said he'd pick it up later.

"*Bisous à Bob.*" Kisses to Bob.

"Bob is dead." *Bob est mort.* The waiter stood, unmoving, taking in the simple, declarative piece of news. *Bob est mort.* He didn't ask Ailene to repeat herself. He didn't ask how or when or where. The questions would have been an evasion, an effort to fill this sudden void with noise.

"*Putain de merde,*" he said finally. A nonsense phrase. Two bad words in one, as though it were the worst thing you could say. Or it was just what you say when you don't have the words.

When you live on a river, you are never not thinking about it. You see it on waking, hear it in nighttime barges that slice through it, feel it in the dampness of the air. It's never the same—rising, rushing, sinking, slow in fog, thick in the summer—and is also always the same. Bob used to throw his unsold baguettes into it. Only now does it occur to me that, with bread that he had made single-handedly, he couldn't do the obvious and put it out with the trash. He seemed to need to replicate the making of it in its unmaking, tossing the baguettes, one by one, as if returning them to nature for the birds and the fish.

Bob had held the quartier together, a community of like-minded food fanatics, and when he died we briefly considered returning to the United States. We didn't, we couldn't, until finally, after five years in Lyon, we went back for many reasons, including the fact that our children, who could read and write in French, were having trouble speaking English.

I returned the following year on my own, to visit Lac du Bourget, the largest lake in France, a piece of unfinished business. I spent the night at La Source, a farmhouse turned into a restaurant with rooms, which was run by a husband-and-wife team, members of the Maîtres Restaurateurs, a chefs' collective committed to making as much as possible from scratch: butter churned by hand, fresh ice cream daily.

At breakfast, I scooped up butter on the tip of my knife and tasted it. It was fatty and beautifully bovine. The bread was curious. It had been sliced from a rectangular loaf and, to my prejudiced eye, looked store-bought and industrial. I had a bite. It wasn't store-bought. *Wow,* I thought. *This is good bread.*

The flour, the owner told me, was from Le Bourget-du-Lac, on the other side of the lake. The name of the miller was Philippe Degrange. I wrote it down. It didn't seem right. A grange is where you store your grains. Degrange? It would be akin to buying milk from a guy named Dairy.

I drove to the town and got a coffee. At the bar, I googled "Degrange"—and there he was. Minoterie Degrange. What was a *minoterie*? I looked it up. "Flour mill." It appeared to be within walking distance. I set off.

After half an hour, my doubts returned. The addresses were erratic, and the street—flower beds, trimmed hedges, garages for the family car—was unequivocally suburban. Was there really an operation here, milling only local grains? But then, just when I decided to turn back, voilà! In the shade of tall trees, half-obscured by thick foliage, was a small letter-slot mailbox, no street number but a name, Minoterie Degrange.

The trees and a high metal gate, covered with graffiti, hid whatever was behind. Next to the mail slot was a speaker box. I pressed a button.

"Oui?" the speaker box said, a woman's voice.

"Bonjour," I told the box. "I have eaten a bread made from your flour, and I would like to meet the owner, Monsieur Degrange?"

Nothing.

"But it's lunchtime," the box said finally.

"Of course. I'm sorry. I'll wait."

Another protracted silence. Then the gate opened and revealed an industrial yard, completely out of keeping with its neighbors. A man emerged, round and robust, with a factory foreman's forthrightness, wiping his mouth with a napkin. He looked at me hard.

"Monsieur Degrange?" I confirmed. "Please excuse me. I ate a slice of bread that was made, I believe, with your flour, and it reminds me of the bread that my friend Bob used to make."

He pointed to a car: "Get in."

I got in.

"It's all about the flour," he said. "I'll take you to Boulangerie Vincent. "

The boulangerie, a few miles down the road, was also a bar and a pub and a restaurant with tablecloths. The door opened directly onto the *four* and a cooling rack built against a wall. The top rows were for *boules* ("balls," the ancient way of bread baking), about 30 of them. On the bottom were *couronnes*, massive, each fashioned into a ring like a crown. A woman, carefully dressed, affluent in manner, was negotiating with the bread guy.

"Mais, Pierre, s'il vous plaît. Just one *boule,* please. I have guests tonight."

"I am very sorry, madame, but every loaf has a name attached to it. You know that. If you haven't reserved, I can't give you one."

"He does two ferments," Degrange whispered, "and starts at seven in the evening. The bread needs ten hours. Or twelve. Sometimes fourteen."

Inside, men were gathered around a bar—electricians, cable people, metalworkers, painters, *mecs.* The room roared with conviviality. Degrange ordered us *diots,* a Savoyard sausage, and a glass of wine, a local Mondeuse. Through the door to a kitchen, I saw hundreds of *diots*, drying in the air, looped by a string. They were cooked in a deep sauté pan with onions, red wine, and two bay leaves, and served in a roll made with Degrange's flour.

It had the flavors that I had tasted at breakfast. I asked for another roll, broke it open, and stuck my nose into *la mie*, the crumb —Frederick's routine. It smelled of yeast and oven-caramelized aromas, and of something else, an evocative fruitiness. I closed my eyes. Bob.

"You recognize it," Degrange said. "It comes from wheat that grew in good soil."

"Where do you get it?"

"Small farms. Nothing more than forty hectares."

Small farms, he explained, are often the only ones in France with soil that hasn't been ruined.

"Where are they?"

"Here in Savoie. And the Rhône Valley. They grow an old wheat, a quality wheat. And the Auvergne. I love the wheat from the Auvergne. Everyone does. The volcanic soil, the iron-rich dirt. You can taste it in the bread."

We drank another glass of Mondeuse. Degrange proposed that we go back: "I want to show you the factory."

A Degrange has been milling flour here, or on a site closer to the river, since 1704. Until modern times, the operation was powered by water; on a wall was an old photo of Degrange's father and grandfather, seated before a mill paddle wheel three times their height. There are no mill paddles today. The process is whirringly hidden in pipes and generators and computer screens—except for the source material, freshly picked wheat that is tipped out from hydraulically raised trailers. I followed Degrange up ladder-like stairs to the third floor, where he opened the cap of a pipe and retrieved a cupful of a bright golden grain.

"Taste."

It seemed to dissolve in my mouth, creamy and sweet and long in flavor. "What is it?"

"Wheat germ."

I wanted to take some home. "You'll have to refrigerate it," he said. "It is like flour but more extreme. It has fat, which spoils rapidly."

He described conventional flour production—the sprawling farms in the French breadbasket or the American Midwest, their accelerated-growth tricks, their soils so manipulated that they could have been created in a chemistry lab. "The bread that you make from it has the right texture. But it doesn't have the taste, the *goût*." He asked an assistant to bring him a baguette, then tore off a piece, smelled it, and looked at it approvingly.

"In the country, we don't change as fast as people in the city," Degrange said. "For us, the meal is still important. We don't 'snack,'" he said, using the English word. "What I learned from my father and grandfather is what they learned from their fathers and grandfathers. There is a handing off between generations." The word he used was *transmettre*. *Le goût et les valeurs sont transmis*. Flavor and value: those are the qualities that are transmitted. Only in France would "flavor" and "value" have the same moral weight.

Degrange gave me a 10-kilo bag of his flour. A gift. I said good-bye, an affectionate embrace, feeling an unexpected closeness to this man I had reached by intercom only a few hours ago, and who instantly knew what I was talking about: *goût*.

I was flying home in the morning and reserved a *boule* at the Boulangerie Vincent. I contemplated the prospect of arriving in New York bearing bread for my children which had been made near Lac du Bourget earlier that very day. On the way to the airport, I stopped to pick it up. It was dawn, and there were no lights on inside, just the red glow from the oven. My *boule* was hot and irresistibly fragrant.

In New York, I cut a few thick slices and put out some butter. "I think you'll like this," I said.

Frederick took a slice and sniffed it and then slammed it into his face, inhaling deeply: "It's like Bob's."

George ate a slice, then asked for another and spread butter on it.

When the loaf was done, I made more from the 10-kilo bag. It was good—not as good as the *boule* from Boulangerie Vincent, but still good. It had fruit and complexity and a feeling of nutritiousness. A month later, it was gone, and I stopped making bread.

Food, It Turns Out, Has Little to Do with Why I Love to Travel

FROM *Eater*

I USED TO LOVE to travel. I'd wander through new cities for days on end, eating and drinking (but mostly eating) in four-seat izakayas, farm-driven pizzerias, southern seafood halls, and boat noodle cafés, talking to locals and walking for miles. Restaurants have always been my joyous entry point to a place and its people. The food, I thought, was what made me love to explore the world.

That slowly fading memory—what it felt like to discover a new city, stomach first—is what excited me about going out on the road again, which I did a couple months ago, driving from Los Angeles to Corsicana, Texas, and back, stopping to eat in places like Albuquerque, Amarillo, El Paso, and Phoenix.

Let me be clear: I absolutely would not and do not recommend frivolous travel. In my case, a looming publishing deadline on *The Bludso Family Cookbook* is what sent me on the long, not-so-winding road to Texas in the midst of a global pandemic, where I would be staying with my longtime friend, mentor, colleague, and big brother Kevin Bludso. Once there, we would be cooking, writing, recipe testing, interviewing, living together, and, in all likelihood, drinking a fair quantity of brown spirits at the end of each night (please, someone get that man a Hennessy sponsorship).

I've spent the better part of the last 15 years working in the food industry in one capacity or another. I've been a bartender, server, chef, culinary director, restaurant consultant, cookbook author, and food writer. My plan since last year had been to continue writing and consulting on the side, but also to finally open my own restaurant. Nothing extravagant. Something small and intimate. A humble, comforting place of my own—clean and well lit, a true neighborhood restaurant where people can get to know each other, where the food and the service are unassuming and genuine, something with no desire for expansion or duplication. I consider myself unbelievably lucky that I didn't open a restaurant right before the pandemic hit.

Instead, I've spent the last several months at home, making a quarantine cooking show with my wife called *Don't Panic Pantry*. It's been a good distraction, but I thought a work-related excuse to drive through the American Southwest and its expansive desert would be a cleansing, meditative, soul-resetting break from what I'd begun to think of as perpetual purgatory.

I took every precaution. A nasal-swab COVID test right before I departed. I also hopefully still had antibodies (my wife and I both had COVID-19 way back in March). It was, at the very least, the polite thing to do: get tested before joining someone in their home for two weeks.

I had planned on driving straight through Arizona from LA, avoiding anything except gas stations until I made it to New Mexico, surviving on a sturdy mix of cold brew and air-conditioning to keep me awake. I'd never been to New Mexico before. I'd pored over Instagram photos of chile-drenched Southwestern Mexican food, enchiladas oozing with melted cheese, their red and green chile sauces popping with Instagram photo-editing exposure. My usual pre-trip Google map was loaded with thoroughly researched restaurants along my route. In earlier times, I'd have peppered each map point with essential info like hours of operation and must-order dishes; now, I was looking up intel like outdoor seating, takeout quality, and, most crucially, whether or not a place had managed to stay open at all.

I left with a bullish heart. But each stop to fuel up took away a notch of my optimism-fueled excitement and replaced it with caution. Each person in a mask made me a little more depressed; each person without, a little angrier.

Ten hours in and I had made it to New Laguna, New Mexico. I stopped at Laguna Burger, an iconic mini-chain inside of a gas station. It's a fast-food place to be sure, but according to old photos online there used to be stools set up against the counter, and even a couple of tables and a few chairs. Those are, of course, gone now—pushed to the side of the room and leaving in their place a vacuous emptiness, even for a gas-station dining room. The staff was nice but appropriately wary. I did not partake in the self-serve Kool-Aid pickle jar. I got my food and then sat in my car, emotionally deflated and no longer very excited to eat my first-ever green chile burger—something I had wanted to try for years.

Ordering a burger at a place like this was supposed to be a tiny gateway into the culture and personality of the place, however small that sampling was going to be. There is an emotional atmosphere, a vibe, that's specific to each and every restaurant, and I had perhaps never been so truly aware that such a thing existed until I noticed it had been zapped entirely from this one. In its place was a blanket of nervous, sad precaution—added to, I'm sure, by my own nervousness.

So I sat in my car with my sack of food, gloomily disappointed even before the first bite. They forgot to salt the fries and it felt oddly appropriate. In this moment, to no fault of the restaurant itself, the food didn't matter. It couldn't have. I had slowly but gradually heaped unreasonable expectations on a green chile cheeseburger, wanting it to justify a 12-hour drive and to somehow soothe an anxious mind. But the food, it occurred to me, wasn't what I was after at all.

Later on, in Albuquerque, I picked up a four-pack of beer from Arrow Point Brewing and received the now-familiar and appropriate treatment: measured, cautious, polite gratitude. It was a transaction, appreciated by both sides, but with a higher degree of precondition from both sides as well. I followed it up with a take-out bag of enchiladas and a taco from the beloved and iconic Duran's Pharmacy, taking them back to the motel room I checked myself into earlier. It was 5:30 p.m. The enchiladas had sloshed in the bag. I took a bite and understood: it was comforting, but not nearly enough. Like being single and reconnecting with an ex, only to both immediately discover that there's nothing there anymore—two empty vessels with no connection beyond a memory.

I took a sip of beer and fell asleep for an hour. When I awoke the city had turned dark and I knew there was no point in going anywhere. The world felt dystopian and deflated. I'd left my redundant, loving, comfortable bubble to experience life alone on the road, and all I wished was that I was right back there with my wife and my dog.

When my wife and I had COVID-19, we lost our sense of smell and taste for a bit. It was, as my wife put it, "a joyless existence." Now I had my taste back, but somehow the joy of eating was still gone.

The enchiladas, in a box, alone, on the floor of my motel, were just enchiladas. Because here's a thing I've come to understand of late: context really does affect flavor. A place, its atmosphere, the people within it, their mood (and ours) genuinely change the way things taste. A restaurant lasagna has to be twice as good as your mother's—or that one you had on that trip to Italy—for it to remind you of it even a little. A rack of smoked pork ribs will never taste as good on a ceramic plate atop a tablecloth as it does from within a Styrofoam box on the hood of your car, downwind from a roadside smoker. I hope that I never find out what Waffle House tastes like while sober, eaten in broad daylight.

So as it turns out, when it comes to my lifelong love of food and travel, the food might not have mattered—not to the degree I thought it did, anyway. Not without everything that goes along with it. The surly bartender in the dark room who fries your chicken behind the bar at Reel M Inn in Portland while a guy two seats down makes fun of you for being from California is a huge part of why that might be my favorite fried chicken in the world. The friend of a friend who abandoned his family (thanks, Marc!) to drive a stranger, me, around Toronto for two days and show off the city's outstanding versions of goat roti (from Mona's Roti) and bún riêu cua (from Bong Lua) makes me realize that yes, the food is outstanding, but that it's the people—excited to show off their hometown, its restaurants, and their community—who make travel worthwhile.

Would Tokyo be my favorite eating city in the world if my now-wife and I hadn't befriended two total strangers in a six-seat dive bar, knocking back cocktails until we both threw up, only to come through to the other side fully bonded over late-night grilled pork skewers with another stranger who gave me his business card and said that he had been eating in this stall for over a decade? What is a bar without a bartender? It's just, well, being home.

The restaurant business can be both horrible and wonderful.

It pays poorly, it requires incredibly long hours, and in many instances, you are going broke while making food for people who complain that it's too expensive. But it is, as Anthony Bourdain often said, the pleasure business. It has always been a place for camaraderie, human connection, and community. Those were the things that made the nearly unbearable parts of our business worthwhile—and that connection, when you can have a genuine one between staff and customer, is what I think everyone really, truly wants out of the transaction. Those things still exist, I suppose, but all at arm's length, or across an app.

I still eventually want to open my own restaurant. I think. But maybe I just want to open my memory of what it would have been in a different, earlier world. I don't want to be a dinosaur, yearning for the good old days. But I also don't want to live in a world where a third-party tech company stands between the restaurant and its customer. I don't want someone to visit my city and think that a robot delivering them a sandwich is the best that we have to offer. I don't want to have to download an app to order a cup of fucking coffee. Human connection, it turns out, is essential, too, and we need to find a way to make it a part of our essential businesses again.

So what, in the midst of a health and humanitarian catastrophe, can we do? Well, we can decide where we spend our money. We support human connection and small businesses. We pick up takeout with our own hands from the places and the people that we love (safely, responsibly). We know that it is just gauze pressed against an open, oozing knife wound, but we try anyway.

So we travel because we have to, whether for work or as a needed break from monotony, and we reset our expectations, we open ourselves up to receiving that connection, we seek out the places that are adapting, and we smile through our masks and ask each other how we are doing, if only to show that somebody cares.

When I eventually made it to Corsicana, Texas, hoisting a large bag of dried red New Mexico chiles, I was greeted with an engulfing hug by Kevin Bludso; it was the first truly comforting thing that happened on the whole trip. I melted into the arms of my friend. I was back in a bubble, connected to something.

I spent two glorious weeks in that bubble, taking turns doing Peloton workouts and then drinking vegetable smoothies, before recipe-testing dishes like Fried Whole-Body Crappie and Ham Hock Pinto Beans; researching Kevin's family history; and then, true to form, sipping rye (me) and Hennessy (him) before I had to head home. Kevin's food was outstanding, but it was made all the better by the time spent together cooking it. So when I readied myself to get out on the road again, my expectations had changed. I knew the food alone could only do so much.

This disease has been a reflection and amplifier of all of our weak points—and the restaurant business is certainly no different. This industry was already ripe with flaws. It has been teetering on the brink of a seismic shift for years—COVID-19 just accelerated it, and all the platitudes, Instagram stories, and false optimism won't fix anything. But there have always been bad restaurants as well as good restaurants. I suppose it's no different now. Yet it is maybe just a little bit harder to give and to be open to receiving the human connection that makes the whole experience worthwhile.

I hit the road early, and after about 10 and a half hours, fueled by caffeine, Christopher Cross, and Bonnie Raitt—with one depressing pit stop in El Paso at the famed H&H Car Wash, where an old curmudgeon out front insisted I take off my mask before going inside—I arrived in Las Cruces, at La Nueva Casita Café. I called ahead, hoping not to have to wait so I could just grab my food and get back on the road. My guard was still up, but then the woman on the other end of the phone was so charming and kind that I was immediately disarmed. She graciously steered me toward the chile relleno burrito ("It'll be the easiest one to eat in the car"). A few minutes later I came inside to pick up my food and the two women behind the counter were, frankly, a delight. I paid, and was promptly handed my food and thanked with genuine, casual appreciation for coming in. The burrito was excellent.

Bolstered by the kindness of strangers, I drove another five and a half hours into Phoenix. As a bit of an obsessive pizza-maker (I had the tremendous fortune to train with Frank Pinello of Best Pizza in Williamsburg, and also had a hand in helping to open Prime Pizza in Los Angeles), I was here to try the new 18-inch New York–style fusion pie by the great Chris Bianco at their Pane Bianco outpost on Central.

Just as at La Nueva Casita Café, the staff was friendly, genuine, helpful, and kind. In retrospect, it took so little but it meant so much. When I expressed a need for caffeine, they sent me next door to Lux Central for a large iced coffee, where the barista talked to me from a responsible distance, wished me a safe drive, and gave me a free blueberry muffin. Even eaten in my car, Chris's pizza was truly outstanding—crisp, thin, and pliable, successfully pulling off the New York–modern Neapolitan (ish) fusion that, in lesser hands, turns into an 18-inch bowl of soup.

I drove the last six hours home, finding myself encouraged by these final two restaurant experiences, excited by what the best in our industry are still somehow capable of in spite of everything. It was, frankly, inspirational to find genuine interaction, care, and kindness in this new reality.

It reminds me of my mother, actually. I remember when I was a kid, she would pick up the phone to call a restaurant, or Block-buster Video, to ask them a question. I would always hear her say something like "Hi, Randy! How are you today?" and I would say, "*Mom!* Do you know him?" and she would shake her head no. Then she would say, "Oh, that's great to hear, Randy. Hey listen, what time do you close today?" My brother and I used to make fun of her for that—for forcing this connection with someone she had no real relationship with beyond an exchange of services. Now I plan to do exactly that, whenever and wherever I can.

AMANDA FORTINI

The People of Las Vegas

FROM *The Believer*

I.

IT'S FEBRUARY IN Las Vegas, and because I have managed to step on my glasses and break them, as I do at least once a year, I have gone to the LensCrafters at the Boulevard Mall, a faux-deco artifact of mid-century Vegas that, like so many malls in America, is a mere husk of its former self. In a faculty meeting a few days earlier, I'd watched as one of my colleagues bent and manipulated a paper clip, then used it to refasten the left bow of his glasses, creating a tiny antenna at his temple. That's not a look I'm after, so I am here, obsessively trying on frame after frame, as the young Iranian man who is helping me on this quiet Monday afternoon patiently nods or shakes his head: yes, yes; no, no, no.

I order two pairs. LensCrafters, the movie-theater chain of eye-glasses, is always offering deals: half off a second set of frames, a su-persize popcorn for 50 cents more. While I wait, I walk around the mall, a 1.2-million-square-foot monstrosity built on 75 acres, with a 31,000-square-foot SeaQuest aquarium and a 28,000-square-foot Goodwill.

Next door to LensCrafters, there's a shop that sells gemstones, crystals, sage, and pink Himalayan salt lamps. The burning sage makes that end of the mall smell musky, animalistic—a strangely fe-ral odor in this synthetic environment. Snaking its lazy way around the scuffed tile floor is an automated miniature train, the sort chil-dren might ride at the zoo, driven by an adult man dressed as a conductor; it toots loudly and gratingly at regular intervals. JCPenney and Macy's and Dillard's closed months and years ago, while Sears is limping along in its fire-sale days. At Foot Locker, I try on black-and-white Vans in an M. C. Escher print. At Hot Topic, I browse the cheap T-shirts printed with sayings like KEEP CALM AND DRINK ON and PRACTICE SAFE HEX. I eat a corn dog, fried and delicious, at a place called Hot Dog on a Stick. (I really do.) The atmosphere is depressing, in all its forced cheerfulness and precise evocation of the empty material promises of my '80s-era youth.

I am almost three miles east of the Strip, but I could be anywhere, at any ailing mall in America. The only clues that I am in Las Vegas are a couple of clothing shops that carry items like six-inch Lucite stilettos and pearl-encrusted crop tops. And then, outside, a well-worn swimsuit someone has discarded on a pedestal near the entrance, where Fleetwood Mac's "Rhiannon" blares. The swimsuit has a built-in corset-like bra, an exoskeleton of sorts—it could probably stand on its own—and it's as if someone has left a part of her body behind. *There's no pool,* I think. *Who undressed here?* Such odd Vegas-y details are everywhere in this city—the Elvis impersonator shopping in full-spangled regalia at my local health food store, the pink vibrator melting on Maryland Parkway in 110-degree heat—and I assume you eventually become blind to them, but after four years here, I still see them.

2.

Las Vegas is a place about which people have *ideas.* They have thoughts and generalizations, takes and counter-takes, most of them detached from any genuine experience and uninformed by any concrete reality. This is true of many cities—New York, Paris, Prague in the 1990s—owing to books and movies and tourism bureaus, but it is particularly true of Las Vegas. It is a place that looms large in popular culture as a setting for blowout parties and high-stakes gambling, a place where one might wed a stripper with a heart of gold, like Ed Helms does in *The Hangover,* or hole up in a hotel room and drink oneself to death, as Nicolas Cage does in *Leaving Las Vegas.* Even those who *would never go* to Las Vegas are in the grip of its mythology. Yet roughly half of all Americans, or around 165 million people, have visited, and one slivery weekend glimpse bestows on them a sense of ownership and authority.

Of course, most tourists stay on the Strip, that 4.2-mile neon stretch of hotels and casinos: an artificial, sealed-off capsule where they remain for the duration of their visit, having some carefully orchestrated corporate fun. The city understands how the mythology fuels the business of tourism, and it does its part to sell it. City of sin, city of vice, of wild abandon and crazy drunk antics. "What happens here stays here," says the infamous official ad slogan—whether that's a lap dance at Spearmint Rhino or an embarrassingly pricey brunch at Giada. Implicit in this unabashed celebration of excess and vice is the notion that nothing that occurs here will be too sinful, too dangerous, or too scary: "Just the right amount of wrong," as one casino ad goes. For the most part, all of this is true. But anyone who has walked along Flamingo Road and observed the Strip's human backwash in the pale gray light of a weekend morning, or who has talked to a gaming lawyer about what happens when a person can't pay their markers (more than $650 is a felony in Nevada, carrying one to four years in prison and up to $5,000 in fines), knows that the fun isn't always without consequences. One might argue that people have ideas about Las Vegas because they have a shit ton of ideas about morality, and a fearful desire to distance themselves from their weaker, more susceptible human counterparts.

All these received narratives, these Vegas hand-me-downs, get recycled by the journalists who parachute in and out of here. These writers (who, it's worth noting, are almost always male) swoop in for a day or two or four, steep themselves in authority and gin at a casino bar, and deliver their pronouncements on the very essence of this "wild and crazy" place. They attach like barnacles to the same tired tropes, even the same language (all the singers in Las Vegas tend to "croon"), and their takes are often hackneyed and snooty at once. They will remind you that Las Vegas, that neon fever dream, is set down smack in the middle of the Mojave Desert. They'll note that the lights of the Strip can be seen from outer space. They'll train their lens on the excessive, the gaudy, the vulgar, and the seedy, of which there is certainly plenty here. There will be a scene from the airport, and it will mention the slot machines there, plus the weirdos playing them—of that you can be sure. It's not that these ideas are wrong, or not exactly; it's more that they're hazy, or half-baked, or tend to conflate the marketing of the Strip with the city itself. Any writer knows that you can't be a years-deep expert on everything you write about, but when you have very little experience of a subject, a single point can look like a line. One colleague perfectly summed up this lazy tourist journalism with the phrase "Let's check in and see how stupid and craven everyone is in Las Vegas."

At its root, such writing is often not about the myths of Las Vegas but about the myths these writers hold about themselves, and how those play out against the backdrop of this city. Las Vegas is the setting, the mise-en-scène, for a rambling, gambling writer, in the now-familiar vein of Hunter S. Thompson and his drug-addled, hallucinatory early-'70s romp through Circus Circus. Other people are merely bit players in a private script. A handful of uncouth, uneducated characters might get a mention—the conventioneers in their Hawaiian shirts sucking on daiquiris as big as prizewinning squash, the alt-right talk radio dummies roaming around a gun show with delusions of heroism in their heads—but it's rare that anyone is actually interviewed. Writing about Las Vegas is inevitably an extreme case of the problem of travel writing more generally: its practitioners forget that the way to understand a place is to get out and see it, and to talk to its people.

In most cases, the parachute writers seem unaware of—or perhaps just uninterested in—the fact that the city *has* people: there are roughly 2.23 million permanent residents of the Las Vegas metropolitan area. These are the bartenders and cooks, the cocktail waitresses and card dealers, the valet parkers and hotel maids, who keep this adult playland in motion, but they are also the doctors and nurses and teachers and lawyers who keep *any* city in motion. The Las Vegas Valley, a vast, sprawling 1,600-square-mile expanse of desert surrounded almost entirely by mountains and foothills, looks like pretty much any other western metropolitan area, with churches, big-box stores, fast-food chains, and strip malls populated by insurance offices and vape shops. Three times as many people live outside the city limits as within them, in one of the area's four other cities (Boulder City, Henderson, Mesquite, North Las Vegas) or in unincorporated Clark County. They live like much of America does: going to church, to work, to school, to bars, to buy garbage bags, to get their teeth cleaned.

Las Vegans who consider themselves culturally sophisticated (like many of my university colleagues) tend to distance themselves from the Strip's uncomplicated and coarse enchantments, emphatically claiming they *never* set foot in any of the restaurants, nightclubs, or overpriced boutiques that populate the casinos. This may be true, but I also think it's a defensive, contrarian reaction to the prevailing clichés—a knee-jerk assertion of individuality in response to years of stereotyping. One could argue that some residents get so caught up in rejecting the clichés that they, too, cease to see the place as it is. Because to say that the world of the casinos and the Vegas beyond them are wholly separate fiefdoms is just as inaccurate as saying that Las Vegas and the Strip are synonymous. As one friend, a gifted writer in his late 20s who was born and raised here, told me, "It's not either/or. To say that is just wrong."

The residents of Las Vegas interact with the tens of millions of tourists who visit each year—around 42 million, according to the Las Vegas Convention and Visitors Authority, three times as many as go to Mecca—in fascinating and complicated ways. This is a company town, after all. The Bureau of Labor Statistics reports that approximately 300,000 people work in the leisure and hospitality sector here, far more than in any other industry. (The next closest, trade, transportation, and utilities, employs 176,000 people.) My students tell me about their jobs on the Strip: as cocktail waitresses at swimming pools and sports bars, where men comment on their uniforms and tourists bet on games; at the Fashion Show mall, where at night they wait on drunk people who have decided to do a little shopping. My female students talk about the male tourists hitting on them at nightclubs, where, even more so than in other cities, every interaction comes freighted with the awareness that it will only ever be temporary. Some weekends, my friends arrange a field trip to a casino buffet, where people from all over the world drink bottomless mimosas. One Friday night, a girlfriend takes me to see the show *Magic Mike Live,* and we sit marooned in a sea of hooting bachelorettes wearing veils. In some ways, Las Vegans are like the permanent crew of a cruise ship—Las Vegas as *The Love Boat,* if you will—and the tourists, the real character actors, stream on and off, week in and week out.

I have often wondered whether the general ignorance about Las Vegas is born of laziness, snobbery, or an altogether more insidious impulse. Las Vegas was, of course, déclassé and embarrassing from the start: founded by the Mafia, the first "unaristocratic" Americans, as Tom Wolfe wrote, "to have enough money to build a monument to their style of life." It's frequently said that Las Vegas

has no culture, but that's not true. My Italian relatives from Illinois
—my aunts with their Carmela Soprano hairdos and long acrylic
nails—love it for a reason. They love playing the slots downtown
at the Golden Nugget and going out for martini dinners at old-
school Italian places. (At one of these, I heard Pia Zadora breath-
ily sing about her "accidents and arrests.") They love Cirque du So-
leil shows, where you can sit and watch first-class acrobats fly across
the stage while you sip from a plastic cup of beer. Las Vegas is
vernacular culture—"prole," Wolfe called it—and thus, he notes,
"it gets ignored, except on the most sensational level." Those who
think of themselves as cultured and educated look down on Las
Vegas as garish and brazen. But concern about "good taste" is often just socially palatable code for classism and racism. This is a
working-class town that's nearly 33 percent Hispanic, 12 percent
Black, and 7 percent Asian. It has one of the largest populations of
undocumented immigrants in the country, and the eighth-highest
rate of homelessness. Consider these demographics, and one starts
to understand why the people of Las Vegas get overlooked.

3.

One of the strangest side effects of moving to Las Vegas is that no
one can remember where I live. I have always divided my time between multiple locales, and my friends and colleagues never had
a problem recalling where I was. I'm convinced this amnesia is an
outgrowth of the fact that no one quite believes *anyone* lives here.
When they do remember, they'll say, fuzzily, confusedly: "Are you
still in Las Vegas? What's *that* like? How's *that* going?" I can't help
but detect more than a little class bias in their incredulity; they
can't seem to understand why someone who has a choice, who
isn't *required* to live in Las Vegas, would choose to do so anyway.

When you say that yes, you do in fact reside in Las Vegas, they'll
say, "I could never live there." They mean on the Strip, with its hec-
tic all-night carousing; its decadent, exorbitant dinners with steaks
as big as your face; its bass-heavy club music that feels like it's rat-
tling your organs. (Once, at XS, the nightclub at the Encore, I became convinced the thudding techno would give me a heart attack
and made my husband leave with me.) Or they'll ask you *where* in
Las Vegas you live—like they'd know if you told them—and with

a little probing you'll realize that they assume you live in a casino hotel. Many people know Las Vegas as the place where entertainers are sent to perform in their dotage, a place populated almost solely by magicians and strippers. One friend told me he thought residents lived in trailers behind the casinos, like on the set of a Hollywood film, or maybe on golf courses, because he'd heard of politicians coming to Las Vegas to golf. People don't grasp that most of the housing here is like housing anywhere—apartments, condos, single-family dwellings in suburban subdivisions—except that the homes are mostly stucco in flat desert shades of dirt, sand, and clay. It's funny to think that one of the most surprising things you can say about a city is that people actually live there.

But a counter-idea is still an idea, an abstraction that doesn't tell you much about the feeling and fabric of life. And if you're playing a game of contrariness or defiance, you're still captive to what's come before. What does it mean, really, to say that people live in Las Vegas? Show me their lives. I say this to a colleague one afternoon as we wait in line to order burritos. He stops talking, cocks his head, and looks stricken. *"Please,"* he says, "tell me you're not writing another thing about 'the real Las Vegas.'"

Oh, but I am, I think. To my mind, there isn't much out there that evokes this so-called "real Las Vegas," that treats it simply as a place some people visit and other people live. Literature should portray, raise questions, and perhaps come to some conclusions about existence, which nobody ever seeks through Las Vegas. People come to Las Vegas looking for their idea of Las Vegas; they don't come here looking for life.

4.

I came here four years ago. I hadn't planned to stay, but I somehow couldn't leave. "This place grows on you like a fungus," one fellow relative newcomer said. My husband had a literary fellowship, and I was haunting around here when a professor, an unassuming connector type who has since become a close friend, suggested I apply for a job at UNLV's journalism school. My husband and I rented an apartment near the university, in the Vegas Towers: two "luxury" high-rise buildings built in 1974 that have some of the worst Yelp reviews I've ever read. "One of the shadiest places to rent in Vegas," reads a typical one. "The staff seem pleasant on first encounter but they are all snakes." My objections were mostly aesthetic: to the wall-to-wall beige '80s-style carpeting whose chemical smell meant we had to keep the windows open at all times, to the dingy hallways that seemed never to be vacuumed —a green M&M once sat there, untouched, for a full three weeks. The airport is 10 minutes away, and at around 5 a.m. each morning, I was awakened by the sound of airplanes ripping holes in the atmosphere. At night, a symphony of construction noises would begin, the players taking up their instruments at 9 p.m. and playing straight through until morning. On Sundays—cleaning day, I guess—someone would walk the hallways and spray an air freshener so cloyingly fragrant I could taste it for hours.

But my students delighted and astonished me. UNLV is the most diverse undergraduate campus in the country, and their families came from all over the world—in Nevada, 38 percent of children live with at least one parent who is an immigrant. Many of these young people had made their way through one of the worst public school systems in the country (Nevada is ranked 50th overall, behind only New Mexico); they were the success stories.

Fierce, tenacious, and hardworking (that's not to say some weren't infuriating or lazy), they were going to college while holding down full-time jobs in retail stores, as waitresses, as substitute teachers. One student, when I asked why he kept nodding off in class, told me he had to get up at 4 a.m. to open the Krispy Kreme at Excalibur. Another student, also always sleepy, told me she worked a 3:30 a.m. to 2 p.m. security shift at the airport. Yet another young woman—a student I became quite close to—was, at 15 years old, kicked out of her home in Pahrump by her mother, who hoped to protect her from her stepfather and his motorcycle-gang friends; she told me she used to steal toilet paper from her job so she didn't have to buy it. She'd read every book I mentioned, even in passing. *The White Album, Battleborn*—I'd see them peeking out of her purse. Each week, she'd arrive at my office hours, where she was joined by other student regulars, who would come to hang out, eat cereal, recite slam poetry, ask advice, and tell me about their lives.

When people wonder what I'm *still* doing in Las Vegas—someone is always asking you to justify your decision to live here, a phenomenon I've never experienced with any other place, and I've

lived in rural Montana—I talk about my students. I mention the
mass shooting here, which I covered for the better part of a year.
But I could also say that in Las Vegas there is, at least in my experience, a curious and refreshing lack of class consciousness, what
the critic Dave Hickey, a former resident, has called "a suppres-
sion of social differences," and that, as a result, I know a wider
and more varied range of people than I do almost anywhere else,
whereas in New York, boringly, I knew mostly writers. I could explain that the creative community here is so small that writers and
artists and intellectuals of all ages and backgrounds mix with one
another. I could mention the arresting variation of the landscape:
the fact that you can drive up the Eastside at dusk and look down
at the city lights glittering like a sequined dress, and that a summer
day in downtown Summerlin feels, save for the palm trees, like a
day in suburban Connecticut. I could say that when I had kidney
surgery last spring, friends took over my classes, offered to bring
groceries, called and texted for updates—and the gestures were
not dutiful but sincere. (You could argue that this would happen
in other cities, but I have lived in those cities, and in my experience it doesn't.) Sometimes I just say that Las Vegas—with its
glossy celebrity-chef outposts, where the meals are painstakingly
perfected, and its off-Strip restaurants, where you can find pretty
much any cuisine you want—has the best food in the country. I
sound like a travel magazine article, but it does.

Yet the deeper truth is something far more complicated. As a
writer, as a human, no place has ever captured my attention, my
imagination, and my concern as this city has. There's certainly
plenty of mundane shit here—I have spent many lonely nights
zombie-ing around the Target on Flamingo and Maryland—but
I have also seen and heard things here that I've never witnessed
anywhere else. Some of them are beautiful, some hilarious, some
perplexing, dark, and disturbing, but they are all blessedly out in
the open. "What is hidden elsewhere exists here in quotidian vis-
ibility," to quote Dave Hickey again.

Why is what's invisible in other cities so visible here? Las Vegas was a place founded on a kind of clarity about human nature,
and it has never pretended otherwise. Starting in 1931—the same
year that gambling was legalized—Nevada passed the most lenient
divorce law in the country, requiring only six weeks of residency
to file, compared to years in some states. Prohibition barely reg-

istered here; alcohol continued to be served on Fremont Street, the town's main gambling drag at the time, and on Block 16, the erstwhile red-light district, where railroad workers, travelers, and, in the 1930s, Hoover Dam laborers would come for the saloons and the prostitutes. Sex work was legal here until 1941, and still is in various brothels around Nevada—the closest to the city are in nearby Pahrump, a little more than an hour away. Indeed, still, today, the whole tourism industrial complex is devoted to serving appetites of all kinds. On top of this, there aren't the same brakes on behavior that exist elsewhere. Joan Didion once called Las Vegas "the most extreme and allegorical of American settlements, bizarre and beautiful in its venality and in its devotion to immediate gratification."

The metropolitan area also is—and, with the exception of the housing crisis in 2008, has long been—one of the fastest-growing communities in the country. In 1950, four years after Bugsy Siegel opened the Flamingo Hotel, the city's first major luxury casino (he stepped in with a mob loan when *Hollywood Reporter* founder and columnist Billy Wilkerson ran out of funds), the population of Las Vegas proper hovered around 24,624; now, a mere 75 years later, it is almost 645,000 and growing. Between 1985 and 1995, in fact, as the lavish resort hotels began to go up and gaming and tourism flourished, the city's population nearly doubled. The entire Las Vegas Valley is relatively young and full of displaced people —in 2018, Nevada was the fourth-most-moved-to state, according to United Van Lines, with many of the transplants fleeing high housing costs in California. People are also drawn by the fact that the entrenched cultural institutions of the coasts, and their rigid mores, simply don't exist here. Whoever you are, whatever you pretended to be back in Boston or New York, you don't have to keep up that pretense. You can let it all hang out, and Las Vegas has long promised to let you. Tourists can be staggeringly drunk on the streets, couples can fight in public—I recently saw a married couple nearly come to blows over the amount of time it took to use a four-dollar coupon at Target—and truly no one will bat an eye. Combine the city's dedication to encouraging shameless self-indulgence and its anything-goes outlaw ethos with seriously light policing outside of the Strip (Clark County's services, like its school system, are, let's just say, a little lacking), and you have human peccadilloes blatantly on display, along with human suffering.

One early morning as I am leaving my apartment, two esoteric sports cars are idling in front of me, bumper to bumper: a man gets out of the rear car holding a giant aspirin-pink designer purse and hurls it, with all the rage in his body, into the first car, which is presumably occupied by the purse's owner. Recently, at a party on the Strip, a four- or five-year-old girl in a mermaid costume posed for photos with partygoers; her parents, also dressed as mermaids, were placing her in people's laps. "I don't think children should be used as props," my friend whispered, after the parents tried to sit the child on her, "but that's just me." I agreed, but the kid seemed to be enjoying herself. Downtown, on a sweltering late-spring afternoon, my husband and I watched as a man in a wheelchair determinedly kicked his way up Fremont Street, backward and uphill, with one leg, his only limb. My heart collapsed in on itself, as it does so often here. Just last Saturday, I saw a woman on the sidewalk outside my apartment bathing her legs in beer. *Well, it's not water,* I thought as I passed her, *but it works.* That's a thought I never would have had before moving to Las Vegas.

It's difficult to generalize about the people of an entire city, but one thing can be said about Las Vegans: they are honest, sometimes bleakly so, and they tend to recognize this quality in others. They believe, to quote Gretel Ehrlich, that "honesty is stronger medicine than sympathy, which may console but often conceals." Sure, there are those whose instinct is to protect, to boost, to paper over the city's problems—I once horrified a colleague by regaling a famous visiting writer with a story of witnessing a robbery in the Walgreens on Flamingo—but most Las Vegans are clear-eyed about the naked human drama taking place around them. In this, they are like the artists I know, and not surprisingly: to live here requires a certain independence of spirit and, to quote F. Scott Fitzgerald, "the ability to hold two opposed ideas in mind at the same time and still retain the ability to function." People here know firsthand that the banal lies alongside the sensational, that just because it's tacky doesn't mean it isn't fun, and that wealth here sits far too close to painful, abject poverty. Las Vegas is as regular a place as any other where people shave their stubble and pay their bills, and as savage, as vulgar, and as glamorous a place as the Las Vegas of lore. Our state legislature votes on insulin pricing and voters elect a dead pimp to office, and when I need my computer fixed, I drive to the Apple store at Caesars Palace, where

tourists are jostling to see water spout from fake Greco-Roman statues. "You laugh," someone here told me, "or you die."

5.

Back at the Boulevard Mall, I return to LensCrafters to pick up
my glasses. I'm anxious because I have one ear that's higher than
the other and a touch of undiagnosed OCD, and getting them to
fit the way I like them—almost floating, not gripping my ears like
tight little baby hands—is always an ordeal. But the young man
who helped me choose the frames bends and shapes them with
such slow and attentive care that I am put immediately at ease. As
he works, we talk. His name is Pouyan. He is 28 years old, bearded
and solidly built, with intense blue eyes and a warm, open manner. He immigrated to Las Vegas three years ago from Fardis, a
city outside Tehran, by way of Turkey, to which he had escaped
by foot, and where he was later met by his parents and younger
brother. He was an optician in Iran, as was his father, but his family is Baha'i, a persecuted religious minority there, and the Iranian
government shut their optical shops down.

In order to practice in the US, he had to go back to school to
get his degree. He learned English from talking with his friends,
he says, none of whom are from Iran, but his parents are struggling with the language. He tells me he's completed his courses
and taken one of five qualifying tests required in Nevada—they
cost $300 each—but wants to help his mom set up an eyebrow-
threading business before he studies for them. He hands me my
glasses. I try them on. They are ever so slightly crooked, so he
gently, delicately, manipulates them some more. I imagine him extending such careful kindness to every customer, day in, day out,
here at this nondescript LensCrafters in the mall.

What does it mean to write about people who are usually overlooked or ignored? I am thinking about this as I walk back to my
office that afternoon, through a corridor on campus where someone often builds little sculpture towers out of rocks—they remind
me of Stonehenge in miniature. I see this found art every day; I
wonder who creates these sculptures, and I marvel that the artist
persists in re-creating them when students or maintenance workers topple them, as they always do. As I walk across the quad, I see

a wire-thin man with close-cropped gray hair placing the rocks, rough-hewn and triangular, one on top of another. They stand as if by some ineffable magic. He tells me his name is Ken; he's part Mi'Kmaq Indian, a civil engineer who ran an environmental re- mediation business for 11 years but is no longer practicing. He says his company removed asbestos from underneath the Statue of Liberty. He became an artist 17 years ago, when he had a vi- sion while planting a garden for his disabled mother in upstate New York, and he moved to Las Vegas in 2013. He calls his pieces "geoglyphs."

I'm always curious what compels people to create art outside the spotlight or the marketplace, so I ask him why he does it. He tells me that he can look at a pile of rocks—he gestures to a river of stones on the grass, an undifferentiated mass to my eye—and see how they could be beautiful. The shapes, angles, planes speak to him. They're puzzle pieces he has to make fit. Every morning when he walks his dog, he will be here, making his towers, one rock precariously balanced on another. When they get knocked down, he will pile them up again. He will do this whether I write about him or not.

In the City of Saints

FROM *Travel + Leisure*

MY FIRST GLIMPSE of Harar was through a late-afternoon haze, a balmy veil that blurred the pinks, blues, and greens of the old city's walls. It was a few days before Ramadan, and around every corner, residents were rejuvenating sun-blanched façades with fresh coats of paint in preparation for the holy month.

Harar Jugol, the labyrinthine walled quarter, seemed to twist the sunlight like a prism, beaming it out into a rainbow of lanes. One colorful path deposited me at a spice market perfumed with frankincense, berbere, cloves, and cardamom. Another led to a mansion with a grand exterior of mahogany and stained glass. It had wood carvings of the Hindu gods Krishna and Ganesh over the threshold, a legacy of the Indian merchant who built the home.

Elsewhere in the medina, I took respite from the heat under a sycamore tree and murmured a prayer at the tomb of Harar's patron saint, Sheikh Abadir. A stroll down Mekina Girgir—a street that gets its onomatopoeic name from the rhythmic rattle of sewing machines—ended at a busy square, where I caught a marching band parading past, led by a baton-twirling majorette.

When I began plotting a side trip from Addis Ababa, Harar hadn't initially been on my radar. I wanted to see the rock churches of Lalibela, the palaces of Gonder, the expanse of the Danakil Depression—but that dream Ethiopian itinerary required two weeks, and I only had two days to spare. Then someone mentioned a millennia-old walled town to the east, said to be Islam's fourth-holiest city. It wasn't what I'd expected to find in one of the oldest Christian countries on the planet, but then, the Muslim world is more of a nebulous idea than a cartographic reality. As a practicing Muslim, I've found that Islam has become one of many lenses through which I see the world, as much a part of my travels as food or art. Whether I'm seeking out peaceful interludes at mosques in Buenos Aires or Minneapolis or exploring predominantly Muslim destinations like Zanzibar or Bosnia, I try to infuse my travels with a bit of local Islamic history and culture.

Many places vie for the title of Islam's fourth-holiest city (after Mecca, Medina, and Jerusalem), but Harar Jugol, founded by Arab traders in the tenth century, has UNESCO credentials bolstering its claim. It is said to have the world's highest concentration of mosques, with at least 82 scattered across 118 acres. The many shrines have earned Harar the nickname City of Saints.

Islam has been woven into the fabric of Ethiopia as long as the religion has existed. Fleeing persecution in 613 CE, followers of the Prophet Muhammad sought refuge in the kingdom of Axum, in northern Ethiopia; when Harar was founded centuries later, it became an important locus for the faith in East Africa.

At sunset, the familiar Arabic summons of the *adhaan* swelled above torrents of Harari and Amharic chatter in the streets. *Hayya as-salah, Hayya al-falah.* Hurry to prayer, hurry to salvation. I felt the joyful flutter of recognition.

At the Sherif Harar City Museum, I browsed coins from Axum, Austria, India, Great Britain, Egypt, and Italy—evidence of Harar's heyday as a trading hub. While the city has a handful of interesting museums, the better way to find traces of its multicultural background is by sampling its street food. One vendor fried falafel under a faded blue awning. Nearby, a woman bent over a basket of glistening samosas. A young boy plucked *bombolini,* piping-hot Italian doughnuts, from a cauldron, stringing them like pearls along a skewer. I had *ful medames,* a fava-bean stew, for breakfast, then stopped at a pharmacy to chase it with a macchiato.

As a crossroads where the Harla tribe, Arab emirs, European explorers, and Indian merchants converged, Harar appears frequently in the footnotes of history. Look up Haile Selassie and you'll find a nod to Harar as the emperor's childhood home (his onetime residence now houses the aforementioned city museum). Read about Richard Francis Burton and you'll learn how the British explorer breached the city—closed to non-Muslims until the late nineteenth century—disguised as an Arab merchant. Search for Arthur Rimbaud and there's a mention of the French poet's turn as a Harar-based gunrunner (the Arthur Rimbaud Center showcases his photos of the city).

On Ethiopia's tourist circuit, Harar has become known for its spotted hyenas—and the "hyena men," who hand-feed raw meat to the wild animals, a tradition that began generations ago as a way to deter attacks on livestock. "Humans and hyenas have been living side by side for centuries," said my guide, Biniyam Fiyato, as he led me to one of the city's feeding grounds to watch the nightly ritual. "Even when the walled city was locked, hyenas would enter through drainage holes and roam the alleys."

At the sound of a whistle, dozens of hyenas slinked out of the darkness, their eyes lit by the headlights of idling vans. These feedings have become the city's tourist calling card, but the spectacle of it all left me wanting a last glimpse of Harar that was free of theatrics or artifice.

I found what I was seeking the next day in the sixteenth-century Jama Mosque, in the quiet hours between Zuhr and Asr, the afternoon prayers, when the hall stood silent. I prayed in solitude amid the white and green arches, reciting words I've repeated everywhere from Hyderabad to Honolulu—and now, Harar. No matter where I am, in a mosque, I'm home.

Reindeer at the End of the World

FROM *Emergence Magazine*

THE FOX COMES out of the willows across the creek. She is nearly invisible at first, standing in the lee of a sunbeam where it breaks over the ravine behind her. Early-morning sun, late in a summer of intense heat. Here, 20 miles north of the Arctic Circle, the light is dilute, low on the horizon and stained orange by forest-fire smoke blown from the Siberian interior. The fox steps into the radiance. Stops. Her blue-gray summer pelt has loosened, tufts of shedding fur blooming a golden corona across her back. Below, a belly slack from recent pregnancy. Something fresh-killed and bloody—a lemming, judging from the short tail—droops from her jaws. She turns, the taut notice of her ears pivoting forward, and, for a moment, I am inside her attention.

I live often in the company of the dead, as historians do. Here, on the Chukchi Peninsula, so far east in Russia it is as close to Boston as to Moscow, I think of what the dead have told me about this place: August snow squalls, whipping cold and wind, ice on still water by September. Eye to eye with the fox, I am not even in a sweater. In this part of the Arctic, it is the hottest summer in recorded memory. All through June and July, people say offhand or with worry or with dark humor, "It's the end of the world," or "It's Armageddon." The first word of a widely read article about climate change is "Doomsday." In a few weeks, scientists will give the world 12 years to reduce carbon emissions or risk warming so great it will be headlined "Climate Apocalypse."

Behind me, the sound of a motor. Alex has started our *uaz,* a Soviet-era van with the soul of a tractor. We are going north, where the Chukchi reindeer brigades run their herds along the Amguema River. Alex has distant relatives there, to whom we are carrying supplies and gifts: biscuits, sugar, candles, bread, tinned butter, evaporated milk, boxes of tea, bags of hard candies. There are hours to go yet on the rutted gravel road. We stopped at this bubbling creek to do something Alex's father taught him: pick a stem of grass and leave it in the water. A *pros'ba*, Alex called it. A request, or a prayer. A supplication to the future.

Then came the fox. The terms of her future, Alex's future, my future, and the future of this place—and all the loved, life-filled places—are given so often now as prophecies of rupture. Years of historical training mean I cannot see the arc of such stories as neutral. They shape the borders of our minds, and our politics. I want to know: Where does it come from, this narrative of absolute end? And what meaning slinks in with a proclamation of apocalypse?

The fox lifts her nose at the engine sound, and turns. I watch her trot back to her kits: paws quick through the bearberries and knots of cotton grass before her path angles among crumbling buildings, cement gone porous with decades of rain, and machinery turned burnt red from rust. The fox does not give us a backward glance as she takes shelter in our ruins.

Building

One of the dead in whose company I have passed some days is a man named Karl Yanovich Luks. He was dark-haired and handsome, from what the photographs tell. The fraying influence of cold winds was just beginning to show around his eyes when he wrote reports from Chukotka to Moscow in the 1920s:

> The Chukchi are the majority of the Native population of the Chukchi Peninsula . . . Under the tsars, these Natives were only of interest as suppliers of furs. Nobody gave a thought to protecting the base of the Native economy, to improving his way of life. As a result, the fur trade was nearly extinguished . . . and reindeer husbandry fell off catastrophically.
>
> To fix this destruction is our task.

In Karl's life is a history of apocalyptic allure, of what sings to us beyond the horizon of a demolished now. He was born on the western edge of the Russian Empire in 1888 to peasants so destitute his father nearly sold an infant Karl to the childless baron who owned the lands his parents worked. As a boy he tended cattle. Around him, most people were confined to agricultural toil on old noble estates or industrial toil in new factories. His parents were unable to afford education beyond basic literacy, so Karl became a deckhand when he was hardly more than a child.

His voyages took him through Baltic ports thrumming with discontent. Strikers protested factories that rent their bodies. Breadlines turned into riots after days of hunger. Students demanded representative government. Tsar Nicholas II, heir to four centuries of autocratic rule, sheltered in his palaces, spent lavishly, and hired more police. The people Karl met outside these aristocratic walls found their present so unjust, so sickly, so impossible, their question was not would it end, but how. Karl heard Baptists preaching hellfire, Orthodox priests invoking the salvation of saints, and a dozen other sects calling down the final judgment.

As the historian Yuri Slezkine explains, these visions all shared a plot: first the apocalypse, then a reign of harmony and perfection. An old story, passed from the Middle East to Europe, from Jewish cosmologies into Christian traditions, going back almost 3,000 years to the prophecies of Zoroaster, who foretold a cataclysmic battle between light and dark. The triumph of light would give the righteous a new life, one without suffering or toil, one where time as meted out in cycles of birth and death ended in a linear, immortal world.

Karl did not become a Baptist or worship saints. He joined a socialist reading circle. In Slezkine's masterful reading of the Russian socialist condition, the plot Karl learned also came from Zoroaster's lineage. Karl Marx and Friedrich Engels foretold how the darkness of capitalist exploitation would become the light of communist utopia. Between these poles was a kind of earthly revelation: what socialists called *revolution*. A word, Slezkine reminds us, promising "the end of the old world and the beginning of a new, just one."

I met Karl in an age-crumpled file in Vladivostok, where I learned what he would give for this new world. At 17, he was arrested for distributing illegal pamphlets. For the next decade, he was in and out of custody. Karl left a four-year term in Orel Central Penitentiary with tuberculosis. In his autobiography, Karl described being bound by a guard in a different prison: "The ropes ate into my body to the bones at hands and feet . . . [which] were swollen and blackened so it was impossible to control them." When Vladimir Lenin brought the revolution to Russia in the bitterly cold and hunger-filled winter of 1917, Karl was in Siberian exile. He joined Lenin's army when it reached the north, then he moved on to Chukotka, tasked by the new Soviet government with "liquidating the consequences of centuries-old historical injustices" from the tundra.

When Karl wrote, "To fix this destruction is our task," what he meant was, "We shall end the unjust world, and beyond it is a life without want." Such a pure vision: Karl went to prison and into exile to help found the kingdom of freedom on earth.

One appeal of the apocalypse is that it can make those on its threshold feel world-historically important.

Back in the *uaz*, we climb through hills of eroding yellow and brown stone, their tops in velvet fog. The road turns out onto green rolling tundra. Somewhere to our north, Alex says, are the reindeer. Like the fox, they are in summer molt, flanks patchy with shedding hair and antlers trailing bloody ribbons of the velvet that nourished their bony growth. Reindeer are almost never alone, and almost never still. They move constantly to find fresh pasture and breezes to keep mosquitoes from tormenting their flesh. With each step the tendons in their hooves move over the sesamoid bone with a soft click. In other summers, on other tundras, I have heard reindeer before seeing them.

Today, the reindeer are with their people. Centuries before the first Russian speaker came here, the Chukchi and wild reindeer struck a bargain, in the relations we call domestication: reindeer who lived as familiars with people were protected from wolves and bears; people who lived as familiars with reindeer were protected from starvation. In the history the Chukchi tell of themselves, a few dozen domesticated reindeer made food and shelter newly dependable. Hundreds or thousands made politics newly potent, as the bodies of many reindeer carried the authority of many gifts and armies fed for war.

Yet to walk out with a herd on a tundra morning was to enter a world where human authority did not extend fully even to
the tame animals shuffling their spade-like hooves and exhaling
great steamy breaths outside Chukchi tents. These hills were home
to many beings, to mushroom-shaped men, and giants with gap-
ing mouths, and wild reindeer people, any of which could steal
a herd. Some were kin, some were foes. Valleys, rivers, reindeer,
foxes, walruses—all bore souls that required entreaty. That required you ask for their favor before you walk. Time itself spooled
out through the land in cycles. A spate of warm years—normal,
for most of the Holocene, each century to half century—brought
intertwined perils. Cold air reduces precipitation, so in warmer
winters herds foundered in deep snow. Sometimes rain fell on the
drifts, then froze again; the resulting ice starved reindeer unable
to paw through it to the lichens and dried grass beneath. Boggy
summers infected their hooves, hindered migration, and left them
vulnerable to anthrax. A family with 5,000 reindeer could in a decade find themselves with only hundreds: enough for food, not
for armies. To walk out on an Arctic morning was always an appeal
to a will-filled universe. For, as one Chukchi man told it not long
after Karl Luks was born, "nothing created by man has any power."

Karl would not have agreed. "Freedom," Engels wrote in *Anti-
Dühring*, "consists in the control over ourselves and over external
nature." Liberation came from bending every resource to human
need, and only humans could be free. It was the fundamental plot
for Marx and Engels: this capacity for progress that drew societies
from hunting and gathering to agriculture, to industrial capitalism, and onward to revolution, beyond which there would be no
suffering or decay. The idea of time Karl brought with him to Chukotka was aggressively linear.

On the tundra, Karl's task was to identify external nature to control. Chukotka was too cold for agriculture, too distant and rugged
for much industry. But there were reindeer with useful meat, and
foxes with valuable pelts. Karl drew up plans to increase the size
of reindeer herds with Soviet farming techniques. Other young
"missionaries of the new culture and the new Soviet state," as one
follower of Marx put it, designed systems of fox pens and barns.
The animals could not be left in the wild: out on the tundra, their
numbers rose and fell every few years, dependent on cycles of lem-
mings. Socialist farms would replace such inconstancy with pre-

dictable growth. Caged foxes required no long days setting traps among the thickets that foxes prowl; the Chukchi could live in town, in apartments with electricity and running water, while their children, Karl wrote, could attend "a first class school not in Native dialect, for a real Soviet education."

Karl did not ask the Chukchi if they wanted this new world. No one did. Nor did anyone ask the foxes about the pens or the reindeer about their corrals; to do so was not thinkable.

Another appeal of the apocalypse: proclaiming it is not an act of supplication, but of certainty.

In 1932, Karl Luks took an accidental bullet while surveying foxes and reindeer and other life on the Chaun River, in Chukotka's northwest. As he bled to death, so Soviet reports go, he begged his fellow revolutionaries to continue their work "in the most remote places inhabited by Natives, . . . no matter the victims, in spite of any cost."

Such certainty can be a kind of madness. In the *uaz*, bumping north, Alex tells me that many of the "victims" who came after Karl were Chukchi. "We did not want to live in the way the Soviets said was correct," Alex explains. Looking west out the *uaz*, I see rocks covered in black lichen breaking through cushions of moss campion. A single white reindeer rib bone curves up from the pink flowers. Across the road, other remains: a *pekaranya*, a bakery, its roof like a broken back, crouched amid low houses charred by old fire. The way of life these structures built into the land—settled, electrified, educated in Russian—did not signal the promised land to Alex's ancestors as it did for Karl. The Chukchi did not want to give their reindeer to Soviet farms and take daylong shifts in dark fox barns. Or give over their visions of creation—the raven that made their land, long ago, or the boy born from a reindeer's ear —for the stories Lenin told.

For two decades after Karl died, war simmered over the tundra. The Chukchi killed their reindeer or killed themselves rather than be part of the new promised land. Around and after the violence, Soviet scientists mapped these hills and rivers, analyzed their plants, plotted migration routes to optimize reindeer nutrition. Veterinarians inoculated herds for anthrax and foxes for distemper, examined hooves for disease, and charted the best time to breed vixens. The tundra was coming under control—was becoming the prophesied human perfection. One reindeer scientist even wrote in the 1950s that the revolution had brought such "new forms of organizing the reindeer herd" that growth would be infinite. The ultimate linear dream, of progress unending: an escape from the limits of moss and lichen, the necessity of relating to other life.

Something else about the apocalypse: its battles only damn or save human beings. In this story, our species has no kin but ourselves.

Falling

We reach the Amguema by midday. A quarter mile or so from its banks is a village, named after the river. A Soviet town, concrete buildings connected by elevated gas pipes shedding insulation. Entropy has taken over on the outskirts, pulling down houses, filling the space between with fireweed. But in the center, there are curtains in open windows and bright paint on the concrete. Somewhere, Pearl Jam is playing, tinny notes floating toward us on the breeze: *A dissident is here. Escape is never the safest path.*

We stop the *uaz* by a group of men in rubber boots and mud-spattered orange overalls. One of them introduces himself as the mayor. They are digging a drainage ditch, he explains. The tundra under the town is seeping. Alex asks if the reindeer brigades are close. The mayor points us west, toward the river. If they have returned, their *yaranga*, their reindeer-hide tents, will be there. He advises that we leave the *uaz* and walk: since the fall, the roads have decayed.

The fall: 60 years after Karl Luks died, the Soviet Union ceased to exist. By then, in the early 1990s, socialist efforts to control this land had changed many things—built these roads and apartments, brought children into schools, herded reindeer with helicopters and snow machines. Chukotka became a Soviet version of the world we now find normal, where lights come on with a switch and airplanes satisfy any need. But the Soviet Union never did mold time into linear form. Even before the USSR sundered, reindeer herds defied Soviet prophecy and declined. Foxes kept dying from rabies. The impossibility of Karl's most apocalyptic promise—the freedom from any natural constraint—was borne out. And then what did change disappeared.

Historians tell stories of why. In Chukotka, the stories of the 1990s bend toward the *how.* How did we survive a civilization in its ending? All that the Soviets brought with them—the gas heat and bakeries, the machinery and medicines—was no more. Alex was a child when the electricity stuttered off. There was no gasoline to move supplies, but there were no supplies to move anyway.

The arrival of the Soviet Union had been terrible for its violence; its dissolution was terrible for its sudden stillness. Towns were emptied as people fled to southern Russia. Older people died without medicine or warmth. Mothers worried that lack of food meant little milk for their infants. Everything was cold. The horizon of time closed: What would summer bring to keep families and whole towns alive during the winter? What would winter do? The fox barns emptied. Untended reindeer went feral or were lost to wolves.

Yet each day came with its small, specific tasks of survival. Chukchi families set up *yaranga* inside their apartments and burned seal oil lamps for warmth and light. Through summer and fall, people picked berries and greens and packed them in seal fat for winter. It was good to know hunters who lived along the coast, in the villages where elders still remembered how to kill bowhead whales without specialized equipment. It was also good to know how to tend reindeer without helicopters, sew reindeer-hide boots, harness a reindeer when the snow machine ran out of fuel. Solidarity, that old socialist refrain, ceased to be a slogan and became a necessity. At the end of a world, there are no damned or saved souls, only people and other kin to share in the work of making life possible.

No one knew what would happen, Alex tells me. The trick to surviving was in knowing something about the land and the animals, and in keeping on without certainty.

The reindeer are still at pasture: none are to be seen as we pick our way over the uneven ground with our parcels of bread and biscuits. Ahead is the Amguema River, bright blue in the midday light, breaking silver in the shallows. On the bank, among low willows, are two *yaranga*, round and white like landed clouds. A dog, waist-high and furred like a bear, rises at our approach and nuzzles my hand. Alex calls out hellos. From within one of the tents, a voice asks if we want tea.

Stooping into the *yaranga*, I am blinded for a moment by smoke, which rises from a small fire, its coals sheltering a blackened pot. Near the coals are an older man and woman: Grigori and Anna, they say. We give our names and sit cross-legged on reindeer skins, passing over our gifts in exchange for tea, brewed oily black and dense with sugar.

The conversation loops between Russian and Chukchi, so I do not understand all of it. There are relatives to discuss. News from wider Russia to pass on: what Putin is doing in Moscow. I catch that Grigori and Anna were born just after the Chukchi and the Soviets ceased killing each other, and were nearly grandparents by the collapse. Their sons work in Amguema part of the year but are out now with the reindeer. They sell some of the meat in Chukotka's larger towns and keep the rest, along with the skins, for their relatives.

The tundra where the reindeer graze has grown strange. There are new insects, Grigori says, beetles the Chukchi have no words for and which eat some of the same plants as reindeer. Anna is worried about chemicals and cancer: from what the Soviets left behind, but also from the garbage she says washes up on the Bering Sea coast after every storm. What does it leech into the fish we all eat from this river? And then there is the weather. Deep snow, rains that come late into fall for the past few years. We all look down at our tea. No one knows what's going to happen, Grigori says. It's probably a good idea to buy more rubber boots, he adds, and laughs.

Today it is hard to say when the reindeer will come back, Anna says. It depends on the winds and the pastures, and if there is rain. The herds have their own plans, so we should eat boiled meat and stay and talk. She puts a larger pot on the fire. Grigori opens a worn Styrofoam cooler, its interior full of red flesh and blood smell, and with a long knife begins to sever reindeer ribs from each other.

When the smoke from the fire begins to sting my eyes, I slip out of the tent and walk toward the river. From the far bank, the country rolls out in a wide plain, lustrous green with summer growth, the hummocks and knots of sedge grass and boggy places smoothed by distance. Far off, low mountains rise purplish. On this afternoon, I am almost the same age Karl Luks was when he wrote "to fix this destruction is our task." We have other things in common. I also came of age—I am of age—in a world too precarious and unjust to continue with impunity. People with power spend lavishly and hire more police. In the United States, where I live, our national politics leads less to the poor selling their children to the wealthy than to the wealthy stealing children's futures, carbon atom by carbon atom. All around are whispers of the end: we live in late capitalism, people say, implying imminent sundown; we live in the sixth extinction, people say, calling up the void with a phrase; we live in a climate emergency, a crisis, a thing terribly more than change. The grimmest of these prophecies tells an old story: the ultimate battle, in which an unlivable climate will drive out the darkness that we have become. As if the end to human failing is our extinction.

The core of apocalyptic thinking is nihilism: this world is too despoiled to continue. The seduction of such stories is how certain they make the teller feel. An apocalyptic narrative is like looking at a horizon with no clouds or hills: the way forward is terribly assured. To walk it, there is no need to mind the lives of others, rendered invisible by the power of imagining they are already gone.

Apocalyptic prophecy is also an escape from contemplating—from seeing in the here and now—how life goes on even through catastrophe. The Chukotkan riverbank where I am standing has borne two world-endings in the past century, the end of a world without socialists and the end of a world with them. The story these endings have etched into this earth bears no relation to Zoroaster's final battle, or the pure cleansing fire of Karl's revolution. What the land here speaks instead is a tale in which rupture is never complete. No revolution excises the quotidian, the need to rise and sleep, to nourish and shelter, to care for new birth and imminent death. This is the insurmountable stuff of being. In the company of Chukotka's dead and living, I have come to believe the most terrifying thing about our future is not just what will change or cease or grow uncanny, but what must continue regardless.

Looking out toward the far mountains, I think of the drive here. Almost a hundred kilometers, the road marked by sequential clots of debris. Rusted things, broken things, shelters opened to the sky. One way to see Chukotka is as unrelentingly scarred, a place befouled by Soviet remnants. Another way is as a site of ongoing restitution. The mayor down in the mud, making another year livable in his town. A reindeer rib, feeding us. The fox raising a new generation inside a lidless, rusted oil barrel. We all live in the company of the dead. What presence will we be for the lives that come after us?

To fix destruction *is* our task. What if that mandate summoned not delusions of escape and human grandeur, but repair? Restoring what has broken is a reminder to be careful with what is here now. It is an entreaty to make things last and to care for what will outlast our small tender lives. Not an easy task. It will take, I think, all of what I find inspiring in Karl Luks's story: how he worked hard and collectively, how he believed justice was possible and equity critical. Our uneasy world needs his courage and his bodily sacrifice. But it also requires trading the temptation of apocalypse escapism for world-historical humility, for perseverance without certainty, for prophecies that hold space for more than people. We must make better ruins. My *pros'ba,* here on this river, is not for a new heaven and a new earth. It is for this earth: I wish to make mends that will hold us.

The sun is rolling toward its setting, late in this summer of intense heat. From inside the *yaranga* comes faint laughter, and then a yell that the meat is ready. I turn and take shelter among the bent alder rafters, snug under the canvas and reindeer skins.

Senegal's Beating Heart

FROM *Westways*

ON A STEAMY night in Senegal's capital, a 64-year-old bald singer and his band were several songs into their set when they launched into *"Dila Beug,"* or "Loving You." Wearing glasses and an elegant plaid tunic, Omar Pene—a West African legend—clutched the microphone and belted out a few lines in the local Wolof. A drummer unleashed a blistering solo. I could feel the room heating up: men in tunics and women in tight, sequined dresses grooved on the dance floor, and, as an electric guitar wailed and the song reached a crescendo, even the cooks in the kitchen gave up any pretense of restraint and gathered around, rocking openly in their pressed chef's whites.

Then one of Senegal's biggest soccer stars, El Hadji Diouf, emerged from the dance floor, grabbed the microphone, and yelled in Wolof: "If you clap your hands, you'll live forever!" The crowd went wild.

Like millions of Americans in the mid-'80s, I got the briefest introduction to Senegalese music thanks to British rocker Peter Gabriel. His hit "In Your Eyes" featured the pyrotechnic backing vocals of a rising Senegalese star named Youssou N'Dour. The song reached its pop-culture zenith in Cameron Crowe's 1989 film *Say Anything,* when a trench coat–wearing Lloyd Dobler (John Cusack) played it from a boombox he held over his head to serenade Diane Court (Ione Skye). The hit helped catapult N'Dour to worldwide acclaim. His silky voice was so expressive, in fact, that *Rolling Stone* declared "the history of Africa seemed locked inside it." N'Dour led me to other West African artists and, over time, to an idea:

some of my most moving travel experiences had involved music —listening to a Moroccan oud player jam in Granada, Spain, for example, or pogoing to Manu Chao and his band in Buenos Aires, Argentina—yet I hadn't even planned those. What if I actually set out to explore Senegal through its music?

I landed in the capital of Dakar at a seemingly promising moment. Not only is Senegal celebrating 60 years of independence from France this year, but just last year, the *New York Times* named Dakar one of its 52 places to visit—right up there with Doha, Qatar, and the islands of Tahiti. The city is "a haven of peace in a region known for unrest," the newspaper proclaimed, and "a siren song for hipsters." And not long before that, the late globetrotting chef Anthony Bourdain heaped praise on the nation. "Even if you've been traveling nearly nonstop for 15 years like me, there are places that snap you out of your comfortable worldview, take your assumptions and your prejudices and turn them upside down," he said. "They lead you to believe that maybe there is hope in this world. Senegal is one of those places." Given the headlines around the world, I could certainly use some hope.

Music City

Happily, I found Dakar to be buzzing with energy when I arrived. Across the sprawling metropolis of more than 3 million people, horse-drawn carts competed for space with taxis and minibuses. Markets overflowed with produce, fish, and other goods—much of which found its way into baskets balanced impressively atop women's heads. Yet communicating was a challenge: Many locals I met spoke French and at least one indigenous tongue, but little English. And my rusty, rudimentary French was of little help. So I was relieved at midday to meet an English-speaking guide for lunch in the cosmopolitan coastal neighborhood of Almadies.

Over the national dish of rice and fish, Adja Kosse Faie told me just how central music is in Senegalese life. "You have music when you get up and when you go to bed," she said. "You hear it everywhere." She pulled out her phone and played YouTube videos of some of her favorite songs. And she raved about an older acoustic musician named Souleymane Faye: "He sings about friendships and life and love, and he sometimes uses proverbs in his songs," she said. Not long after our conversation, she sent me a WhatsApp message (everyone I met, it seemed, used WhatsApp). As luck would have it, Faye was performing tonight. Would I like to go?

So that evening, we headed to a small restaurant-nightclub called Ubuntu in the upscale neighborhood of Ngor Virage. The club was nearly empty when we arrived at 9 p.m.—I was beginning to realize that nightlife in the capital doesn't really start until about midnight. But as Adja and I chatted over dinner near framed photos of Michael Jordan and Che Guevara, people trickled in, and by the time Faye took the stage hours later, the place was hopping. The singer wore a bright vest and cap, and a long silver necklace. Accompanied by a bass player and a dreadlocked drummer on the traditional Senegalese *sabar,* Faye strummed a jangly electric guitar and sang in Wolof. The result was a kind of hypnotic folk-rock, with Faye's resonant voice reminding me of Marvin Gaye one moment and Van Morrison the next. After the show ended around 2 a.m., Adja and I chatted with the gregarious musician, who wistfully recalled playing years ago in New York City. In fact, Faye is one of many local stars whose music has found an enthusiastic audience overseas.

Whether or not they're aware of it, many Americans have heard Senegalese superstar Baaba Maal. Blessed with a golden voice, Maal has not only recorded and toured with British folk rockers Mumford & Sons, but he also sang in his native Pulaar on the Oscar-winning soundtrack to the 2018 hit Marvel movie *Black Panther.* A member of the Fulani tribe, one of West Africa's largest ethnic groups, Maal grew up in northern Senegal in the 1950s and '60s surrounded by music. "Our country was coming into independence," he once said, "was opening to the rest of the world, and it was easy to see where the connection was between the traditional music we were doing and the opportunities the rest of the world was giving us." The confluence of politics and globalization would prove to be a powerful catalyst. Both Maal and N'Dour would become global stars, but neither forgot about home. N'Dour later opened a nightclub and launched a TV network in Dakar. And from 2012 to 2013, after attempting a run for the presidency, he served as Senegal's minister of tourism, culture, and leisure.

The more time I spent in Dakar, the more I realized just how right Adja had been: music really *was* everywhere—good music, too. One evening, as a warm breeze blew off the Atlantic and the sun began to set, I relaxed by the swimming pool at the Radisson Blu hotel and watched a trio set up: a saxophonist, a drummer, and a musician with a kora—the round-bodied West African harp with 21 strings. I didn't expect much; I've rarely been bowled over by poolside musicians. But as the sky turned a burnt peach and the lights of Dakar flickered on, I watched in awe as the group launched into a gorgeous, sometimes haunting, set. The kora player sang in Wolof, his stirring voice rising and falling over the gentle drums, and the saxophonist riffed at just the right moments.

Such acoustic music is often played around Senegal, but the most popular style, by far, is *mbalax*, a high-energy fusion of influences, from Senegalese and Cuban rhythms to soul, rock, and Congolese rumba. Much of Senegal's music has its roots in the country's centuries-old ethnic traditions, including *mbalax*, which exploded in the 1970s with the rise of groups such as Étoile de Dakar, which featured N'Dour, and Super Diamono, starring Pene. To this day, *mbalax* groups generally include keyboardists, drummers, electric guitarists, and a singer. In recent decades, Senegalese music has continued to evolve, with younger artists blending traditional styles with rap and hip-hop.

Woman Power

Late one afternoon at the oceanfront Terrou-Bi hotel, I met up with a popular all-woman trio called Safary, which formed in Dakar in 2007. Back then, the group's three young members were defying convention, said singer Khadija Bayo. "Traditionally, girls in Africa are expected go to school, if they're lucky, and then find a husband and make a family," she said. "Now things are changing a little." The group performs Afrobeat—a percussive blend of rap, hip-hop, Cuban *son*, and other influences—and sings about relationships, societal expectations, and challenges of modern life. They also take pains to celebrate African culture, which they say gets short shrift in much of the international media in Senegal. Because of what they see on the internet and TV, for example, Senegalese women think they should look like Kim Kardashian, Bayo said. "Every woman wants to look like her."

"Really?" I said. "Even here?"

"Of course," she said, grinning.

I shook my head. "I'm so sorry."

Bayo and her fellow bandmates laughed. "Our idea of beauty is to keep our African values," she said. "We don't need to buy Versace to look beautiful. Even tonight, we're all wearing clothes made here in Senegal." And, in fact, the group was working on its first album devoted to traditional *mbalax* music.

I wanted to meet other artists fusing musical genres and soon found myself trading WhatsApp texts with Amadou Barry, a rap star better known as Duggy Tee, who replied to my first message with "Welcome home."

Duggy Tee picked me up in an SUV and drove me to a dusty street corner in Dakar's Sacre Coeur neighborhood, where he often hangs out under shady trees with friends. There, he told me about his childhood in Paris and Dakar. His father was a flight attendant for the now-defunct Air Afrique, he said, and as a kid, he spent countless hours listening to his dad's records. He loved Pink Floyd's *The Wall* and often studied the lyrics on the album jacket. "That," he said, "was one of my first English lessons."

As we talked on, a horse clopped past pulling a buggy, and Duggy Tee described taking up break dancing in his early teens after seeing American dance movies. Later, he started rapping, and, with a former rival turned friend, he established the group Positive Black Soul. At first, some Senegalese accused the pair of imitating American music. "We said, 'No, you're fooling yourselves,'" he recalled. "'Rap is rooted in ancient African traditions.'" The group sang about social issues and celebrated African pride, and they spent years touring the world. Duggy Tee said he was working on a solo album, but he also wanted to produce TV shows for Senegalese children. He thought kids in the country watched too many shows produced in the US and France. "Why don't we make something like *The Simpsons* here?" he said.

Soon it was time for lunch, and he invited me to join him and several friends. We ate rice and fish in the traditional Senegalese style, out of a large communal bowl. "Here, it's considered selfish to eat on your own plate," Duggy Tee said. "This way, you have to be careful to leave enough food for everyone." I'd read that Senegal was famous for its hospitality— *teranga,* in local parlance. "Is this *teranga*?" I asked. Duggy Tee nodded. "It's part of our culture," he said. "It's almost a sin not to feed people when they come to your house."

Our time was winding down. That night, I'd have to catch a flight out of Senegal. As Duggy Tee drove me back to my hotel, we talked about the joys of travel. "You learn so much from it," he said. "Sometimes you see people in extreme poverty, but who have a lot of dignity. And sometimes you meet people who have everything they could want, but they're so mean. The more you travel, the more you realize how little you know."

Of course, he was right. But after a week in Senegal, there were a few things I *did* know: Music can offer a kind of secret passage to the heart of a country. Also, music transcends language, and you don't need to speak a word of Wolof or Pulaar to appreciate the essence of an artist or song. And, finally, thanks to the mysterious alchemy that can occur in a packed Dakar nightclub, for the briefest moment, music can almost make you believe you'll live forever.

Five Oceans, Five Deeps

FROM *The New Yorker*

SEA LEVEL — perpetual flux. There is a micromillimeter on the surface of the ocean that moves between sea and sky and is simultaneously both and neither. Every known life-form exists in relation to this layer. Above it, the world of land, air, sunlight, and lungs. Below it, the world of water, depth, and pressure. The deeper you go, the darker, the more hostile, the less familiar, the less measured, the less known.

A splash in the South Pacific, last June, marked a historic breach of that world. A crane lowered a small white submersible off the back of a ship and plonked it in the water. For a moment, it bobbed quietly on the surface, its buoyancy calibrated to the weight of the pilot, its only occupant. Then he flipped a switch, and the submarine emitted a frantic, high-pitched whirr. Electric pumps sucked seawater into an empty chamber, weighing the vessel down. The surface frothed as the water poured in—then silence, as the top of the submersible dipped below the waterline, and the ocean absorbed it.

Most submarines go down several hundred meters, then across; this one was designed to sink like a stone. It was the shape of a bulging briefcase, with a protruding bulb at the bottom. This was the pressure hull—a titanium sphere, five feet in diameter, which was sealed off from the rest of the submersible and housed the pilot and all his controls. Under the passenger seat was a tuna-fish sandwich, the pilot's lunch. He gazed out of one of the viewports, into the blue. It would take nearly four hours to reach the bottom.

Sunlight cuts through the first thousand feet of water. This is the epipelagic zone, the layer of plankton, kelp, and reefs. It contains the entire ecosystem of marine plants, as well as the mammals and the fish that eat them. An Egyptian diver once descended to the limits of this layer. The feat required a lifetime of training, four years of planning, a team of support divers, an array of specialized air tanks, and a tedious, 13-hour ascent, with constant decompression stops, so that his blood would not be poisoned and his lungs would not explode.

The submersible dropped at a rate of about two and a half feet per second. Twenty minutes into the dive, the pilot reached the midnight zone, where dark waters turn black. The only light is the dim glow of bioluminescence—from electric jellies, camouflaged shrimp, and toothy predators with natural lanterns to attract unwitting prey. Some fish in these depths have no eyes—what use are they? There is little to eat. Conditions in the midnight zone favor fish with slow metabolic rates, weak muscles, and slimy, gelatinous bodies.

An hour into the descent, the pilot reached 10,000 feet—the beginning of the abyssal zone. The temperature is always a few degrees above freezing, and is unaffected by the weather at the surface. Animals feed on "marine snow": scraps of dead fish and plants from the upper layers, falling gently through the water column. The abyssal zone, which extends to 20,000 feet, encompasses 97 percent of the ocean floor.

After two hours in free fall, the pilot entered the hadal zone, named for the Greek god of the underworld. It is made up of trenches—geological scars at the edges of the earth's tectonic plates—and although it composes only a tiny fraction of the ocean floor, it accounts for nearly 50 percent of the depth.

Past 27,000 feet, the pilot had gone beyond the theoretical limit for any kind of fish. (Their cells collapse at greater depths.) After 35,000 feet, he began releasing a series of weights, to slow his descent. Nearly seven miles of water was pressing on the titanium sphere. If there were any imperfections, it could instantly implode.

The submarine touched the silty bottom, and the pilot, a 53-year-old Texan named Victor Vescovo, became the first living creature with blood and bones to reach the deepest point in the Tonga Trench. He was piloting the only submersible that can bring a human to that depth: his own.

For the next hour, he explored the featureless beige sediment, and tried to find and collect a rock sample. Then the lights flickered, and an alarm went off. Vescovo checked his systems—there was a catastrophic failure in battery one. Water had seeped into the electronics, bringing about a less welcome superlative: the deepest-ever artificial explosion was taking place a few feet from his head.

If there were oxygen at that depth, there could have been a raging fire. Instead, a battery junction box melted, burning a hole through its external shell without ever showing a flame. Any instinct to panic was suppressed by the impossibility of rescue. Vescovo would have to come up on his own.

Seven miles overhead, a white ship bobbed in Polynesian waters. It had been built by the US Navy to hunt Soviet military submarines, and recently repurposed to transport and launch Vescovo's private one. There were a couple of dozen crew members on board, all of whom were hired by Vescovo. He was midway through an attempt to become the first person to reach the deepest point in each ocean, an expedition he called the Five Deeps. He had made a fortune in private equity, but he could not buy success in this—a richer man had tried and failed. When the idea first crossed his mind, there was no vehicle to rent, not even from a government. No scientist or military had the capacity to go within two miles of the depths he sought to visit. Geologists weren't even sure where he should dive.

Vescovo's crew was an unlikely assemblage—"a proper band of thieves," as the expedition's chief scientist put it—with backgrounds in logistics, engineering, academia, and petty crime. Some on board had spent decades at sea; others were landlubbers. For more than a year, they faced challenges as timeless as bad weather and as novel as the equipment they had invented for the job. They discovered undersea mountain ranges, collected thousands of biological samples that revealed scores of new species, and burned through tens of thousands of gallons of fuel and alcohol.

In 1969, when Vescovo was three years old, he climbed into the front seat of his mother's car, which was parked on a hill outside their house. He was small and blond, the precocious, blue-eyed grandson of Italian immigrants who had come to the United States in the late nineteenth century and made a life selling gelato in the South. Vescovo put the car in neutral. It rolled backward into a tree, and he spent the next six weeks in an intensive care unit. There were lasting effects: nerve damage to his right hand, an interest in piloting complex vehicles, and the "torturous compulsion," he said, to experience everything he could before he died.

He grew up reading science fiction, and aspired to be an astronaut; he had the grades but not the eyesight. As an undergraduate, at Stanford, he learned to fly planes. Afterward, he went to MIT, for a master's degree in defense and arms-control studies, where he modeled decision-making and risk—interests that later converged in overlapping careers as a reserve naval intelligence officer and a businessman. Vescovo was deployed as a targeting officer for the NATO bombing of Kosovo, and, as a counterterrorism officer, he was involved in a hostage rescue in the Philippines. He learned Arabic and became rich through finance and consulting jobs, and, later, through a private equity firm, Insight Equity, in the suburbs of Dallas, where he lives.

Vescovo started going on increasingly elaborate mountaineering expeditions, and by 2014 he had skied the last hundred kilometers to the North and South Poles and summited the highest peak on every continent. He had narrowly survived a rock slide near the top of Mount Aconcagua, in the Argentinean Andes, and had come to embrace a philosophy that centered on calculated risk. Control what you can; be aware of what you cannot. Death, at some point, is a given—"You have to accept it," he said—and he reasoned that the gravest risk a person could take was to waste time on earth, to reach the end without having maximally lived. "This is the only way to fight against mortality," he said. "My social life was pretty nonexistent, but it just wasn't a priority. Life was too interesting." He grew his hair down to his shoulders, and touched up the color, even as his beard turned white. On weekends, he used his private jet to shuttle rescue dogs to prospective owners all over the US. At sea, according to members of his expedition team, he spent hours in his cabin alone, playing *Call of Duty* and eating microwaved macaroni and cheese.

But every age of exploration runs its course. "When Shackleton sailed for the Antarctic in 1914, he could still be a hero. When he returned in 1917 he could not," Fergus Fleming writes, in his introduction to *South*, Ernest Shackleton's diary. "The concept of heroism evaporated in the trenches of the First World War." While Shackleton was missing in Antarctica, a member of his expedition

cabled for help. Winston Churchill responded, "When all the sick
and wounded have been tended, when all their impoverished &
broken hearted homes have been restored, when every hospital is
gorged with money, & every charitable subscription is closed, then
& not till then wd. I concern myself with these penguins."

A century later, adventurers tend to accumulate ever more
meaningless firsts: a Snapchat from the top of Mount Everest; in
Antarctica, the fastest mile ever traveled on a pogo stick. But to
open the oceans for exploration without limit—here was a mean-
ingful record, Vescovo thought, perhaps the last on earth. In 1961,
John F. Kennedy said that "knowledge of the oceans is more than
a matter of curiosity. Our very survival may hinge upon it." Yet, in
the following decades, the hadal trench nearest to the US became
a dumping ground for pharmaceutical waste.

In September 2014, Vescovo sent an inquiry to Triton Submarines, a small manufacturer in Vero Beach, Florida. He noted that
he was a jet and helicopter pilot familiar with the "procedure-
driven piloting of complex craft," and outlined what became the
Five Deeps Expedition.

Patrick Lahey, the president of Triton, took up scuba diving when
he was 13 years old, and discovered that he felt more at home underwater than he did on land. The muted silence, the slow, deep
breaths—diving forced him into a kind of meditative state. "I love
the feeling of weightlessness," he told me. "I love moving around
in three dimensions, instead of two." Lahey attended commercial
diving school, to learn underwater welding and construction for
dams, bridges, and oil-and-gas installations. "Just about anything
you might do out of the water you could do underwater," he said.
"You bolt things, you cut things, you weld things together, you
move things, you recover things." Water conducts electricity, and
sometimes, he added, "you can feel it fizzing in your teeth."

In 1983, when he was 21, he carried out his first submarine
dive, to 1,400 feet, to inspect an oil rig off the coast of Northern
California. He was profoundly affected by the experience—to go
deep one hour and surface the next, with "none of the punitive
decompression," he said. By the time Vescovo contacted him, Lahey had piloted more than 60 submersibles on several thousand
dives. An expedition leader who has worked with him for decades

told me that he is, "without question, the best submarine pilot in the world."

Lahey cofounded Triton in 2007. The business model was to build private submersibles for billionaires, including a Russian oligarch and a member of a Middle Eastern royal family. (In the years leading up to the first order, Lahey used to be laughed at when he attended boat shows; now there are companies that build support vessels for yachts, to carry helicopters, submarines, and other expensive toys.) But his deeper aspiration was to make other people comprehend, as Herman Melville wrote, in *Moby-Dick,* that in rivers and oceans we see "the image of the ungraspable phantom of life; and this is the key to it all." After a few dives, many of Lahey's clients started allowing their vehicles to be used for science and filming.

Vescovo didn't care if Lahey sent him to the bottom of the ocean in a windowless steel ball; he just wanted to get there. But Lahey declined to build anything that didn't have a passenger seat, for a scientist; a manipulator arm, for collecting samples; and viewports, so that the occupants could appreciate the sensation of submergence. Such features would complicate the build, possibly to the point of failure. But Lahey has a tendency to promise the reality he wants before he's sure how to deliver it. "It wasn't really a business decision," a Triton engineer told me. "He wanted to build this. Giving up was not an option." Lahey saw Vescovo's mission as a way to develop and test the world's first unlimited hadal exploration system—one that could then be replicated and improved, for scientists.

Vescovo flew to the Bahamas, and Lahey took him for a test dive in Triton's flagship submersible, which has three seats and is rated to a depth of 3,300 feet. The third seat was occupied by an eccentric British man in his 30s, named John Ramsay, who didn't seem to enjoy the dive; he was preoccupied with what he didn't like about the submersible—which he had designed.

"I never really had a particular passion for submarines," Ramsay, who is Triton's chief submarine designer, told me. "I still don't, really." What he does love is that he gets to design every aspect of each machine, from the central frame to the elegant handle on the back of the hatch. Car manufacturers have entire teams design a seat or a fender, and then produce it at scale. But nearly every Triton submarine is unique; Ramsay determines how he wants things to be, and a dozen or so men in Florida start building.

Ramsay, who works out of a spare bedroom in the wilds of southwest England, has never read a book about submarines. "You would just end up totally tainted in the way you think," he said. "I just work out what it's got to do, and then come up with a solution to it." The success or the failure of Vescovo's mission would rest largely in his hands.

"If Victor dies, and it's your fault, you've got to kill yourself," he told his wife, Caroline.

"Would you, though?" she replied.

"Of course!"

A submariner thinks of space and materials in terms of pressure, buoyancy, and weight. Air rises, batteries sink; in order to achieve neutral buoyancy—the ability to remain suspended underwater, without rising or falling—each component must be offset against the others. The same is true of fish, which regulate their buoyancy through the inflation and deflation of swim bladders.

Ramsay's submarines typically center on a thick acrylic sphere, essentially a bubble; release it underwater and it will pop right up to the surface. But acrylic was not strong enough for Vescovo's submersible. At the bottom of the deepest trench, every square inch would have to hold back 16,000 pounds of water—an elephant standing on a stiletto heel.

Ramsay settled on titanium: malleable and resistant to corrosion, with a high ratio of strength to density. The pressure hull would weigh nearly 8,000 pounds. It would have to be counterbalanced by syntactic foam, a buoyant filler comprising millions of hollow glass spheres. For the submarine to stay upright, the foam would have to go above the hull, providing upward lift—like a hot-air balloon, for water. "As long as the heavy stuff hangs in balance below the buoyant stuff, the sub will always stay upright," Ramsay explained.

The hull required the forging of two slabs of titanium into perfect hemispheres. Only one facility in the world had a chamber that was sufficiently large and powerful to subject the hull to pressures equivalent to those found at full ocean depth: the Krylov State Research Center, in St. Petersburg, Russia. Lahey attended the pressure test. There was no backup hull; an implosion would end the project. "But it worked—it validated what we were doing," Lahey told me.

It was the middle of summer, 2018, in South Florida, and Triton's technicians were working 15 hours a day, in a space with no air-conditioning. Lahey paced the workshop, sweating, trying to encourage his team. The men who were building the world's most advanced deep-diving submersible had not attended Stanford or MIT; they were former car mechanics, scuba instructors, and underwater welders, hired for their work ethic and their practical experience. The shop foreman used to be a truck driver. The hydraulics expert had a bullet in his abdomen, from his days running cocaine out of Fort Lauderdale, in the '80s. One of the electricians honed his craft by stealing car radios, as a teenager. ("I was really good at it," he told me.) Lahey, for his part, said that he was named—and later exonerated—by the federal government as an unindicted co-conspirator in a narcotics-trafficking operation involving a Soviet military submarine and a Colombian cartel.

Every major component of Vescovo's submarine had to be developed from scratch. The oil-and-gas industry had established a supply chain of components that are pressure rated to around 6,000 meters—but that was only half the required depth. Before assembling the submarine, the Triton team spent months imploding parts in a pressure chamber, and sending feedback to the manufacturers. "You're solving problems that have never existed before, with parts that have never existed before, from venders who don't know how to make them," Ramsay said.

The rest of the expedition team was on a ship docked in the harbor at Vero Beach, waiting. Vescovo remained at home in Dallas, training on a simulator that Triton had rigged up in his garage. On Lahey's recommendation, he had hired Rob McCallum, an expedition leader and a cofounder of EYOS Expeditions, to inject realism into a project that might otherwise die a dream.

For every Vescovo who goes to the South Pole, there is a McCallum making sure he stays alive. (McCallum has been to Antarctica 128 times.) "I love it when clients come through the door and say, 'I've been told this is impossible, but what do you think?'" he said to me. "Well, I think you've just given away your negotiating position. Let's have a glass of wine and talk about it."

McCallum—who is trim but barrel-chested, with a soft voice

and a Kiwi accent—grew up in the tropics of Papua New Guinea, and became a polar guide. He is a trained medic, dive master, fire-fighter, aircraft pilot, and boat operator, a former New Zealand park ranger who has served as an adviser to the Norwegian navy. He speaks three Neo-Melanesian languages, and can pilot a Zodiac boat standing up, in 16-foot waves. He is the subject of a Modern Love column, in the *Times*. ("My father warned me about guys like you," the author recalls telling him, before marrying him anyway.) McCallum and his associates have discovered several high-profile shipwrecks, including Australian and American warships and an Israeli military submarine. A few months ago, he showed me on his computer an object on a sonar scan, which he believes to be Amelia Earhart's plane.

Vescovo asked what McCallum required from him. "The first thing I need is for you to triple the budget," he replied. He also shot down several of Vescovo's proposals, from the antiquated (no alcohol or spouses on board) to the insane (installing fake military hardware on the bow; bringing his dog to the deepest point on earth).

Five oceans, five deeps—a journey around the world and to both poles. McCallum explained that the expedition would have to be anchored by the polar dives. The likely dive spot in the Arctic Ocean is covered by ice for much of the year, but there is a two-week dive window, beginning in late August. The Antarctic, or Southern Ocean, dive could be done in February, the height of summer in that hemisphere. The team would have to avoid hurricane season in the Atlantic, and monsoon season in the Pacific, and otherwise remain flexible, for when things inevitably went wrong.

Lahey persuaded Vescovo to buy the USNS *Indomitable*, a 220-foot vessel that he had found at a dry dock in Seattle. It was built as an intelligence-gathering ship, in 1985, and spent much of the next 15 years prowling the world's oceans, towing an undersea lis-tening device. "It was owned by the navy but operated by civilians," McCallum told me. He winked. "I didn't say CIA—I just said civil-ians." Vescovo renamed it the *Pressure Drop*, for a spaceship from the Culture series of science fiction novels by Iain M. Banks.

The Arctic-dive window was fast approaching, and it seemed un-likely that the submersible would be ready. "That's when Patrick Lahey's overflowing optimism went from being an incredible, endearing personality trait to being a huge issue," Stuart Buckle, the *Pressure Drop*'s captain, said. "Every day, Patrick would say, 'Oh, yes, it'll be ready in one or two days.' And then two days pass, and he'd say, 'It'll be ready in two days.'"

The final step in building a submarine is to put it in a swimming pool or in the water at a marina. "You need to know how much it weighs and how much it displaces," Ramsay said, because the average density of the craft and its passengers must be equal to that of the water in which it is submerged. "You've only calculated the volume of each object through computer models, which can't possibly represent the actual thing, with all its tolerances. Things are a bit bigger, things are a bit smaller, cables are fatter."

But there was no time to do this before loading it onto the ship and setting off for sea trials in the Bahamas. They left Florida without knowing how much the submarine displaced. "It had never even touched the water," Ramsay said. "It was just 'Right, off we go. Let's see if it works.'"

Sea Trials

"When people talk about sea trials, they always think about testing a ship or testing a sub," McCallum told me. "But, really, what you're doing is you're testing people. You are testing systems, processes, conditions, and teams."

Buckle, the captain, dropped anchor near Great Abaco Island, in the Bahamas, and immediately became alarmed by the Triton crew's cavalier approach to safety. He had grown up in the Scottish Highlands, and gone to sea when he was 17 years old. "Me and my guys were trying to adjust from the oil-and-gas industry, where you need a signed bit of paper to do anything, and to go out on deck you have to have your overalls, hard hats, goggles, earmuffs, and gloves," Buckle said. "Whereas a lot of the Triton guys were used to walking around in shorts and flip-flops, like you watch on *American Chopper*. They were grinding and drilling and using hydraulic awls, looking at it, sparks flying everywhere, not wearing safety glasses or anything. To them, if something catches fire, it's funny—it's not an issue."

Vescovo named the submarine the *Limiting Factor*, for another spaceship from the Culture series. It was secured to a custom-built cradle, which could be rolled backward on metal tracks, to lower the sub into the ocean from the aft deck of the ship. During launch operations, the Triton crew attached it to a hook that hung down from a crane, known as an A-frame, shaped like an enormous hydraulic swing set. Buckle had asked Vescovo to buy a larger A-frame—one that was "man-rated" by a certification agency, so that they could launch the submersible, which weighs around 26,000 pounds, with the pilot inside and the hatch secured. But there was no time to install one. So the Triton crew lowered the empty submersible into the water, and the ship's crew, using a different crane, launched a Zodiac boat over the starboard side. McCallum climbed into the Zodiac, and drove the pilot to the sub as it was being towed behind the ship.

The ship had no means of tracking the submarine underwater. "Once he left the surface, I had no idea where he was," Buckle said. "All we had at that point was one range." Buckle could see, for example, that the *Limiting Factor* was 500 meters away, but he didn't know in which direction. "As long as that number was getting bigger, that meant he wasn't surfacing directly under me," he said. "If it just kept getting smaller and smaller, I'm in trouble."

"The thing about driving a ship is that unless you know how to drive a ship you never see the bad stuff," McCallum told me. "It's only when the captain's going 'Christ, that was close!' that you go 'Really? Was it?'"

Other incidents were unambiguous. "I was seeing Triton guys bouncing up the ladders without holding the handrails, wanting to jump on top of things while they were still swinging from the crane," Buckle recalled. Ropes failed, deck equipment snapped under stress. "One of the big ratchet hooks blew off the top of the hangar, and missed Patrick's head by that much," McCallum said, holding his fingers a couple of inches apart. "Just missed him. And he wasn't wearing a helmet, so that would have killed him."

Lahey piloted the sub on its earliest dives—first to 20 meters, then 50, then 1,000. Electronic systems failed. The hatch leaked. Emergency lights malfunctioned, and drop weights got stuck. Pre-dive checklists labeled several switches "inoperable." Post-dive checklists noted critical components lost and fallen to the seafloor.

"In a sea trial, you're trying to break stuff—you're trying to work out where your weakest link is," McCallum said. "It's incredibly demoralizing. You never feel as if you're making any mean-ingful forward progress." Each morning, he delivered a pre-dive briefing to members of the ship and submarine crews. "Don't be disheartened by the long list of things that broke," he told them. "Rejoice, because those are things that are not going to fail in the Southern Ocean—and if they did fail in the Southern Ocean we'd be fucked."

On September 9, 2018, Patrick Lahey piloted the *Limiting Factor* to the bottom of the Abaco Canyon, more than three miles down. It was the ninth time that the submersible had been in the water. Everything worked. The next day, Lahey repeated the dive, with Vescovo as the lead pilot. When they reached the bottom, Vescovo turned on the control unit that directs the manipulator arm. Something wasn't right. He and Lahey glanced at each other. "Do you smell that?" Lahey asked.

"Yes."

There was a puff of smoke in the capsule. Vescovo and Lahey grabbed the "spare air"—scuba regulators, with two-minute compressed-air cannisters—so that they wouldn't pass out while preparing the emergency breathing apparatus. A circuit breaker tripped, automatically switching off the control unit for the manipulator arm, and the acrid smell dissipated. Lahey, who was training Vescovo to handle crises underwater, asked what they should do.

"Abort the dive?" Vescovo said.

"Yes." They were two hours from the surface.

Ramsay and Tom Blades, Triton's chief electrical designer, had devised numerous safety mechanisms. Most systems were duplicated, and ran on separate electrical circuits, in case one of the batteries failed. The thrusters could be ejected if they became entangled; so could the batteries, to drop weight and provide buoyancy. The 550-pound surfacing weight was attached by an electromagnet, so that if the sub lost electricity it would immediately begin its ascent. There was also a dead-man switch: an alarm went off if the pilot failed to check in with the ship, and if he failed to acknowledge the alarm the weights would automatically drop.

"Whenever we had any significant failure of some kind, the only thing that mattered was why," Vescovo said. "If you can identify the problem, and fix it, what are you going to do? Give up? Come on. That didn't even cross my mind. Maybe other people get freaked out. I've heard of that happening. But if you're mountain climbing and you fall, are you not going to climb again? No. You learn from it, and keep going."

By the middle of September, the sea trials had given way to "advanced sea trials"—a euphemism to cover for the fact that nothing was working. The Arctic Ocean dive window had already passed. Buckle was especially concerned about the launch-and-recovery system. The cranes were inadequate, and poorly spaced. One of the support vessels, which had been selected by Triton, was 18 years old, and its rubber perimeter was cracking from years of neglect in the Florida sun. "I was pretty pissed off at that point," Buckle told me. "I had put my guys in a difficult situation, because they were trying to compensate for structural issues that you couldn't really work around. You can only piss with the dick you've been given."

McCallum redesigned the expedition schedule to begin with the Puerto Rico Trench, in the Atlantic Ocean, in December, followed by Antarctica, in early February. The adjustment added cost but bought time.

When Alan Jamieson, the expedition's chief scientist, contacted Heather Stewart, a marine geologist with the British Geological Survey, and told her that Vescovo wanted to dive to the deepest point of each ocean, she replied that there was a problem: nobody knew where those points were.

Most maps showing the ocean floor in detail are commissioned by people looking to exploit it. The oil-and-gas and deep-sea-mining industries require extensive knowledge, and they pay for it. But, with a few exceptions, the characteristics of the deepest trenches are largely unknown. As recently as the 1960s, ocean depths were often estimated by throwing explosives over the side of a ship and measuring the time it took for the boom to echo back from the bottom.

It may appear as if the trenches are mapped—you can see them on Google Earth. But these images weren't generated by scanning the bottom of the ocean; they come from satellites scanning the top. The surface of the ocean is not even—it is shaped by the features beneath it. Trenches create mild surface depressions, while underwater mountain ranges raise the surface. The result is a vaguely correct reading—here is a trench!—with a ludicrous margin of error. Every pixel is about 500 meters wide, and what lies below may be thousands of feet deeper or shallower than the satellite projects, and miles away from where it appears on the map.

Vescovo would have to buy a multibeam echo sounder, an advanced sonar mapping system, to determine precise depths and dive locations. He chose the Kongsberg EM-124, which would be housed in a massive gondola underneath the ship. No other system could so precisely map hadal depths. Vescovo's purchase was the very first—serial number 001.

That November, Buckle sailed the *Pressure Drop* to Curaçao, off the coast of Venezuela, to have the EM-124 and a new starboard crane installed. But there was still no time to order a man-rated A-frame—its purchase, delivery, and installation would require that they miss the Antarctic dive window, adding a year to the expedition. "He's a wealthy dude, but he's not like Paul Allen or Ray Dalio," Buckle said of Vescovo. "He hasn't got that kind of money. This is a huge commitment of his resources."

Stewart prepared a list of possible dive locations, which earned her a spot on the expedition. For others, participation was largely a matter of luck. Shane Eigler had started working at Triton the previous year, after Kelvin Magee, the shop foreman, sent him a Facebook message asking if he'd like to build submarines. They had met in the 2000s, after Eigler had saved up enough money by growing marijuana to pay for dive lessons. Magee was his instructor. Later, Eigler worked as a car mechanic. "Building submarines—this shit is exactly the same as cars, just different components," Eigler told me.

On December 14, the *Pressure Drop* set off for the Puerto Rico Trench, from the port of San Juan. "Been feeling a little queasy ever since we got underway," Eigler wrote that night, in an email to his wife. It was his first time at sea.

The Starting Gun

Vescovo and Lahey went for a test dive down to a thousand meters. It was Lahey's last chance to train Vescovo in the *Limiting Factor* before he would attempt an 8,000-meter dive, solo, to the bottom of the Puerto Rico Trench. A scientific goal for the expedition was to collect a rock sample from the bottom of each trench, so Lahey switched on the manipulator arm.

Seconds later, on the *Pressure Drop,* a transmission came up from below. "Control, this is L.F.," Lahey said. "We have lost the arm. It has fallen off."

It was December 17. After surfacing, Vescovo and Lahey walked into McCallum's office, toward the stern of the ship. "Patrick was under immense pressure that would have crushed almost anybody else I know," McCallum said. "He had applied a huge amount of his team's intellectual capital to this project, at the expense of all other projects, and yet things were just not quite where they needed to be."

Vescovo called off the expedition. "I think I'm just going to write this whole thing off as bad debt," he said. The manipulator arm had cost $350,000, and there was no spare.

Lahey begged for more time. "Give my guys one more day," he said. Vescovo relented, and went up to his cabin. No one saw him for the next 32 hours. "The more time I spend with Victor, the more I think he is Vulcan in his decision-making but not in his emotions," Buckle told me. "He's one of those guys who has a veneer of calm, but then probably goes into his cabin and screams into his pillow after he's been told the fifth bit of bad news that day." (Vescovo denies screaming into his pillow.)

Lahey pulled his team into the submarine hangar. "Do you think you can fix this fucking thing?" he asked.

Blades noted that the loss of the manipulator arm had freed up an electrical junction box, creating an opportunity to fix nearly everything else that was wrong with the electronics. "Basically, Tom Blades hot-wired the sub," Lahey explained. "There was literally a jumper cable running through the pressure hull, tucked behind Victor's seat."

On December 19, Vescovo climbed into the *Limiting Factor* and began his descent. "The control room was just packed, and you could cut the atmosphere with a knife the entire way down," Stewart told me. "Patrick was just in his chair, ear to the radio, just wringing sweat."

At 2:55 p.m., Victor Vescovo became the first person to reach the deepest point in the Atlantic Ocean, 8,376 meters. It was his first solo dive, and it was flawless.

That night, "Victor was wandering around, drinking out of a bottle of champagne," McCallum said. "It was the first time we'd seen Victor relax. It was the first time we'd seen Victor touch alcohol. And from that point we knew we were going to take this around the world."

"Puerto Rico was the starting gun," Vescovo told me. "The Southern Ocean was the forge."

The Forge

Waves are local—the brushing of the ocean by the wind. Swells roll for thousands of miles across open water, unaffected by the weather of the moment.

On January 24, 2019, the *Pressure Drop* set off from the port of Montevideo, Uruguay, to dive the South Sandwich Trench, the deepest point of the Southern Ocean. Buckle and his crew had loaded the ship with cold-weather gear, and provisions for more than a month. There was a 5,000-mile journey ahead of them, and the ship could barely go nine knots.

"Captain, can I have a word?" Peter Coope, the chief engineer, asked. "Is this ship going to be okay?"

"Yes," Buckle replied. "Do you think I would invite on board all the people I like working with most in the world, and then sail us all to a certain death?"

But Buckle wasn't so sure. A year earlier, when he'd first walked up the gangplank, he wondered why Triton had chosen this ship. The *Pressure Drop* hadn't been in service in several years. The hull was watertight, but there were holes in the steel superstructure, and the shipyard had stripped every functional component. The steering system had been wired in reverse; turn one way and the ship went the other. "It's a classic case of people who have spent a lot of time on boats thinking they know boats," Buckle told me. "I've spent a lot of time on planes, but if Victor said, 'I want to buy a 747,' I wouldn't go up and say, 'Yes, that one is great—buy that one.' I'd get a pilot or a flight engineer to do it." Buckle's first officer recalled, "The ship was fucking breaking apart."

After the purchase, Buckle and a small crew of mostly Scottish sailors spent two months living near a dockyard in Louisiana, refitting and repairing the ship. "Stu took a huge risk—not only for himself but for all his officers," McCallum told me. "He handpicked the guys, pulled them off of very well-paying oil-and-gas jobs, and got them to follow him to bumfuck nowhere." In the evenings, Buckle and his crew drank beer on the top deck, and tossed pizza slices to alligators in the bayou. The ship came with no manuals, no electrical charts. "It was just a soul-destroying, slow process," Buckle said.

Now Buckle was steering the *Pressure Drop* into the Southern Ocean, the site of the most reliably violent seas in the world. After a few nights, Erlend Currie, a sailor from the Orkney Islands, shoved a life jacket under the far side of his bunk, so that the mattress would form a U shape, and he wouldn't fall out.

"You get these nasty systems rolling through, with just little gaps between them," McCallum told me. McCallum has seen waves in the Southern Ocean crest above 90 feet. He had carefully mapped out a dive window, between gales, and brought on board an ice pilot and a doctor. "If something goes wrong, there's no port to go to, and there's no one to rescue you," he said.

Albatross trailed the ship for the first several days. Soon they disappeared and the crew began seeing whales and penguins. "Filled with trepidation, we steamed into the teeth of the area where, on the old maps, they used to write, 'Here Be Monsters,'" Vescovo told me.

On the forecastle deck, in the control room, a cheerful, brown-haired Texan named Cassie Bongiovanni sat before four large monitors, which had been bolted to the table. Bongiovanni, who is 27 years old, was finishing a master's degree in ocean mapping at the University of New Hampshire when Rob McCallum called and said that he needed someone to run a multibeam sonar system for one and a half laps around the world. She graduated at sea while mapping Vescovo's dive location in the Puerto Rico Trench.

As the head sonar operator, Bongiovanni had to make perfect decisions based on imperfect information. "The sound is generated from the EM-124, housed inside the giant gondola under the ship," she said. "As it goes down, the width of each sound beam grows, so that in the deepest trenches we're only able to pick up one point every seventy-five meters or so." In these trenches, it takes at least seven seconds for sound to reach the bottom, and another seven seconds to return. In that gap, the ship has moved forward, and has pitched and rolled atop the surface of the sea. Bongiovanni also had to account for readings of sound speed at each dive site, as it is affected by variations in temperature, salinity, and depth.

The purchase and installation of the EM-124 cost more than the ship itself, but its software was full of bugs. Each day, Bongiovanni oscillated between awe and frustration as she rebooted it, adjusted parameters, cleaned up noisy data, and sent emails to Kongsberg, the maker, to request software patches. The expedition wasn't merely the first to dive the South Sandwich Trench but the first to map it as well.

Buckle positioned the ship over the dive site. A Triton mechanic named Steve Chappell was assigned the role of "swimmer," meaning that he would balance atop the *Limiting Factor* as it was lowered into the water, and disconnect the towline before it went down. He wore a dry suit; polar waters can rapidly induce involuntary gasping and vertigo, and even talented swimmers can drown within two minutes. For a moment, he lay on a submarine bucking in the middle of the Southern Ocean, fumbling with wet ropes, fingers numb. Then a Zodiac picked him up and took him back to the *Pressure Drop,* where he warmed his hands by an exhaust vent. Vescovo started the pumps, and the *Limiting Factor* began its descent.

Dive protocols required that Vescovo check in with the surface every 15 minutes and announce his depth and heading and the status of his life-support system. But, after 4,500 meters, the communications system failed. The ship could still receive Vescovo's transmissions, but Vescovo couldn't hear the replies.

Abyssal critters drifted past the viewports. It is customary to abort a dive 30 minutes after losing communications, but Vescovo knew that he might never have another chance to reach the bottom of the Southern Ocean, so he kept going. He liked the sensation of being truly alone. Sometimes, on the surface, he spoke of human nature as if it were something he had studied from the outside. Another hour passed before he reached the deepest point: 7,433 meters. The point had never been measured or named. He decided to call it the Factorian Deep.

That night, Alan Jamieson, the chief scientist, stood on the aft deck, waiting for biological samples to reach the surface. "Most marine science is gritty as fuck," he told me. "It's not just 'Look at the beautiful animal,' or 'Look at the mysteries of the deep.' It's all the weird vessels we end up on, the work of hauling things in and out of the water." Jamieson, a gruff, 42-year-old marine biologist, who grew up in the Scottish Lowlands, is a pioneer in the construction and use of hadal landers—large, unmanned contraptions with baited traps and cameras, dropped over the side of a ship. In the past two decades, he has carried out hundreds of lander deployments in the world's deep spots, and found evidence of fish and critters where none were thought to be. Now, as snow blew sideways in the darkness and the wind, he threw a grappling hook over the South Sandwich Trench and caught a lander thrashing in the waves.

There were five landers on board. Three were equipped with advanced tracking and communications gear, to lend navigational support to the sub underwater. The two others were Jamieson's— built with an aluminum frame, disposable weights, and a sapphire window for the camera, to withstand the pressure at depth. Before each dive, he tied a dead mackerel to a metal bar in front of the camera, to draw in hungry hadal fauna. Now, as he studied the footage, he discovered four new species of fish. Amphipods scuttled across the featureless sediment on the seafloor, and devoured the mackerel down to its bones. They are ancient, insect-like scavengers, whose bodies accommodate the water—floating organs in a waxy exoskeleton. Their cells have adapted to cope with high pressure, and "they've got this ridiculously stretchy gut, so they can eat about three times their body size," Jamieson explained. Marine biologists classify creatures in the hadal zone as "extremophiles."

The following night, one of Jamieson's landers was lost. "Usually, things come back up where you put them, but it just didn't," Buckle said. "We worked out what the drift was, and we then sailed in that drift direction for another three or four hours, with all my guys on the bridge—searchlights, binoculars, everyone looking for it. And we just never found it."

The second one surfaced later that night. But during the recovery it was sucked under the pitching ship and went straight through the propeller. By now, there was a blizzard, and the ship was heaving in 18-foot waves. "I lost everything—just fucking everything—in one night," Jamieson said. Vescovo suggested naming the site of the lost landers the Bitter Deep.

The *Pressure Drop* set off east, past a 30-mile-long iceberg, for

Cape Town, South Africa, to stop for fuel and food. Bongiovanni left the sonar running, collecting data that would correct the depths and the locations of key geological features, whose prior measurements by satellites were off by as much as several miles. (Vescovo is making all of the ship's data available to Seabed 2030, a collaborative project to map the world's oceans in the next 10 years.) Meanwhile, Jamieson cobbled together a new lander out of aluminum scraps, spare electronics, and some ropes and buoys, and taught Erlend Currie, the sailor from the Orkney Islands, to bait it and set the release timer. Jamieson named the lander the Erlander, then he disembarked and set off for England, to spend time with his wife and children. It would take several weeks for the ship to reach its next port stop, in Perth, where the Triton crew would install a new manipulator arm.

At the time, the deepest point in the Indian Ocean was unknown. Most scientists believed that it was in the Java Trench, near Indonesia. But nobody had ever mapped the northern part of the Diamantina Fracture Zone, off the coast of Australia, and readings from satellites placed it within Java's margin of error.

The *Pressure Drop* spent three days over the Diamantina; Bongiovanni confirmed that it was, in fact, shallower than Java, and Currie dropped the Erlander as Jamieson had instructed. When it surfaced, around 10 hours later—the trap filled with amphipods, including several new species—Currie became the first person to collect a biological sample from the Diamantina Fracture Zone.

Pirates

The Java Trench lies in international waters, which begin 12 nautical miles from land. But the expedition's prospective dive sites fell within Indonesia's exclusive economic zone; according to UN conventions, a country has special rights to the exploration and exploitation of marine resources, as far as 200 nautical miles from the coast. McCallum had spent much of the previous year applying for permits and permissions; he dealt with 57 government agencies, from more than a dozen countries, in order to plan the Five Deeps.

For several months, the Indonesian government ignored Mc-Callum's inquiries. Then he was bounced among 10 or more agencies, to which he sent briefing materials about the submersible, the ship, the crew, and the mission. Between the Atlantic and the Antarctic dives, Vescovo flew to Jakarta to deliver a lecture, and he offered to bring an Indonesian scientist to the bottom of the trench. But when the ship arrived in Bali, McCallum still hadn't received permission to dive.

Officially, this meant that the team could not carry out any scientific work in the Java Trench. But the international law of the sea allows for the testing of equipment, and, after Java, the next set of dives, in the Pacific Ocean, would be the deepest of all. "So we tested the sub a few times," McCallum said, smiling. "We tested the landers, we tested the sonar—we tested everything."

The Java Trench is more than 2,000 miles long, and the site of violent seismic activity. Surveys in the northern part show evidence of landslides, from the 2004 earthquake that triggered a tsunami with hundred-foot waves that killed a quarter of a million people across Southeast Asia. Farther south, satellites had detected two deep pools, several hundred miles apart. The *Pressure Drop* mapped both sites, and Bongiovanni discovered that, in fact, the deepest point was between them, in a small pool that had previously gone unnoticed. It may be a new rupture in the ocean floor.

Buckle positioned the *Pressure Drop* over the pool, and turned off the ship's tracking and communications equipment. McCallum hoisted a pirate flag. The climate was tropical, 86 degrees, the ocean calm, with slow, rolling swells and hardly a ripple on the surface. On the morning of April 5, 2019, the Triton crew launched the *Limiting Factor* without incident, and Vescovo dived to the deepest point in the Java Trench.

Mountaineers stand atop craggy peaks and look out on the world. Vescovo descended into blackness, and saw mostly sediment at the bottom. The lights on the *Limiting Factor* illuminated only a few feet forward; the acrylic viewports are convex and eight inches thick. Whatever the true topography of the rock underneath, hadal trenches appear soft and flat at the deep spots. Flip a mountain upside down and, with time, the inverted summit will be unreachable; for as long as there has been an ocean, the trenches have been the end points of falling particulate—volcanic dust, sand, pebbles, meteorites, and "the billions upon billions of tiny shells and skeletons, the limy or silicious remains of all the minute creatures that once lived in the upper waters," Rachel Carson wrote, in *The Sea Around Us,* in 1951. "The sediments are a sort of epic poem of the earth."

Vescovo spent three hours at the bottom, and saw a plastic bag through the viewports. In the Puerto Rico Trench, one of the *Limiting Factor*'s cameras had captured an image of a soda can. Scientists estimate that in 30 years the oceans will hold a greater mass of plastic than of fish. Almost every biological sample that Jamieson has dredged up from the hadal zone and tested in a lab has been contaminated with microplastics. "Does it harm the ability of these animals to feed, to maneuver, to reproduce?" McCallum said. "We don't know, because we can't compare one that's full of microplastics with one that's not. Because there aren't any."

The walls of trenches are filled with life, but they were not Vescovo's mission. "It's a little bit like going to the Louvre, putting your running shoes on, and sprinting through it," Lahey said. "What you really want to do is to go there with someone who can tell you what you're looking at." The next day, Vescovo told Lahey that he could take Jamieson to the bottom of the trench. "I don't want to go to the deepest point, because that's boring," Jamieson said. "Let's go somewhere really cool."

Four and a half miles below the ship, the Australia tectonic plate was being slowly and violently subsumed by the Eurasia plate. Bongiovanni had noticed a staircase feature coming out of a fault line, the result of pressure and breakage on a geological scale. It extended more than 800 feet up, beyond vertical, with an overhang—an outrageously difficult dive. Lahey would have to back up as they ascended, with no clear view of what was above the sub.

The hatch started leaking during the descent, but Lahey told Jamieson to ignore it—it would seal with pressure. It kept dripping for more than 90 minutes, and stopped only at 15,000 feet. "I fucking told you it would seal," Lahey said.

The *Limiting Factor* arrived at the bottom just after noon. Lahey approached the fault-line wall, and headed toward some bulging black masses. From a distance, they looked to Jamieson like volcanic rock, but as Lahey drew closer more colors came into view —brilliant reds, oranges, yellows, and blues, cloaked in hadal darkness. Without the lights of the submarine, the colors might never have been seen, not even by creatures living among them. These were bacterial mats, deriving their energy from chemicals emanating from the planet's crust instead of from sunlight. It was through this process of chemosynthesis that, billions of years ago, when the earth was "one giant, fucked-up, steaming geological mass, being bombarded with meteorites," as Jamieson put it, the first complex cell crossed some intangible line that separates the non-living from the living.

Lahey began climbing the wall—up on the thrusters, then backward. Jamieson discovered a new species of snailfish, a long, gelatinous creature with soft fins, by looking through a viewport. The pressure eliminates the possibility of a swim bladder; the lack of food precludes the ossification of bones. Some snailfish have antifreeze proteins, to keep them running in the cold. "Biology is just smelly engineering," Jamieson said. "When you reverse engineer a fish from the most extreme environments, and compare it to its shallow-water counterparts, you can see the trade-offs it has made."

The wall climb took an hour. When the last lander surfaced, Jamieson detached the camera and found that it had captured footage of a dumbo octopus at 23,000 feet—the deepest ever recorded, by more than a mile.

The *Pressure Drop* set off toward the Pacific Ocean. McCallum lowered the pirate flag. Seven weeks later, Jamieson received a letter from the Indonesian government, saying that his research-permit application had been rejected "due to national security consideration."

A Daily Flight to the Moon

Buckle sailed to Guam, with diversions for Bongiovanni to map the Yap and Palau Trenches. Several new passengers boarded, one of whom was unlike the rest: he had been where they were going, six decades before. Hadal exploration has historically prioritized superlatives, and an area of the Mariana Trench, known as the Challenger Deep, contains the deepest water on earth.

On January 23, 1960, two men climbed into a large pressure sphere, which was suspended below a 40,000-gallon tank of gasoline, for buoyancy. One of them was a Swiss hydronaut named Jacques Piccard, whose father, the hot-air balloonist Auguste Piccard, had designed it. The other was Don Walsh, a young lieutenant in the US Navy, which had bought the vehicle, known as a bathyscaphe, and modified it to attempt a dive in the Challenger Deep.

The bathyscaphe was so large that it had to be towed behind a ship, and its buoyant gasoline tank was so delicate that the ship couldn't travel more than one or two miles per hour. To find the dive site, sailors tossed TNT over the side of the ship, and timed the echo reverberating up from the bottom of the trench. There was one viewport, the size of a coin. When the bathyscaphe hit the bottom, stirring up sediment, "it was like looking into a bowl of milk," Walsh said. A half century passed before anyone returned.

The bathyscaphe never again dived to hadal depths. Jacques Piccard died in 2008. Now Don Walsh, who was 88, walked up the gangway of the *Pressure Drop.* It was a short transit to the Mariana Trench, across warm Pacific waters, over six-foot swells.

Above the Challenger Deep, Vescovo pulled on a fire-retardant jumpsuit, and walked out to the aft deck. A gentle wind blew in from the east. Walsh shook Vescovo's hand. Vescovo climbed into the *Limiting Factor,* carrying an ice axe that he had brought to the summit of Mount Everest.

Hatch secured, lift line down, tag lines released, towline out —pumps on. Vescovo wondered, *Is the sub able to handle this?* He didn't think it would implode, but would the electronics survive? The thrusters? The batteries? Besides Walsh and Piccard, the only other person to go to the bottom of the Challenger Deep was the filmmaker James Cameron, in 2012. Multiple systems failed at the bottom, and his submersible never dived deep again.

The depth gauge ticked past 10,900 meters, 36,000 feet. After four hours, Vescovo started dropping variable ballast weights, to slow his descent. At 12:37 p.m., he called up to the surface. His message took seven seconds to reach the *Pressure Drop:* "At bottom."

Outside the viewports, Vescovo saw amphipods and sea cucumbers. But he was two miles beyond the limits of fish. "At a certain point, the conditions are so intense that evolution runs out of options—there's not a lot of wiggle room," Jamieson said. "So a lot of the creatures down there start to look the same."

Vescovo switched off the lights and turned off the thrusters. He hovered in silence, a foot off the sediment bottom, drifting gently on a current, nearly 36,000 feet below the surface.

That evening, on the *Pressure Drop*, Don Walsh shook his hand again. Vescovo noted that, according to the sonar scan, the submarine data, and the readings from the landers, he had gone deeper than anyone before. "Yeah, I cried myself to sleep last night," Walsh joked.

The Triton team took two maintenance days, to make sure they didn't miss anything. But the *Limiting Factor* was fine. So Vescovo went down again to retrieve a rock sample. He found some specimens by the northern wall of the trench, but they were too big to carry, so he tried to break off a piece by smashing them with the manipulator arm—to no avail. "I finally resorted to just burrowing the claw into the muck, and just blindly grabbing and seeing if anything came out," he said. No luck. He surfaced.

Hours later, Vescovo walked into the control room and learned that one of the navigation landers was stuck in the silt. He was in despair. The lander's batteries would soon drain, killing all communications and tracking—another expensive item lost on the ocean floor.

"Well, you do have a full-ocean-depth submersible" available to retrieve it, McCallum said. Lahey had been planning to make a descent with Jonathan Struwe, of the marine classification firm DNV-GL, to certify the *Limiting Factor*. Now it became a rescue mission.

When Lahey reached the bottom, he began moving in a triangular search pattern. Soon he spotted a faint light from the lander. He nudged it with the manipulator arm, freeing it from the mud. It shot up to the surface. Struwe—who was now one of only six people who had been to the bottom of the Challenger Deep—certified the *Limiting Factor*'s "maximum permissible diving depth" as "unlimited."

The control room was mostly empty. "When Victor first went down, everyone was there, high-fiving and whooping and hollering," Buckle said. "And the next day, around lunchtime, everyone went 'Fuck this, I'll go for lunch.' Patrick retrieves a piece of equipment from the deepest point on earth, and it's just me, going, 'Yay, congratulations, Patrick.' No one seemed to notice how big a deal it is that they had already made this normal—even though it's not. It's the equivalent of having a daily flight to the moon." McCallum, in his pre-dive briefings, started listing "complacency" as a hazard.

Vescovo was elated when the lander reached the surface. "Do you know what this means?" McCallum said to him.

"Yeah, we got the three-hundred-thousand-dollar lander back," Vescovo said.

"Victor, you have the only vehicle in the world that can get to the bottom of any ocean, anytime, anywhere," McCallum said. The message sank in. Vescovo had read that the Chinese government had dropped acoustic surveillance devices in and around the Mariana Trench, apparently to spy on US submarines leaving the naval base in Guam; he could damage them. A Soviet nuclear submarine sank in the 1980s, near the Norwegian coast. Russian and Norwegian scientists have sampled the water inside, and have found that it is highly contaminated. Now Vescovo began to worry that, before long, non-state actors might be able to retrieve and repurpose radioactive materials lying on the seafloor.

"I don't want to be a Bond villain," Vescovo told me. But he noted how easy it would be. "You could go around the world with this sub, and put devices on the bottom that are acoustically triggered to cut cables," he said. "And you short all the stock markets and buy gold, all at the same time. Theoretically, that is possible. Theoretically."

After a maintenance day, Lahey offered to take John Ramsay to the bottom of the trench. Ramsay was conflicted, but, he said, "there was this sentiment on board that if the designer doesn't dare get in it then nobody should dare get in it." He climbed in, and felt uncomfortable the entire way down. "It wasn't that I actually needed to have a shit, it was this irrational fear of what happens if I do need to have a shit," he said.

Two days later, Vescovo took Jamieson to the bottom of the Mariana Trench. They returned with one of the deepest rock samples ever collected, after Vescovo crashed into a boulder and a fragment landed in a battery tray.

Buckle started sailing back to Guam, to drop off Walsh, Vescovo, and the Triton crew. "It's quite mind-blowing, when you sit down and think about it, that, from the dawn of time until this Monday, there were three people who have been down there," he said. "Then, in the last ten days, we've put five more people down there, and it's not even a big deal."

*

It was early May, and there was only one ocean left. But the deepest point in the Arctic Ocean was covered by the polar ice cap, and would remain so for several months. The *Pressure Drop* headed south, toward Tonga, in the South Pacific. Bongiovanni kept the sonar running 24 hours a day, and Jamieson carried out the first-ever lander deployments in the San Cristobal and Santa Cruz Trenches. "The amphipod samples are mostly for genetic work, tracking adaptations," he told me. The same critters were showing up in trenches thousands of miles apart—but aren't found in shallower waters, elsewhere on the ocean floor. "How the fuck are they going from one to another?"

Bongiovanni mapped the Tonga Trench. The sonar image showed a 40-mile line of fault escarpments, a geological feature resulting from the fracturing of an oceanic plate. "It's horrendously violent, but it's happening over geological time," Jamieson explained. "As one of the plates is being pushed down, it's cracking into these ridges, and these ridges are fucking huge"—a mile and a half, vertical. "If they were on land, they'd be one of the wonders of the world. But, because they're buried under ten thousand meters of water, they just look like ripples in the ocean floor."

Bongiovanni routinely stayed up all night, debugging the new software and surveying dive sites, so that the *Limiting Factor* could be launched at dawn. "Day Forever," she dated one of her journal entries. "Sonar fucked itself." Now, before taking leave, she taught Erlend Currie, who had launched Jamieson's makeshift lander in the Diamantina Fracture Zone, how to operate the EM-124.

"When you give people more responsibility, they either crumble or they bloom, and he blooms," Buckle said. In the next month, Currie mapped some 6,000 nautical miles of the ocean floor, from the Tonga Trench to the Panama Canal. "Erlend's doing a good job," another officer reported to Bongiovanni. "He's starting to really talk like a mapper. He just hasn't quite learned how to drink like one."

Norwegian Candy

I boarded the *Pressure Drop* in Bermuda, in the middle of July, seven months into the expedition. The crew had just completed another set of dives in the Puerto Rico Trench, to demonstrate the equipment to representatives of the US Navy and to the billionaire and ocean conservationist Ray Dalio. (Dalio owns two Triton submarines.) Vescovo hoped to sell the hadal exploration system for $48 million — slightly more than the total cost of the expedition. During one of the demonstrations, a guest engineer began outlining all the ways he would have done it differently. "Okay," McCallum said, smiling. "But you didn't."

We set off north, through the turquoise waters of the Gulf Stream. It would take roughly three weeks, without stopping, to reach the deepest point in the Arctic Ocean. But the Arctic dive window wouldn't open for five more weeks, and, as Vescovo put it, "the *Titanic* is on the way." For several nights, I stood on the bow, leaning over the edge, mesmerized, as bioluminescent plankton flashed green upon contact with the ship. Above that, blackness, until the horizon, where the millions of stars began. Sometimes there was a crack of lightning in the distance, breaking through dark clouds. But most nights the shape of the Milky Way was so pronounced that in the course of the night you could trace the earth's rotation.

The air turned foggy and cold. Buckle steered out of the Gulf Stream and into the waters of the North Atlantic, a few hundred miles southeast of the port of St. John's, Newfoundland. After midnight, everyone gathered on the top deck and downed a shot of whiskey — a toast to the dead. We would reach the site of the *Titanic* by dawn. At sunrise, we tossed a wreath overboard, and watched it sink.

A few years ago, Peter Coope, Buckle's chief engineer, was working on a commercial vessel that was affixing an enormous, deepwater anchor to an oil rig off the coast of Indonesia. The chain slipped over the side, dragging down one side of the ship so far that the starboard propeller was in the air. Water poured into the engine room, where Coope worked. It was impossible for him to reach the exit.

British ship engineers wear purple stripes on their epaulets. Many of them think of this as a tribute to the engineers on the *Titanic*, every one of whom stayed in the engine room and went down with the ship. Now Coope, whose father was also a chief engineer, resolved to do the same. "I saw my life blowing away," Coope recalled. "People say it flashes in front of you. I was just calm. I felt, *That's it—I've gone.*" The bridge crew managed to right the ship after he had already accepted his fate.

The next day, Vescovo piloted the *Limiting Factor* down to the *Titanic*, with Coope's epaulets, and those of his father, in the passenger seat. The debris field spans more than half a mile, and is filled with entanglement hazards—loose cables, an overhanging crow's nest, corroded structures primed to collapse. ("What a rusting heap of shit!" Lahey said. "I don't want the sub anywhere near that fucking thing!") Large rusticles flow out from the bow, showing the directions of undersea currents. Intact cabins have been taken over by corals, anemones, and fish.

That evening, Vescovo returned the epaulets, along with a photograph of him holding them at the site of the wreck. Coope, who is 67, had come out of retirement to join this expedition—his last.

The *Pressure Drop* continued northeast, past Greenland and Iceland, to a port in Svalbard, an Arctic archipelago about 600 miles north of Norway. Huge glaciers fill the inlets, and where they have melted they have left behind flat-top mountains and slopes, crushed and planed by the weight of the ice. Most of the archipelago is inaccessible, except by snowmobile or boat. The population of polar bears outnumbers that of people, and no one leaves town without a gun.

McCallum brought on board two EYOS colleagues, including a polar guide who could smell and identify the direction of a walrus from a moving ship several miles away. By now, McCallum had adjusted the expedition schedule 97 times. The *Pressure Drop* set off northwest, in the direction of the Molloy Hole, the site of the deepest point in the Arctic Ocean. The least-known region of the seafloor lies under the polar ice cap. But scientists have found the fossilized remains of tropical plants; in some past age, the climate was like that of Florida.

It was the height of Arctic summer, and bitterly cold. I stood on the bow, watching arctic terns and fulmars play in the ship's draft, and puffins flutter spastically, barely smacking themselves out of the water.

The sun would not set, to disorienting effect. When I met John Ramsay, he explained, with some urgency, that the wider, flatter coffee cups contained a greater volumetric space than the taller, skinnier ones—and that this was an important consideration in weighing the consumption of caffeine against the potential social costs of pouring a second cup from the galley's single French press.

Ice drifted past; orcas and blue whales, too. Buckle sounded the horn as the ship crossed the 80th parallel. One night, the horizon turned white, and the polar ice cap slowly came into view. Another night, the ice pilot parked the bow of the ship on an ice floe. The *Pressure Drop* had completed one and a half laps around the world, to both poles. The bow thruster filled the Arctic silence with a haunting, mechanical groan.

Bongiovanni and her sonar assistants had mapped almost 700,000 square kilometers of the ocean floor, an area about the size of Texas, most of which had never been surveyed. Jamieson had carried out 103 lander deployments, in every major hadal ecosystem. The landers had traveled a combined distance of almost 800 miles, vertically, and captured footage of around 40 new species. Once, as we were drinking outside, I noticed a stray amphipod dangling from Jamieson's shoelace. "These little guys are all over the fucking planet," he said, kicking it off. "Shallower species don't have that kind of footprint. You're not going to see that with a zebra or a giraffe."

The earth is not a perfect sphere; it is smushed in at the poles. For this reason, Vescovo's journey to the bottom of the Molloy Hole would bring him nine miles closer to the earth's core than his dives in the Mariana Trench, even though the Molloy is only half the depth from the surface.

On August 29, Vescovo put on his coveralls and walked out to the aft deck. The ship and submarine crews had so perfected the system of launch and recovery that, even in rough seas, to an outsider it was like watching an industrial ballet. The equipment had not changed since the expedition's calamitous beginnings—but the people had.

"'This is not the end,'" Vescovo said, quoting Winston Churchill. "'It is not even the beginning of the end. But it is, perhaps, the end of the beginning.'"

He climbed inside the *Limiting Factor*. The swimmer closed the hatch. Vescovo turned on the oxygen and the carbon dioxide scrubbers. "Life support engaged," he said. "Good to go."

For the first few hundred feet, he saw jellyfish and krill. Then marine snow. Then nothing.

The Triton crew piled into the control room. Lahey found a

box of licorice from Svalbard, took a bite, and passed it around. "Just fucking heinous," he said, grimacing. "Who the fuck makes candy like that? Tastes like frozen shit."

There was a blip on the communications system. For a moment, the room went silent, as Vescovo called in to report his heading and depth. Then Kelvin Magee, the shop foreman, walked into the control room.

"Try it, Kelvin, you bastard!" Lahey said. "It's from Svalbard. It's local. It's a fucking Norwegian candy."

"Get it while there's still some left!"

"It's that ammonium chloride that really makes it—and that pork gelatin," Buckle said.

"Pork genitals?"

McCallum stood quietly in the corner, smiling. "Look at these fucking misfits," he said. "They just changed the world."

Water or Sky?

FROM *Hazlitt*

LAST WINTER, I took a train to Höchst im Odenwald, a small town an hour south of Frankfurt. Clusters of white rooftops poked above the trees, spindly pines scraping the pale blue sky. The air smelled of chimney smoke. Forests gave way to wide pastures, where cows and sheep grazed and starlings swooped low in search of seeds. Elke Hilbert picked me up at the train station in a wheezing stick shift and told me families took summertime boat trips on the nearby Main River. Her family took a boat there once, when her son Max was a child. She thinks about that trip often.

We took a roundabout route to Elke's home. She showed me Max's primary school, the traveler's hostel where he worked as a teenager, the soccer pitch where he used to practice. Later, in the house, I sat at the kitchen table, and Elke brought me coffee and a tray of heart-shaped muffins she'd baked for Valentine's Day. A neighbor rang the doorbell and gave Elke a basket of black and white cookies. "Please, eat them," Elke said, pushing the treats toward me.

I pulled out my recorder, and for the next five hours we talked about Max. He died in 2015 at 19, an apparent drowning in a Galician fishing village. When I visited Elke, he would have been 23. My age.

I learned about Max after I walked the Camino de Santiago to Fisterra, a village on Galicia's Costa da Morte. Fisterra means "End of the Earth" in Gallego, the local language. The landscape there is austere. Rugged cliffs cut into choppy water. During the wintertime, waves can reach up to 40 feet high. The regional delicacy is a barnacle called *percebe*, and *percebeiros* risk their lives scrambling down rocks to collect them. Residents told me Fisterra saw a handful of drownings a year—most often pilgrims who underestimated the power of the current, but sometimes fishermen and *percebeiros*, too. The rocky coast was also notorious for shipwrecks. With any tragedy on the sea, the first to arrive on the scene were fishermen, the people who knew the coast best. Later, a local poet would tell me, "We know death well here."

After I left Galicia, I spent a few hours browsing the internet for reports of drownings in Fisterra. One web page provided a list of people who died walking the Camino each year—heatstroke, heart attack, a 26-year-old run over by a train. Further searching led me to a news article about a young German man named Max who had gone swimming in frigid water, and the fisherman who had spent weeks searching for him when he disappeared. I googled images of Max, and photos popped up: bright blond hair, piercing blue eyes. More searching got me his mother's email address, and a month later, Elke responded to my interview request.

"I think that speaking with you about my beloved son Max could be a kind of 'psychotherapy' for me, an effective medicine for both my soul and my heart," she wrote.

We spoke by Skype in October of 2018. I took the call in my pajamas. It was 2 a.m. in California, where I was visiting my family, and I spoke quietly from a dim corner of the living room, wary of waking my parents. Elke had white-blond hair and blue eyes like her son, and she apologized repeatedly for her English, though it was near-perfect. As we talked, she told me about Max's penchant for philosophy and his lust for traveling. She was more reticent to speak of his mental health problems. She mentioned a "psychotic break" and marijuana use but didn't want to say more.

People usually have a personal reason for walking the Camino de Santiago, a ready-made answer to the question "Why are you walking?" Some people walk because they have quit their jobs; others quit their jobs to walk. One man I met while walking had just broken up with a longtime girlfriend. The summer I walked, I walked because I didn't want to do anything else. I wanted to think of nothing but my surroundings. I wanted to be in motion.

Max's friend Jenny Gast told me he walked because he felt

stifled at home. He'd lived there the year after graduating high school, uncertain about his future. He'd excelled in school and considered studying philosophy or literature at university. But after he graduated, his sense of self and purpose began to deteriorate.

Sometimes, Jenny told me, Max would come over to her house. They would sip tea on the balcony and talk about the future, their families. His parents were strict, suspicious that his friends were bad influences. They didn't know how to help him. During one of his examinations the year before, he felt his mind go blank and bolted from the classroom. After disappearing for several hours, he showed up at home, soaking wet, his cell phone damaged. He'd taken a train to a nearby town and stood in the river, contemplating drifting away with the current.

Just before he left for Spain, in April of 2015, Max and Jenny, who then lived in Munich, took a meandering drive through Höchst. Why don't you move to Munich, where doctors could help you? Jenny asked. She thought it was a bad idea to walk the Camino de Santiago, given his mental health. But Max felt that nothing was helping: not the pills doctors made him take, not the time spent resting at home. He was stuck in his head. I need to do something with my body, he told her. I need to walk.

I visited Fisterra again in December. It rained every day, a pounding rain whose roar blended with the crashing surf. The pilgrims were gone, the hotels shuttered, the only remaining people locals. The town was a dreary shell of its summer self. I met Guillermo Traba, a fisherman who had searched for Max and who claimed he could hold his breath underwater for 15 minutes. When we met for coffee at a dim restaurant on the port, he told me the water was murky the day he started searching for Max. Shadows of algae on the seafloor had looked like ghostly bodies, rocking in the current.

Guillermo spent his days diving for razor shell clams and suddenly found himself leading the search for a missing German pilgrim, spending every morning swimming and scanning the water for clues. That search ended, two weeks later, with the discovery of a body floating in the sea.

This wasn't the first time I had become obsessed with drowning. A few years before, I had spent a summer writing about deaths on the Kern River in central California, following a rescue team around the valley as they raced to save stranded swimmers and search for bodies. I saw the power and terror of water firsthand. Water could snatch a life away. Bodies sank, released gases, then floated. Professional divers were trained to recover corpses. They trawled the sea, sped down rivers in boats.

It was divers like this who had recovered the body of my friend Haley Rue when she drowned. She had fallen into a whirlpool the summer after our first year in college. We'd been backpacking in Europe—she in Austria, Hungary, and Germany, I in Spain and Portugal. We talked every day. I would send her messages from bars and cafés, recounting to her the day's adventures and the interminable loneliness I felt while traveling from city to city. Once, I wrote her from a corner store in Ibiza. A few hours earlier, I had missed the last bus from the north side of the island and walked 20 kilometers along the side of the highway, arriving back to my hostel just as night fell. You're crazy, Haley wrote me, then asked how I was doing. She, in turn, would tell me about the quirky people she met in her hostels and her favorite foods from each city—schnitzel, chocolate cake, cherries.

One day in July the conversation stopped. That evening, I read about her death on Facebook. There was a post from a family friend. It said something about prayers, and a river, and Haley. The word "drowned."

In the years after, I couldn't stop imagining my friend's death. I had a running list of questions. How long did it take for her to die? Had she been conscious? Did she know what was happening? Did she struggle? What was the last thing she saw—water or sky?

After I spoke to his mother, I started thinking about Max as though he were alive. As I wrote alone in my small bedroom, staring at the walls when I felt stuck, I would speak to Max. I'd sit in the gray morning light and throw my questions into the air—Why didn't you go to Munich like Jenny asked? Why did you keep swimming when the water was so cold? His presence in my life was a constant.

I had just moved to Barcelona, my fifth city in two years. I had no friends, no sense of direction. I sort of just ended up here, I'd say when people asked—explanations are always too long. When I wasn't sending story ideas to editors, I walked around the port of

Barcelona and watched the boats come in and out, trying to keep my mind off my loneliness.

Writing about Max gave me purpose, a way to spend my days. I turned to his friends, his text messages, his diary, spoke with the last people who saw him alive.

Natalie Kapahnke, who had walked for a week with Max through Cantabria, wrote me an 1,800-word email. Max felt like a little brother, she wrote, "the little brother you look after and care for." They walked with a group, exploring lighthouses along the coast and talking deep into the night. On one of their last evenings together, they made pizza and salad at a hostel. "Max told me that he understood that he has to change and that he misses his family," she wrote. "Still, he knew that the Camino and the distance was the best for him at this moment."

Asli Hanci, Max's girlfriend at the time of his death, sent me a few of their last Facebook messages. The messages are quotidian updates, small windows into Max's mind. In one, Max describes finishing 40 kilometers in one day—his longest stretch of walking—and going to eat a quarter-pounder as a celebration. In another, he feels homesick and ambivalent about having left Höchst. He tells Asli to call his parents and let them know he's fine. He sent his last message to Asli on May 28, arranging to meet her back in Frankfurt or Höchst once he finished walking. He did not mention he planned to go to Fisterra the following day.

Juan Mayan had been in Fisterra the day Max disappeared. That evening, while relaxing on the beach, Juan and his wife had seen a young man sitting nearby, smoking a cigarette and staring out to the water. After a while, the man left his backpack on shore and waded into the sea. He swam farther and farther until his body became a speck. When daylight began to fade, Juan and his wife left. The next morning, Juan took a stroll along the beach and saw the backpack untouched. Later, he would learn that though the sea had been calm on May 29, the water was frigid: 12 degrees Celsius —cold enough to cause a body to go into shock.

I got a coffee with Max's friend Jakob. We sat on a terrace in a village north of Frankfurt, drinking in the late-afternoon sunlight. Jakob rolled a cigarette and told me that during high school, he and Max would walk through the forest. They'd sit under a peach tree, or climb a tall oak and lounge in the branches, talking.

Jakob still struggles with Max's death. Did Max want to die? Did he have a psychotic break when he was alone on the beach? Jakob shrugged. It didn't matter—nothing would change Max's death. But he wanted to know everything. He wanted to go to Fisterra, see what Max saw. I told Jakob about Haley, how I wanted to know what she'd seen, too.

As we talked, I thought about one of the first times I'd written about death, when I was a freshman in college and a student had killed himself. After we published the story in the student newspaper, I kept speaking with his friends, even though their quotes would never leave my notebook. It was nice, we thought, just to have someone to talk to, someone who would listen.

After a few hours at the table with Elke as she recounted the worst days of her life, I felt I owed her an explanation. Why did I want to write about her son? she asked.

I told her about Haley.

We had met in our first year of college and would have been roommates the following year. We were both from the West Coast and, that first college spring, had experienced a shapeless sense of loss. We missed home and who we had been at home, a world away from the pressure of academics and college social life. On a sunny April day, we skipped class and went to a park. As we were looking at the sky, Haley told me she wanted to move to the Grand Canyon. She liked how big it was, how it was so far away. What would you do there? I asked, and she was quiet for a minute. Maybe be a guide, she said. That sounds nice, I said. An escape. She smiled with her whole face. I like the way you talk, she said. That's the only sentence I remember in her voice.

In July, when I was in Lisbon, Haley went to Innsbruck, Austria. She was in love with everything: the job, the food, the landscape, the people. In Innsbruck, Haley bought a carton of cherries and ate them, one by one, as she walked barefoot on the hot asphalt back to her hostel. In Innsbruck, Haley hiked up a mountain, ate strudel at the top, and tripped a few times on her way down. "In Innsbruck," Haley wrote on her blog, "I'm a little girl."

A week later, I sat on my hostel bed fanning my face. It was 11 p.m. and hot. I opened my laptop to check Facebook. I saw the post.

I couldn't close my laptop. I tiptoed to the hostel kitchen for a glass of water and screamed. I lay facedown on the wood floor and breathed dust until I choked. I texted Haley but the messages didn't go through. They appeared on my phone screen with a red exclamation point. A few days later, I learned she had fallen into a whirlpool in Germany. She was 19.

In 2018, I went to Munich to visit the place where Haley died. A friend who had been with her at the river picked me up and drove me to the mountains. We stopped at a forest. The earth was damp from a recent rainstorm, and lightning had felled several large trees. A guide showed up, and he gave me a wet suit. The friend went to read in a restaurant, and the guide took me up the river.

As I clambered and slipped, he showed me how to look out for dangerous rapids. A safe rapid was formed by a pillow of water that rushed against a rock's surface. A dangerous rapid looked like nothing special: a rock wedged in the current. But moving water needs somewhere to go. If a water pillow wasn't there, that meant there was a hole in the rock. A hole sucks things—twigs, leaves, animals—with a crushing force. I didn't want to think about the rocks, but they surrounded us, on the banks, on the riverbed, under my feet.

I heard it before I saw it. Crashing water. A wall of sound thundering against my ears. The sound was hidden behind a mass of rock. The whirlpool. There was a hole in the rock, at the bottom.

As I sat with Elke, I thought about rivers, and currents, and water that steals young lives. I'd outlived Max and Haley by four years. I told Elke I wanted to write about her son because I was figuring out how to live without Haley. Writing was a way to process, to understand, to mourn. Speaking was, too. Over pizza that night, Elke said that Max and I would have been friends.

I started writing about Haley. Piecing together nearly five years, recounting all the times I thought about her: when I was hot and facing an open window and a breeze cooled my skin; while lying on grass and staring at the sky; while eating a handful of M&Ms or waffles with whipped cream. I thought of Haley at the beach, in the mountains, on dusty paths that cut through the countryside. I thought of Haley when I stole packets of hazelnut cream from hostels. I thought of Haley when I bought cartons of cherries. I thought of Haley when I wore my traveler's backpack, when my sandals gave me tan lines, when I sat at a bar alone, when I craved a piece of cake, when I went for long walks. Haley Haley Haley Haley Haley Haley Haley Haley.

The story never felt finished. But I thought by letting those words live outside of my head, something else might start. Maybe a stranger would send me an email and we would speak on the phone about the friends we had lost. Perhaps someone would ask for Haley's mother's email, or Elke's email, and they could start correspondences with people around the world. They could discover new ways to think about their children. Strangers could know about Max. They could know about Haley.

Imagine: a dozen of us talking into the early morning, across time zones, in our pajamas, making new meaning. The dead could keep on living.

Last summer, when the air grew humid in Barcelona, I left Spain. In Berlin, I walked 20 miles in a single day. In Bratislava, I walked down a path until I ran out of road. Being in motion distracts me. I think I'm going somewhere.

Fisterra. Fin de Tierra. End of the Earth. Max Hilbert had heard of the town before he began walking the Camino de Santiago in April of 2015, but he didn't know much about it. As with most good things on the Camino, like the best places to spend the night and the mysterious water fountains that poured red wine, Max had heard about the town through word of mouth. He had been walking for a month and felt stronger than he had in a long time. He wanted to keep going.

"I have the feeling, somehow, that I have not finished walking," Max wrote in his journal. "So I'll go to Fisterra."

Every year, on the anniversary of Haley's death, I send an email to her mother. I write to her about all my new cities, all the places I've visited and people I've met these past five years. She writes to me about life in Tacoma, where Haley was raised, and the hours she spends in the garden, thinking about her daughter. During the springtime, after her mother had picked fresh fruit, the two had a ritual. "The first ripe radish, raspberry or cherry tomato," Haley's mother once wrote to me, "would always be divided down the middle to share."

A few years ago, I caught a plane to Seattle. Haley's mother picked me up at the airport and took me to Tacoma. Puget Sound glinted under the late-afternoon sun and the lavender Mount

Rainier hovered in the distance. At the house, I put my backpack in Haley's room, and her mother drove me to Haley's elementary school, the boardwalk where she had liked to walk, the places where she used to go running.

The next morning, I woke up late. I sat at the kitchen table and looked out the window. Haley's mother, wearing a pink bathrobe, was in the garden, crouched over a bush. When she returned to the kitchen, she set a bowl of blueberries on the counter and searched the cupboard for flour. I haven't made blueberry pancakes in years, she told me.

We sat at the table and ate slowly. I took another pancake, relishing the long, quiet morning, the way the sun streamed through the window, the sweet smell of butter and fruit. I wished I could stay at that table forever. For the first time in a long time, I didn't need to walk away. I didn't need to move. There was nowhere else to be.

JACKIE BRYANT

California's Weed Country Is Lit

FROM *Cannabitch*

ONE NIGHT I was coughing so hard I woke myself up. It was one of those dry, insidious coughs that started with a sinus tingle and ended with dry heaving once my body realized there was nothing more to expel. Then, moments later, it started again, not letting up until my eyes fully bugged out.

I had been in one of those sleeps that was so deep and disorienting that someone could have told me I was anywhere in the world at all and I would have believed them. I looked around, remembered I was in my tent, and pulled a jagged rock out from under my butt. I hacked again. "Fuck!" I said out loud to nobody.

Rather than waking up in a comforting place, I was instead in southern Mendocino County, camping on a semi-legal cannabis grow operation. Seeing as this was only a month or so ago, it also meant I was there during the August Complex fires, which are still burning and, as of this writing, 74 percent contained, despite recently converting to what's now called a "gigafire" (that's not a good thing).

Mendocino County is part of what's called the Emerald Triangle. The name refers to the cannabis-growing region in Northern California that is made up of three counties, officially—Mendocino, Humboldt, and Trinity—and others in its vicinity that are equally rural and therefore provide cover for a variety of less-than-legal operations, such as growing cannabis.

The Emerald Triangle is the historic home of cannabis cultivation in the present-day United States. It's where most of the country's black market weed comes from, no matter if it's from a plug in San Diego or from "a guy" in New York. It's where all the good bud that wasn't Mexican brick weed has always come from. These days, plenty of legal cannabis is grown and sold there, too. I'm sure many reading this have seen *Murder Mountain,* the documentary series that showed up on Netflix about two years ago. That takes place in the Emerald Triangle. It's kinda *the* place, as far as weed is concerned.

So, it shouldn't be surprising that I've found myself up there a lot in recent years. This year, in particular, I received invitations from farmers, legal and illegal alike, to see the cannabis harvest firsthand, which begins in September and continues throughout the rest of the year. Not to be, you know, *whatever* about it, but it's a big deal to be invited! Even with legal grows, there are a lot of security concerns, so people can't just show up and say, "Where the weed at?!" One must be asked to show face. If I'm honest, I've never even asked to visit. It always seemed like a narc move. At best, it was deeply uncool. I've always waited for the invite.

So, when I received some invites this past August, the origins of which spanned varying legalities, I knew I had to head north. At the same time, California's wildfires began and quickly burned out of control, threatening not only the immediate areas I was due to visit but also the industry I make a living covering and partake in as a consumer. I sent a bunch of texts to my contacts all over the Triangle.

"How are you guys? Evacuation plans? Still harvesting? Still want me to come?" my messages read. I got enthusiastic "yes" responses from everyone.

"It's really gnarly up here, but we are safe. We have a good evac plan. We will take care of you. Come see what we're up against . . . ps have some fire for you to try," one of the texts from a grower read. Imminent danger, a good story, a long road trip, cataclysmic earth happenings, and really killer weed? I couldn't say no. I drove up one day in September, a straight 13-hour shot from my home in San Diego.

To turn an adage on its head and make it painfully literal: Where there's fire, there's smoke. The smoke is what woke me up in my tent at 3 a.m. that night, despite the nearest blaze being about 20 miles away. I remember quietly saying out loud to myself, "You're a fucking idiot, Jackie," before readjusting my sleeping pad and blankets, coughing a few more times, lighting a joint because, truly, *who cares anymore?* and eventually flipping my zip-up hoodie backward. I fell back asleep with the hood over my face as a makeshift smoke shield, deciding that the risk of suffocating myself with my own hood was worth it for a decent night's rest.

Camping on grows is required in many cases—often, because the work is temporary and sometimes illegal, it makes no sense for the owner and/or grower to build permanent structures on the land. Whatever permanent or semipermanent structure that does pop up quickly turns into storage for clones, drying plants, and equipment.

Plus, a human presence is required near the plants at all times, especially near harvest, for security reasons. It's a popular moneymaking pastime for the most hard-core of outlaws to rob grows of product and cash just before harvest, when plants are mature and ready to be cured and processed into the street product we all know and love. That's why I was outside, sleeping alone in a secluded part of the property. Others on the grow staff bedded down elsewhere on-site—in a garage, their cars, or in their tents.

It's been exceptionally hard on the farmworkers, who are spending months at a time on grows—much longer than the handful of nights I spent in the area. If they don't work, they don't get paid. If they bolt, they will most likely not be invited back to work for future harvests. There are always more bodies to take their places.

"The hill and farm have been covered in smoke for about a month," Andrea A., a trimmer near Ukiah, in Mendocino County, tells me over text. "The smoke has literally BARELY lifted, we had to harvest in the smoke because of how urgent it was to save the plants," she says.

"Because of [the smoke], some of the plants are dying," Andrea says. "Browning at the stem or budding too early—like three weeks too early. Our farm was set to produce a good amount. The most they've ever produced," she says.

Andrea's boss, let's call him Jake, who is the head grower in charge of the whole operation, confirmed this to me. "We were expecting to average around 5–7lbs [of saleable dried cannabis flower] per plant. Looking like it's gonna be 1–3lb average," he said to me over text. Jake noted that he has 99 plants, which meant they were expecting 500 to 700 pounds and will now only get 100 to 300. He believes the heavy, consistent smoke blocked out the light—something other growers have commented to me, which caused the plants to yield less overall.

This echoes what I've heard from other Triangle growers throughout the 2020 growing season. This was set to be a record year, many of them said. Now, faced with crop loss and taint, it's poised to be one of the most devastating ever.

Every grower I talked to—10, in total—also knows a few people who have lost everything. Their farms completely burned. Most of these farms are, at best, only partially legal. In Mendocino County, in particular, it has become common for farms to become licensed only at the county level, stopping short of state oversight and licensing. County officials overlook the lack of state permitting, seeing as it's not their jurisdiction, and tend to not see much incentive in blowing the whistle at the state level. They're getting paid, so who cares?

It's much cheaper for these small farms to stay illegal, thanks to the mountain of permitting fees, taxes, and expensive tweaks they'd have to make, like making the farm Americans with Disabilities Act compliant, which would require putting in bathrooms. I went to the bathroom in a hole in the ground the entire time I was there, among other mild inconvenient indignities for me that are prohibitive for many others. This is one effect of operating in the shadows. Needing to put up with smoke inhalation during working is another.

Another shadow effect is that if a farm isn't legal, there aren't many ways to be insured. Forget about federal disaster aid, too. Even if a farm is legal, that's only at the state level. Cannabis, as a Schedule I narcotic, is still federally illegal. Major insurers won't touch it with a 10-foot pole. Some cannabis insurance companies specifically cover cannabis operations, but there is only one I know of that covers outdoor growers, and I have been unable to confirm their efficacy.

Even the most legit of the legit—hemp, a federally legal cash crop—lacks access to insurance. In California, qualifying as a fire-safe property worthy of insurance is becoming increasingly elusive as everything seems to exist in a fire zone nowadays.

There isn't really a silver lining here, save for the fact that cannabis is, blessedly, an annual crop. It will be a new year next year, regardless of what else happens between now and then. That's a helpful reminder for us humans, too. The August Complex fires, which were tempered over the weekend by much-needed rain, are still burning as of today, October 12, 2020. The complex, which was ignited by a lightning strike, comprises 38 fires that have, so far, burned 979,386 acres. Many of the farms in that land were so off-the-grid that their losses won't be publicly known, though they will be felt in the cannabis markets.

For those who like to jump ahead, your suspicions are correct: there will be a squeeze on supply, both legal and illegal, across the nation and local to California.

"2021, at least the first six months before greenhouse starts to flip, is going to be a really dry year," says Julia Jacobson, CEO of Aster Farms, a licensed farm in Lake County that sits just over the Mendocino County line. "Many cultivators were not able to get their licenses renewed, now add the fires to it? We're losing some of the best farms in California who are growing outdoors," she says to me while we sit in the shadow of her flowering plants. Jacobson and her business partner and husband, Sam Ludwig, speak from experience. In 2018, Aster Farms lost a house and several structures during the Mendocino Complex fire.

One of the striking things about experiencing a disaster in real time is that, for slower-burning ones, it isn't all panic and pain. There are moments of genuine levity, like the hug I received from Andrea after emerging from 13 hours in my car alone. There is the fat joint filled to the brim with Do-Si-Do that her co-trimmer, who I had never met before, rolled for me so it would be ready for my arrival. He even uses water, rather than spit, to seal it, to keep it COVID safe. There are the conversations about the killer sushi joint in Ukiah, the garbanzo aguachile Andrea and her partner whipped up. There are the countless joints we individually take to the face as we all decide to press pause on the literal world on fire —during a pandemic!—that surrounds and threatens to consume us at the hint of a wind change. In a myriad of ways both big and small, we all decide to quietly push on.

"Just another speed bump in life," Jake says to me over text just this morning. "You can only do what you can, and you can't change the weather. We've replanted our greenhouses and gonna keep moving forward."

Youtopia

FROM *Outside*

I'VE HEARD MANY strange things from Uber drivers. But this was a new one.

"Are you sure?" she asked, questioning my destination as I hopped into her car at Atlanta's Hartsfield-Jackson airport one night last fall. "I've been driving Uber to and from the airport for five years now, and I've only taken someone south twice." North is the city proper and Atlanta's endless suburban expanse. South is deep country. The crickets get louder and the sidewalks vanish.

Tucked into Georgia's remote Chattahoochee Hills, a mere 30 miles from one of America's biggest urban centers, is Serenbe (pronounced "saren-be"), a 750-resident, 1,400-acre "agrihood" founded in the early 2000s. Billed as a premium-living paradise —in its own literature and in *Architectural Digest* and *O, The Oprah Magazine,* among others—it allows residents to connect with nature while surrounded by award-winning architecture. When I arrived, an employee handed me the keys to my lodging and an electric golf cart to use for the duration of my five-day stay. But after a pause she reconsidered. "Maybe I should drive you," she said, skeptical of my ability to navigate to my temporary home in the dark. We drove by a rustic-chic farmhouse restaurant and down a winding country road, past a stylized rusted-metal signpost displaying the quote ALL BEAUTY IS AN OUTWARD EXPRESSION OF IN-WARD GOOD. I found the language pretentious, self-satisfied, and utterly irresistible. Still, I felt a vague sense of panic rising within as we drove through the darkened woods: Where was the award-winning architecture?

Just as my concerns began to peak, we reached Serenbe's residential area, a fully formed, cleverly constructed community like something out of a Narnian fantasy. Currently divided into three large "hamlets," the development is a whimsical hodgepodge of more than 300 minimalist-modern homes, town houses, cottages, and farmhouses. We passed a general store, a florist, a high-end bike-repair shop, a school, and a playhouse before reaching my two-bedroom townhome in the hamlet of Grange. The 1,500-square-foot lodging was nearly three times the size of my New York apartment and had the ambiance of a premium Airbnb, with elegant decor, a library of self-help books, and Serenbe-branded glass water bottles. I stepped out onto the back deck overlooking a wooded expanse and was met with silence; even Serenbe's dense neighborhoods are free from the sounds of traffic and commerce. Many residents have electric vehicles, and Serenbe rents out golf carts like mine to visitors in an effort to reduce noise pollution. Even during the busy day and evening hours, you can hear a pin drop.

I came to Serenbe to observe the transcendentalist antidote it offers to the modern ills that plague many Americans. In the last several years, I had tried numerous tactics to neutralize the exhausting effects of my fast-paced, exhausting, digital urban life —meditation apps, yoga retreats, limited screen time, knitting, devouring books like Jenny Odell's *How to Do Nothing*. Unplugging had begun to feel like another full-time job.

But at Serenbe, you don't have to try so hard. A balanced life can be your full-time reality. You can drive 40 minutes to work in the city and return to the community's idyllic confines in the evening. You can replenish yourself with hyper-local vegetables and woodsy hikes without sacrificing your livelihood or access to cosmopolitan life. In theory it's heaven. So why was my stay so unsettling?

The following morning, I tried, like other journalists before me, to get my bearings with a tour led by Serenbe's founder, Steve Nygren. A 74-year-old former restaurateur, Nygren is spry and trim, with a thicket of white hair and a light southern drawl. As Serenbe's chief spokesman and mascot, he can often be found walking the property with a smile on his face, waving to residents while carrying one of his young grandchildren. Today, Nygren was doing what he often does: explaining this little community to a group—mine consisted primarily of baby boomers who worked in financial services—trying to understand what exactly Serenbe *is*.

Serenbe is not a gated enclave sealed off from the rest of Georgia. There is no formal application process to live there, only a willingness to sign a lease or hand over a down payment. It's not a resort, nor is it a cult, a retirement community, or a crunchy commune ruled by dogma. It's not a smallholding, either, although it does have a 25-acre organic farm and offers a community-supported agriculture program to residents.

Nygren stumbled upon the lush landscape that would eventually become Serenbe in the early 1990s. At the time, he was living in Atlanta with his wife and three daughters, experiencing the numbing bustle of running a constellation of 36 successful restaurants. One weekend, the family took a day trip to the rural farms south of the city, resulting in the impulse purchase of a country home on 60 acres. The open space made Nygren realize that he was ready to get off "the treadmill of life," as he likes to say. In 1994, he sold his business and moved the family out of Atlanta.

By the late '90s, Nygren decided to create a bed-and-breakfast on the property, bestowing it with the name his wife had coined for their rural escape, Serenbe—a mash of "serenity" and "being." When, in 2000, development threatened to encroach on Serenbe's surrounding areas, Nygren bought up 600 neighboring acres. He worked with the local government to craft zoning laws to encourage conservation-minded, village-like developments rather than a sea of McMansions.

"Everybody thought I was this crazy liberal," Nygren announced to the tour group, reminiscing about Serenbe's early days in the 2000s, when suburban developments were growing and sustainability was less mainstream. "Now I've become a visionary." He led us deeper into the wooded property, with the sound of roosters echoing in the distance.

Today, Serenbe is a hub of innovation with local, national, and global influence. It currently houses around 750 residents, but the community's final plans can accommodate roughly 3,500 Serenbeites. Now that its first two hamlets, Grange and Selborne, are built and populated, it's developing Mado, the third of its planned five residential and commercial zones. Serenbe's population includes intellectuals, workaholics, Hollywood heavyweights, hippies, and politicos on both sides of the aisle. Even with this heterogeneous populace, it strives to facilitate thoughtful conversation, in part by avoiding political messaging in its marketing. When residents meet, they're more likely to gripe about the recent armadillo invasion than their neighbors.

All this growth has made Nygren a leader in the wellness-community trend. Every year, Serenbe hosts a "placemaking" conference, where developers and urban planners convene for inspiration. Today there are wellness-oriented communities outside Seattle, London, multiple Florida cities, and Tulum, Mexico.

Twenty minutes into the tour, Nygren led our group past the farmhouse that was his original home at Serenbe. The conversation fell on the weather. It was an unusually hot September, even by Georgia standards, which would typically bring out swarms of mosquitoes. But not here, Nygren explained to the group. At Serenbe, where workers don't use harsh chemicals for landscaping, natural predators keep bugs in check. (I was skeptical, but then again I didn't see a single mosquito during my stay.)

Serenbe is most frequently described using the phrase "new urbanism," a movement to resist suburban sprawl and develop walkable, citylike neighborhoods. But Nygren doesn't agree with this label, since he claims Serenbe has a stronger environmental focus than new urbanists generally do. The term Nygren likes to use to characterize Serenbe is "biophilic," an idea popularized in the '80s by the biologist Edward O. Wilson, who believes that humans have an innate tendency to connect with the natural world. While this thesis seems obvious, tech-addled urban and suburban life has all but suffocated the average American's connection to nature, causing us to lose out on its benefits. Research suggests that exposure to greener urban spaces can improve mental health, reduce cardiovascular disease and diabetes, boost immunity, and even possibly help patients recover from surgery.

Nature as therapy is the founding principle of biophilic design and, by extension, Serenbe. By developing the Mado hamlet, Serenbe is signaling its focus on health. Perhaps more than anything previously built, it speaks to the bedrock of Serenbe's promise: wellness. One of its buildings, which houses the gym, the spa, and a suite of offices that will eventually be filled with doctors, nutritionists, and New Age practitioners, displays the slogan that underlies everything Nygren has believed in since he conceived of Serenbe: "Be here, be well."

As we walked by carefully maintained rows of produce near the farmhouse, Nygren addressed the tour group. "That's the vegetable garden, designed by Ryan Gainey."

A developer from North Carolina turned to me. "Do you know who Ryan Gainey is?"

I didn't.

"He was this really eccentric, flamboyant guy who charged to think about your garden—$5,000 just to *think* about your garden."

We passed an area described as the animal village, consisting mostly of goats. Nygren pointed in the distance. "They're doing goat yoga up there. Do you see that? The goats are trained, and the people are trained, and then they put the goat on your back. They walk on your back, and so . . . It's a rage. She sells out every class. People come from all over."

Walking away from the animal village, Nygren talked about a Serenbe employee who had recently become an expert in forest bathing, originally a Japanese practice that involves mindfully engaging with nature. Met with some quizzical looks, he summarized the concept: "Basically, it's spending quiet time in nature."

One participant raised his eyebrows and turned to his friend. "So when you were a little kid and you walked around in the woods, you never knew you were forest bathing."

In the Selborne hamlet, Nygren pointed out the lack of visible garbage cans—all residential waste at Serenbe is disposed of in underground vessels just outside each front door. The main directive to the community's builders, who must go through a detailed design-review process, is restraint. Large swaths of manicured grass are nowhere to be found, and most cottages must have a front porch that's at least seven feet wide. "We try to put buildings in a garden, versus gardens around buildings," Nygren told the group. Occasionally, an Amazon Prime truck would pass by, jolting us back to reality.

To end the excursion, Nygren led the group into Serenbe's real estate office to distribute paperwork and answer any questions. Like a museum tour that culminates at a gift shop, it was a reminder: utopia is also a business. Nygren continued to reel off Serenbe's perks. He mentioned that as part of the Mado neighborhood's wellness efforts, the community has three on-site death doulas to help the elderly. One man from the tour group smiled and turned to Nygren. "When you figure that they're going to live forever at Serenbe," he said, "you'll have to plan for that."

As a temporary Serenbe resident, I wanted to fully immerse myself in its way of life. I saw a playhouse production (*The Sleepy Hollow Experience*), did goat yoga (which lived up to my Instagram expectations), took long walks (through a wildflower meadow and a stone labyrinth), and ate plenty of farm-to-table salads (my favorite was the Nordic salmon on mixed greens and haricots verts). On my third day, I signed up for a horseback ride around the property, where our young guide, Emma, highlighted some notable vegetation and explained the temperament of the horses, some of which had not been getting along. I was hoping that fellow riders would be able to share some of the unvarnished realities about living at Serenbe. But, as was true of many of my experiences there, all my cohorts were interlopers from out of town.

I asked Emma how often Serenbe's residents go on her trail rides. She paused for a moment. "You know," she said, "I don't think that I've ever given one to a resident. Most of our customers are visitors." This was the case at goat yoga as well, an activity advertised prominently on Serenbe's social media. (A portion of the class is dedicated to taking selfies with the goats.) And although Nygren talks profusely about Serenbe's giant stone labyrinth, I never saw anybody walk through it. The whole place reminded me of New York, where permanent residents rarely willingly visit Times Square or the Statue of Liberty. And like New York, Serenbe relies on the substantial revenue that outsiders provide. Because many people have tried to use the property for photo shoots, there are signs along the trails reminding visitors that shooting commercial photos and video footage is allowed only with a permit. For most, the Serenbe way of life is still only a photo op, a temporary respite.

Living this fantasy full-time can come at a steep cost. Serenbe's 800-square-foot one-bedroom lofts start at around $275,000, and four-bedroom houses can go for up to $1.8 million, exceeding local home prices many times over. Although some employees rent apartments at Serenbe, its high prices make living there out of reach for others. Atlanta is one of the most diverse cities in the country, but Serenbe feels like a liberal arts college in New England, touting diversity as an ideal rather than a practice. One major challenge is the lack of well-funded, quality public schools in the area. (Serenbe residents helped launch the Chattahoochee Hills Charter School in 2014, but it's not large enough to guarantee Serenbe residents spots. There's currently a long waiting list to attend.)

Still, what can appear as upper-class elitism is rooted in real concerns, at least about our well-being. After years of upward climb, the life expectancy of Americans experienced a troubling dip between 2015 and 2017, influenced in part by rising drug overdoses and suicide, while obesity has skyrocketed. Currently we're witnessing the emergence of a $4.5 trillion global wellness industry, spurred by lifestyle-obsessed Americans who want to biohack and self-quantify themselves into well-oiled longevity machines.

Serenbe—and its new wellness neighborhood, Mado, in particular—is an outgrowth of these trends. What it offers is more about prevention than remedies, facilitating a wholesome lifestyle aimed at rendering modern health issues irrelevant. "I walk to the CSA and walk back, and I eat vegetables all week long that have never been in a car and were grown by somebody I know," says Garnie Nygren, Steve Nygren's daughter and Serenbe's chief operating officer. Then she told me the story of Cathy Gailey, a middle-aged woman who moved to Serenbe with her husband. When they first arrived, Gailey was told there was a waterfall on the property, but the people she met encouraged her to find it on her own, without guidance, as a means of exploration. Months of walking—and the fresh produce—led her to drop 30 pounds. (When I spoke to Gailey after my visit, she told me that she later gained some of it back when a knee surgery prevented her from taking daily walks.)

Given the financial advantages of its residents, you could argue that Serenbe is likely appealing to the converted, creating a kind of bubble. One tagline used frequently in the wellness industry is "Health is wealth," but the inverse is more true—as a 2017 study in *The Lancet* puts it, "Low socioeconomic status is one of the strongest predictors of morbidity and premature mortality worldwide."

I ask Garnie Nygren about my bubble concern. "We're building a thousand homes, not ten thousand or a million," she says. "We can't change everything in the world." She notes that Serenbe is surrounded by affordable housing in Chattahoochee Hills, with access to all of Serenbe's stores and nature paths. (And Serenbe's tax base continues to greatly support various municipal services, including medical facilities and the fire department.) Garnie likens Serenbe's high-cost premium lifestyle to a Tesla—a luxury product that has helped influence an entire marketplace. "Someone who's selling houses at a lower price point will look to what we're doing and say, *If I just change this and this, people will buy them,*" she says. "They're aspiring to live in a Serenbe-like community. Like it or not, no one changes the conversation by providing products at a lower price point. That's just market forces."

If you spend enough time reading about Serenbe or walking around its properties, you start to believe that it really is a singular, pioneering kind of paradise. But former Chattahoochee Hills councilman Ricky Stephens put it in perspective for me a few months after I visited. Beyond Serenbe's confines, the region still abides by the agricultural and conservationist principles that Serenbe is known for, just without all of the headline-grabbing quirks and designer elements. "We want to protect the rural life that so many people outside Serenbe have lived their whole life," he told me. "The area was rural and agricultural before Serenbe ever got here."

I enjoyed most of my stay at Serenbe. And yet, as I prepared to leave, something seemed off. I couldn't shake the spooky feeling that it was too pristine, too isolated, and too good to be true. A new Serenbe homeowner named Jessica Jacobson summed up the sensation for me when I spoke to her during my stay: "When we first came out here, I was like, *Am I on a set right now? What is happening?*"

It was a lazy Sunday afternoon, and Jessica and her husband, Jon, were loafing around a friend's house, getting ready to watch football. They'd just signed the paperwork on a home in the Mado neighborhood, but Jon could vividly recall the slight skepticism he felt when he first visited a friend who lived there five years earlier. After repeated trips, the skepticism began to fade away. Eventually, the couple didn't just acclimate to the pace and way of life, they started to crave the much-needed respite from their lives and jobs in New York City. "We were returning a wedding gift at Macy's, and everything was forty-five minutes out of the way," Jon said, recalling one of his frustrations with the city. "How hard is it to return something at Macy's?"

I constantly experience frustration like this in my own life, which is filled with habits that feel verboten at Serenbe. I order delivery filled with preservatives, I rarely seek out nature, I often drift down the sidewalk in an iPhone haze. I stand on crowded subway platforms awaiting trains that never come and pick through rotting vegetables at the convenience store. I hardly know anything about most of my neighbors, some of whom I share walls with. Yet I still feel connected to the world in a way that might be impossible at Serenbe. I'm in constant, unavoidable dialogue with its grossness and weirdness. After a few days at Serenbe, I realized that, despite its insistence that it's not a gated community, it felt like one. Maybe I'd feel differently if I spent months or even years there. But right now, the small gestures I make in the name of tranquility in New York City, be it shopping at the farmers' market, choosing plant-based meals over red meat, or incorporating meditation into my daily routine, bring me greater satisfaction than an all-inclusive ticket to purity.

For their part, Jessica and Jon are not planning to move to Serenbe full-time. Like other homeowners in the community, they'll visit their new residence on vacations but rent it out most of the year. Right now a permanent shift feels too dramatic. When they told me this, I felt relieved, as if my own life choices were being validated.

This part-time Serenbe existence preserves the tantalizing appeal of escape. "I come back from these weekends so energized," Jessica explained. "My colleagues are like, *What? We want to go.*"

NATALIE STOCLET

Can Travel Become an Addiction?

FROM *Playboy*

MORE THAN A century ago, wanderlust wasn't a desirable trait. Instead it was considered a psychological condition.

As Ian Hacking traces in *Mad Travelers: Reflections on the Reality of Transient Mental Illnesses,* Albert Dadas was the first man diagnosed for "traveling obsessively, often without identification or a specific reason for why he was traveling," in France in the 1890s. Dadas would become one of many in an epidemic of French men who were locked up for wandering, be it across borders or continents, with no apparent destination or set plan in mind. These men, when caught, would be put into a jail or mental asylum, and were eventually diagnosed amongst professionals as "pathological tourists."

These diagnoses would continue in France for 23 years, from 1886 to 1909. As Hacking tells it, the epidemic would eventually have cultural repercussions for its misuse as a convenient diagnosis rather than a true psychiatric condition. Doctors would label men as pathological tourists for any behaviors that were seen as outside of social norms. Left your wife? Pathological tourist. Left the army? Pathological tourist. Quit your job? You get it. While the diagnoses were misguided, it guided me to question the relevance of this case study today. Mainly, what is the collective psychology behind our society's obsession with #wanderlust?

As I sat to write this, I had just gotten home from vacation. When I woke up from my routine post-plane nap, I felt hazy and disoriented. I wiped my eyes, looked around my room, and was reminded I was back to reality. I had a physical reaction to this realization. A rush in my chest, followed by absolute nothingness. The escapism I had sought and found when I was away would now be a memory. Before I could muster the attention to write the first word in this article, I found myself online imagining where my next escape would be. When could I take my next day off? Should I just pack up and hit the road? I began wandering through the travel sites with no apparent destination in mind. I was today's pathological digital tourist.

Ever since I can remember, I've been on the move. I'm what you would call a third culture kid—the quintessential expat. I grew up moving every two to three years, born in New York City and raised in Tunisia, Morocco, Argentina, England, and the United Arab Emirates. Changing environments was pretty much the only thing that didn't change throughout my life. This year, I've taken over 30 flights for pleasure, and business here and there. And I had never stopped to consider the intent behind my travels. I believe travel makes us interesting. But is that the reason we're interested?

In Mark Manson's *Everything Is Fucked,* he describes how "any active participant in modern-day society is prone to a series of low-level addictive behaviors, checking our phones, finishing shows we don't like, traveling not because we want to but because we want to be able to say that we went. We are looking for diversions.

Freedom is not having more brands of cereal to choose from, or more beach vacations to take selfies on." Ninety percent of young travelers share their vacation photos on social media during their trip. #Wanderlust has over 108 million posts on Instagram. I'm of the opinion that travel is an entirely beautiful and enriching facet to life. But I'm also ready to question the intent behind why so many of us travel today, and whether we could be addicted to those kinds of behaviors or ideas.

I talked to Dr. Gwilym Roddick, a psychotherapist and addiction specialist at the Ross Center, to better understand addictive behaviors and if, in fact, someone could be addicted to travel itself. First was understanding the process of how addiction is diagnosed. Roddick explained that "the assessment process involves asking the questions: What is the function of the behavior, and how is it both detrimental and benefiting a person's life, well-being, and what's important to them?"

Because of the nature of addiction, and it's cultural repercussions, he says that "it is important to note that 'addiction' is a word or term, like all mental health diagnoses, that is made up and contextual. The word has so much attached to it, in both unhelpful and helpful ways." He continues, "It should be said that mental health diagnoses are based on behavioral and cultural norms and attitudes, often dictated by who or what culture is in power and who is attempting to enforce those ideas to attain influence. They do not take everyone and everything into consideration."

When we think of addictive behaviors, we often look toward the subject of the addiction rather than what underlying causes it might be rooted in. Roddick dissects this further in saying, "By assessing the issue using two evidence-based therapeutic modalities, cognitive behavioral therapy and acceptance and commitment therapy (ACT), behaviors we call 'addictions' are attempts to enhance pleasure or avoid suffering, which essentially is one thing, the avoidance of suffering.

"Suffering, in this context, is a word used to describe what human beings have designated as the unwanted, undesirable, bad, or wrong things one should experience and therefore often try to avoid. This could be anything from anxiety to boredom. Most mental health conditions involve some form of avoidance, and from an ACT perspective, the specific type of avoidance is what creates a 'diagnosis.' Compulsively using substances, gambling, or compulsive shopping, for example, all have aspects of avoidance, just in different forms. This makes the exploration and attention to the multiple factors necessary."

So, could this same avoidance of suffering be applied to an individual's perceived addiction to travel? Roddick weighs in: "Not in regards to traveling, moving perhaps, but I wouldn't use the term 'addiction' to describe their behavior. I would explore the function of the many moves: Is it an avoidant behavior, and why are they doing it so often? For example, in recovery programs, a common term used is called 'doing a geographic.'

"Many people with a substance use disorder have compulsively relocated when their circumstances become too emotionally and psychologically difficult, as a way to avoid the problem and hope the problem will go away by being in a different environment. In some cases, an environment is extremely unhelpful to a person's well-being so they should leave, but in several cases I have seen, a 'geographic' is simply an avoidant strategy to deal with working through your problems. It's a quick fix that provides immediate relief, which is experienced in the brain the same as pleasure."

I thought back to my year in travel. How I sought to escape relationships or office life. How it helped with the pain of considering my life mundane. How it made me feel validated to have others call me well traveled. "I usually tell clients who have or are intending to move to have a 'fresh start,' meaning their symptoms or suffering would go away completely, that I bet it will only be a few weeks, perhaps longer, before their anxiety or depression or substance use returns to exactly as it was or worse," Roddick notes.

If you're traveling in hopes that being somewhere new will fix all of your problems, think again. I've done so, many times, and while you may have moments of peace or distraction while you're away, when you decide to return or settle into your new place, those suffering points are sure to resurface. Just like anything in life, there are positive and negative reasons to do something. Luckily with travel, whether you do it for a positive or negative reason, there is always much to be gained. So maybe we don't use the word "addiction" when thinking of travel. Perhaps the better way to look at it is to check in with the intent behind your travel. If you find yourself traveling often with no apparent reason, not even an interest in the destination, maybe ask yourself: Is there a form of suffering you're trying to avoid?

If you came to this article looking for an answer, change what you're looking for. Don't look for the answers, look for the questions. The more you ask yourself, the more you'll learn about yourself. Keep traveling. Go far, explore often, meet new people and make new friends. Just do so not to escape life, but to enrich it. Catch flights, and feelings. You can't avoid pain and suffering. But you can upgrade and embrace it.

On the Complicated Questions Around Writing About Travel

FROM *Literary Hub*

JAKARTA, 1994: I wanted to write a story about magic slippers that would take me anywhere. I ended up writing a novel about demonic red shoes as an adult, with more complex reasons than fulfilling my simple wish to go to Singapore, but there were times when travel was an unattainable obsession. I thought of Singapore because my imagination as a Third World '90s teen did not stretch far enough. Japan was too costly, Cambodia was unthinkable, and America only existed on TV. Singapore was the place where my wealthy friends would go shopping, although they also visited other countries. In one girl's house, I saw a family photo in Dutch costume taken in Volendam, and in another girl's mansion, photos of a family vacation to Disneyland California were hung on the wall. Our friendship lasted long, despite being occasionally haunted by the not-so-ghostly presence of different classes. My parents lived in Jakarta as common people, raising two kids who would be common people, doing whatever common people do.

What does it mean to travel? Does writing about it from where I stand make a difference? The question of moving has never ceased to be relevant, and it is, to borrow from Baudelaire, the one "I discuss incessantly with my soul." "Questions of Travel" is the title of Michelle de Kretser's novel about travel, home, and belonging; Caren Kaplan's scholarly book on the modern and postmodern discourses of travel and displacement; and the famous poem by Elizabeth Bishop that both writers allude to. "Should we have stayed at home and thought of here?" asked Bishop. Questions of travel are many and have become more complicated, especially when we think about the global conditions that shape travel today.

Interrogating the socioeconomic and environmental impacts of travel can be challenging because the romanticized images of travel have been sustained in narratives, via literature and the media. Thus here is the first question to begin with: Why do travel stories fascinate us, and why do people keep telling them? We want to know every path, every yellow brick road trodden by our favorite characters, on the pages or screen. What will Dorothy discover when the on-screen image shifts from black-and-white to Technicolor? In *The Wizard of Oz*, excitement is always somewhere else, somewhere unknown, over the rainbow. Stories of travel speak to us because we, too, desire to venture into the unfamiliar. Perhaps in our journey, our troubles will melt like lemon drops, and we are eager to find out what awaits us. What kind of world is there to see? What souvenirs to bring home? Will we ever return home?

Travel narrative has a long tradition in both Western and non-Western cultures, from Odysseus, who faces various obstacles and temptations that lure him away from his goal to return home in Homer's *The Odyssey*, to the Mahabharata, in which the Pandavas are sent into exile for 12 years after losing a dice game. Stories of exile, return, and conquest have been told many times. Messages are often deeply embedded in the dominant social norms, from "See the world and seize the day" to "Home is where the heart is," and they are both strong and shaky. The mantra "There's no place like home" in *The Wizard of Oz*, as Salman Rushdie writes, ambivalently coexists with the portrayal of Oz as a magnificent place where Dorothy savors her freedom.

History constructs how travel is imagined in my Third World backyard. Indonesian children know the song "My Ancestors Were Sailors" by heart. It is a celebration of travel within the archipelagic imagination—sailing the vast ocean with delight, against the waves, without fear—but here is the irony: most of us do not travel, or even if we do, stories of our travel are insignificant. We have always been the place traveled, the people written about, the picture painted. We are the bare-breasted Balinese women in paintings, a paradise, a heart of darkness, a perfect setting for a thriller in *The Year of Living Dangerously*. My hometown, Jakarta, despite being less charming than Bali, appeared in Baudelaire's poem when it was Batavia, described as a tropical beauty wedded to the spirit of Europe. In 1869, certainly this was not the way we the natives, the half-naked, lazy, and unsophisticated *Inlanders,* perceived the city. The grand tour, the seventeenth- and eighteenth-century travel for education, was not part of our tradition. When we *Inlanders* traveled, we became the exhibits in the colonial expositions.

Questions of travel must consider the unequal power relations that characterize present global encounters and how they are enmeshed in the historical processes in the past. Travel was embedded in the colonial exploitation of empires, and cosmopolitanism —at least the dominant version of it—has always been capitalist driven. Knowledge about other cultures has been used to validate colonialism, as we have learned from Edward Said, and to create infrastructure for neo-imperialist market expansion. The traveler has been wearing the colonizer's cloak since Prospero claimed an island and enslaved the "hag-seed." *The Tempest* exemplifies travel as a narrative of discovery, and Prospero is not the only one who understands that knowledge is power.

Narratives of discovery, which involve discovering the Other and the self in a dialectic fashion, frame many stories about travel. How do I write about travel without taking into account the historical construction of my home, my people? In these stories, we are the ones being discovered: the smiling Calibans. In contemporary travel memoirs such as *Eat Pray Love,* the external journey is a vehicle for the internal journey, a journey to discover oneself. Abuse and economic hardship suffered by Wayan in *Eat Pray Love* allows the New York traveler to understand her feminist agency. The smiling Calibans are the catalyst for self-recognition in global tourism.

Should we seize Prospero's pen and write our own stories of travel and discovery? There is a problem there. What we will discover is determined by a map that already exists. We can read the map, but the map has read us first, locating us based on where we come from and the color of our skin. Elizabeth Bishop writes, "Continent, city, country, society: the choice is never wide and never free." Your option as a traveler is certainly not wide and free especially if your body, class, or gender does not fit quite right. Your name is not "universal" enough. Your passport determines your status, access, and even the length of time you will spend at the immigration counter.

Travel was and will always be about exclusion. Instead of unpacking the idea, many contribute to strengthen the demarcating lines. Social hierarchies are maintained through attempts to promote that certain traveling practices are more prestigious than others. In *Abroad: British Literary Traveling Between the Wars,* first published in 1979, Paul Fussell historicizes travel and outlines the distinction between the explorer, the traveler, and the tourist: "All three make journeys, but the explorer seeks the undiscovered, the traveler that which has been discovered by the mind working in history, the tourist that which has been discovered by entrepreneurship and prepared for him by the arts of mass publicity." Fussell's elitist view exposes a nostalgia for certain ideals. In idealizing the age of Renaissance exploration, Fussell deodorizes travel from colonialism. He also suggests that masculinity constitutes the "real" travel; exploration, in his term, involves "the athletic paramilitary activity" and results in knighthood.

For centuries, travel stories have always been male stories, and women occupy the roles as objects of desire or the loved ones at home receiving letters. The nineteenth-century figure of the flâneur, or the wanderer in the Parisian streets, was male, while unchaperoned women in the city were not considered respectable. Literature and cinema are packed with stories of male travelers who discover freedom on the road, such as Jack Kerouac's *On the Road* and the 1969 film *Easy Rider.* Looking back to my own history, not everyone in the Dutch East Indies was *njai* (concubines) or *baboe* (maids), confined to beds and kitchens. A few select people went to the Netherlands: the upper-class men. *Student Hidjo,* a 1918 novel by Marco Kartodikromo, tells the story of a Javanese student sent to the Netherlands to study. While offering a critique of colonialism, the novel presents self-discovery in gendered terms: the male protagonist's awareness of his cultural identity emerges as he distances himself from morally loose Dutch women (of course, after some passionate love affairs).

Jakarta, 2008: The pair of red shoes I was wearing have traveled. I was a PhD student at NYU, after living in San Diego for two years, and I visited Jakarta for a summer break. Travel was disorienting; I had been everywhere, but I felt that I belonged to nowhere. In the Indonesian language there is a word we use for wandering spirits who are no longer in our world but have not crossed to the world of the dead: *gentayangan,* being in between, neither here nor there,

a common symptom of border crossing. The Third World woman
had a travel story to tell. But what kind of story?

I did not want to talk about freedom on the road like in *Easy
Rider* without considering the exclusion of women. Unlike men's
travel stories, stories of women who traverse are usually haunted
by guilt and punishment. In Hans Christian Andersen's *The Red
Shoes,* the girl cannot stop dancing with her red shoes, so she
asks for God's forgiveness and begs an executioner to cut off her
feet. Good girls go to heaven, but the red shoes keep wandering.
I wanted to write about *gentayangan* women, but I could not relate to stories of women's travel in which self-discovery is achieved
through financial independence and consumption, like in *Eat Pray
Love.* I could not write about New York from the perspective of the
elites, like *Sex and the City,* and glorify the Emerald City sanitized
by Rudy Giuliani.

The *Sex and the City* ladies drink cosmopolitans, but the stories
of privileged globe-trotters were not mine. A brown version of neoliberal cosmopolitan narrative felt like ill-fitting shoes. I lived in
Queens, a borough of migrants that smells of tacos and masala,
juggling teaching jobs in Staten Island and Bronxville to pay the
rent. My story would be inspired by my Asian landlords, one of
which is a Vietnamese American who picked me up from a shady
motel when I first arrived in the United States. He came as a refu-
gee as a teenager, and although he was doing well, he would tell
me stories of daily micro-aggressions such as people patronizing
him to speak better English (he would reply: "You speak better
English!"). My other landlords were Chinese immigrants, whose
interactions with me were mediated by their children acting as in-
terpreters. They had many properties, and they would only accept
cash payment.

My story as a traveler was more precarious than glamorous. In
times of troubles, the idea of borrowing money from my parents
was a joke because they had nothing to lend. Yet I kept traveling
to conferences to maintain a professional network that I was afraid
of being excluded from, and this made me aware of my privilege
compared to friends and neighbors who overstayed their visas and
therefore could not travel freely. Undocumented migrants, however, do not see themselves as victims. They engaged in gatherings
and lively conversations, easily switching topics from food from
home to Obama, though the subject of paperwork was delicate

and perhaps irrelevant. Some were politically conscious, and to-day, they remind me of writer and migrant worker Yuli Riswati, who was deported after covering Hong Kong protests to raise awareness among the migrant community. Migrants are actively looking for shared experiences, connections, and solidarity. This is a different version of cosmopolitan life and sensibility: cosmopoli-tanism of the common people.

Openness to other cultures that marks cosmopolitanism is of-ten understood in a narrow sense as taste, made possible by ac-cess to mobility entangled in social and economic privileges. But let's not forget that Diogenes, who claimed that he was "citizen of the world" (*kosmopolitês*) was a hobo. The categories produced by global travel discourse—expats, exiles, migrants, refugees, tour-ists—contribute to how they experiences mobility, whether they would encounter bridges or barriers, hospitality or displacement. Those who make the bed when travel bloggers/influencers go on vacation have their own travel stories; their lives are shaped by na-tional and transnational structures as they juggle between making their ends meet in their new home and sending money to families in the old home. Yet when neoliberal cosmopolitanism becomes the dominant frame, some traveling bodies are erased, and certain forms of mobility do not count as stories of travel, or stories *that* travel.

Travel is about the desire to cross boundaries as well as tangible encounters with walls and borders. Questions of travel should go beyond the rainbow, digging deep into the greasy moments, dis-juncture, power relations, and social inequalities.

I decided to write a story that puts you in the shoes of a Third World woman who, after making a Faustian deal with the Devil, re-ceives a pair of red shoes to roam the world. Getting off the plane (or a flying house) is one thing, but to stay in a place without secu-rity—social connection, cultural capital, or First World privileges —is another animal. Unfortunately, no magic slippers can help you with that.

Out There, Nobody Can Hear You Scream

FROM *Outside*

IN THE SPRING of 2019, right before I leave for my writing residency in Great Smoky Mountains National Park, my mama tries to give me a gun. A Ruger P89DC that used to belong to my daddy, it's one of the few things she kept after his death. Even though she doesn't know how to use it, she knows that I do. She's just had back surgery, and she's in no shape to come and get me if something goes wrong up in those mountains, so she tries to give me this. I turn the gun over in my hand. It's a little dusty and sorely out of use. The metal sends a chill up my arm.

Even though it is legal for me to have a gun, I cannot tell if, as a Black woman, I'd be safer with or without it. Back in 2016, I watched the aftermath of Philando Castile's killing as it was streamed on Facebook Live by his girlfriend, Diamond Reynolds. Castile was shot five times at close range by a police officer during a routine traffic stop, when he went to reach for his license, registration, and permit to carry a gun. His four-year-old daughter watched him die from the back seat. In his case, having the proper paperwork didn't matter.

I'll be in the Smokies for six weeks in early spring, the park's quiet season, staying in a cabin on my own. My local contact list will be short: the other writer who had been awarded the residency, our mentor, maybe a couple of park employees. If something happens to me, there will likely be no witnesses, no one to stream my last moments. When my mother isn't looking, I make sure the safety is on, and then I put the gun back where she got it. I leave my fate to the universe.

Before I back out of our driveway, my mama insists on saying a protective blessing over me. She has probably said some version of this prayer over my body as long as I've been able to explore on my own.

In 2018, I wrote an article for this magazine titled "We're Here. You Just Don't See Us," about my family's relationship to nature and the stereotypes and obstacles to access that Black people face in the outdoors. As a journalist, that piece opened doors for me, like the residency in Great Smoky Mountains National Park.

It also inspired people to write me.

Two years later, the messages still find me on almost every social media platform: Twitter, Instagram, even LinkedIn. They come through my Gmail. Most of them sound the same—they thank me for writing the article and tell me how much it meant to them to see a facet of the Black experience represented in a major outdoor magazine. They express apprehension about venturing into new places and ask for my advice on recreating outside of their perceived safety zone. They ask what they can do to protect themselves in case they wind up in a hostile environment.

Folks have their desires and dreams tied up in the sentences they send me. They want to make room for the hope that I cautiously decided to write about in 2018.

Back then, as a realist, I didn't want my essay's ending to sound too optimistic. But I still strayed from talking about individual discrimination in the parks, often perpetrated by white visitors, like the woman who recently told an Asian American family that they "can't be in this country" as they finished their hike near Mount Tamalpais in Marin County, California, this past Fourth of July. Or the now-famous "BBQ Becky," who called the police on two Black men at Lake Merritt in Oakland, California, in 2018, for using a charcoal grill in a non-charcoal-grill-designated area. Nor did I mention that when I venture into new spaces, I am always doing the math: noting the lengths of dirt roads so I know how far I have to run if I need help, taking stock of my gas gauge to ensure I have enough to get away.

I have been the target of death threats since 2015, when I started writing about race. I wasn't sure if magazine readers were ready for that level of candid conversation, so in 2018 I left that tidbit out.

There are risks to being Black in the outdoors; I am simply willing to assume them. And that's why I struggle to answer the senders of these messages, because I don't have any tips to protect them. Instead I invoke magical thinking, pretending that if I don't hit the reply button, the communication didn't happen. Sometimes technology helps: when I let the message requests sit unaccepted in Instagram, the app deletes them after four weeks.

I deem myself a coward. I know I am a coward.

There are two messages that still haunt me.

The first is an email from a woman who wanted to know what she and her brown-skinned husband should do if they encounter another campground with a Confederate flag hanging in the check-in office. She described to me a night of unease, of worrying if they and their daughter would be safe. I filed her email so deep in my folders that I don't even think I can find it anymore. I was dying to forget that I had no salve for her suffering.

The second was even more personal. It came via Facebook Messenger, from a woman named Tish. In it she says: "I came across a read of yours when I was searching African Americans and camping. I want to rent an RV and go with my family. I live in Anderson S.C. Had a daughter that also attended SCGSAH. Is there a campground you recommend that is not too far and yes where I would feel comfortable? Thank you."

The signaling in it, of tying me to her daughter, examining my background enough to offhandedly reference the South Carolina arts high school I attended, and saying, *Please, my daughter is similar to you.*

I leave her message in the unread folder.

These women have families, and they, too, are trying to pray a blessing over the ones they love while leaving room for them to play, grow, and learn—the same things their white peers want for their offspring. In their letters, they hang some of their hopes for a better America on me, on any advice I might be able to share.

I haven't written back because I haven't had any good advice to offer, and that is what troubles me. These letters have been a sore spot, festering, unwilling to heal.

Now, in the summer of 2020, there are bodies hanging from

trees again, and that has motivated me to pick up my pen. Our country is trying to figure out what to do about racial injustice and systemic brutality against Black people. It's time to tell those who wrote to me what I know.

Dear Tish, Alex, Susan, and everyone else:

I want to apologize for the delayed reply. It took a long time to gather my thoughts. When I wrote that article back in 2018, I was light on the risks and violence and heavy-handed on hope. I come to you now as a woman who insists we must be heavy-handed on both if we are to survive.

I write to you in the middle of the night, with the only light on the entire street emanating from my headlamp. Here in upstate South Carolina, we are in the midst of a regional blackout. My time outdoors has taught me how to sit with the darkness—how to be equipped for it. Over the years, I have found ways to work within it, or perhaps in spite of it. If there's anything I can do, maybe it's help you become more comfortable with the darkness, too.

But before I tell you any more, I want you to understand that you and I are more than our pain. We are more than the human-rights moment we are fighting for.

It isn't an exaggeration to say that the *Outside* article changed my life. People paid me for speaking gigs and writing workshops. They put me on planes and flew me across the country to talk about equity, inclusion, and accountability. I know the statistics, the history, the arguments that organizations give about why they have no need to change. I call them on it.

I have to apologize for not being prepared for the heaviness of this mantle at the time. I have to admit my hesitation back then to call white supremacy and racism by their names. The unraveling of this country in the summer of 2020 has forced me to reckon with my actions, my place in the natural world, and the fact that as a Black woman writer in America, I am tasked with telling you a terrible truth: I am so sorry. I have nothing of merit to offer you as protection.

I am reluctant to inform you that while I can challenge white people to make the outdoors a nonhostile, equitable space where you can be your authentic selves, when the violence of white supremacy turns its eyes toward you, there's nothing I can give you to protect yourself from its gaze and dehumanization.

I do not wish to ask you to have to be brave in the face of inequality. This nation's diminished moral capacity for seeing Black people as human beings is not our fault. Their perception of you isn't your problem—it's theirs, the direct result of the manifest destiny and "anybody can become anything in America" narratives they have bought into. We are made to suffer so they can slake their guilt. I want you to be unapologetically yourselves.

I check with my fellow Black outdoor friends, and they say they've gotten your email and messages, too. They also waffle on what to say, telling y'all to carry pepper spray or dress in a non-threatening way. I am troubled about instructing people who have already been socially policed to death—to literal, functional death—to change the way they walk, talk, dress, or take up space in order to seem less threatening to those who are uncomfortable with seeing our brown skin.

I have no talisman that can shield you from the white imagination. The incantation "I'm calling the police" will be less potent coming from your mouth, and will not work in the same way. In the end, your utterance could backfire, causing you more pain.

I want to tell you to make sure you know wilderness first aid, to carry the 10 essentials, to practice leave no trace, so no one has any right to bother you as you enjoy your day. I want to tell you to make sure you know what it means not to need, to be so prepared that you never have to ask for a shred, scrap, or ribbon of compassion from anybody.

But that is misanthropic—maybe, at its core, inhumane.

I resist the urge to pass on to you the instinct my Black foremothers ingrained in me to make ourselves small before the denizens of this land. I have watched this scenario play out since I was a child: my father, a tall 50-year-old man with big hands, being called "boy" by some white person and playing along, willing to let them believe that they have more power than he does, even though I have watched him pin down a 400-pound hog on his own. I have seen my mother shrink behind her steering wheel, pulled over for going five miles above the speed limit on her way to her mom's house. She taught me and my brother the rules early: only speak when spoken to, do not ask questions, do not make eye contact, do not get out of the car, keep your hands on the wheel, comply, comply, comply, even if it costs you your agency. Never, ever show your fear. Cry in the driveway when you get to your destination alive. Those traffic stops could've ended very differently. The corpses of Samuel DuBose, Maurice Gordon, Walter Scott, and Rayshard Brooks prove that.

I will not pass on these generational curses; they were ways of compensating for anti-Black thinking. They should never have been your burden.

It would be easy to tell you to always be aware of your surroundings, to never let your guard down, to be prepared to hit record in case you run into an Amy Cooper or if a white man points an AR-15 at you and your friends as you take a break from riding your motorcycles, hoping to make the most of a sunny almost-summer day in Virginia.

These moments—tied to a phone, always tensed in fear—are not what time in nature is supposed to be. Yet the videos seem to be the only way America at large believes us. It took an 8-minute-and-46-second snuff film for the masses to wake up and challenge the unjust system our people have had to navigate for more than 400 years. They are killing us for mundane things—running, like Ahmaud Arbery; playing in the park, like Tamir Rice. They've always killed us for unexceptional reasons. But now the entire country gets to watch life leak away from Black bodies in high definition.

I started writing this on the eve of what should have been Breonna Taylor's 27th birthday. The police broke into her home while she was sleeping and killed her. I write to you during a global pandemic, during a time when COVID-19 has had a disproportionate impact on Black and brown communities. I conclude my thoughts during what should have been the summer before Tamir Rice's senior year of high school. All the old protective mechanisms and safety nets Black people created for ourselves aren't working anymore. Sometimes compliance is not enough. Sometimes they kill you anyway.

Having grown up in the Deep South, I have long been aware of the threat of racial violence, of its symbolism. In middle school, many of my peers wore the Dixie Outfitters T-shirts that were in vogue in that part of the country during the late '90s. The shirts often featured collages of the Confederate flag, puppies, and

shotguns on the front, with slogans like STAND AND FIGHT FOR
SOUTHERN RIGHTS and PRESERVING SOUTHERN HERITAGE
SINCE 1861 printed on the back.

I was 11 years old, and these kids—and their commitment
to a symbol from a long-lost war—signaled that they believed I
shouldn't be in the same classroom with them, that I didn't belong
in their world.

But that was nothing compared with the routine brutality perpetrated upon Black people in my home state. In 2010, years before the deaths of Trayvon Martin, Michael Brown, and Sandra
Bland, there was the killing of Anthony Hill. Gregory Collins, a
white worker at a local poultry plant not far from my family farm,
shot and killed Hill, his Black coworker. He dragged Hill's body
behind his pickup truck for 10 miles along the highways near my
grandmother's house, leaving a trail of blood and tendons. Abandoned on the road, the corpse was found with a single gunshot
wound to the head and a rope tied around what remained of the
body. Collins was sentenced for manslaughter. Five years ago, a
radicalized white supremacist murdered nine Black parishioners
as they prayed in Mother Emanuel African Methodist Episcopal
Church in Charleston. South Carolina is one of three states that
still do not have a hate-crime law.

Before my writing residency, I did not own a range map. Traditionally, these are used to depict plant and animal habitats and
indicate where certain species thrive. Ranges are often defined by
climate, food sources, water availability, the presence of predators,
and a species' ability to adapt.

My friend J. Drew Lanham taught me I could apply this sort of
logic to myself. A Black ornithologist and professor of wildlife ecol-
ogy, he was unfazed by what happened to bird-watcher Christian
Cooper in Central Park—he's had his own encounters with white
people who can't understand why he might be standing in a field
with binoculars in his hand. Several years ago he wrote a piece for
Orion magazine called "9 Rules for the Black Birdwatcher."

"Carry your binoculars—and three forms of identification—
at all times," he wrote. "You'll need the binoculars to pick that
tufted duck out of the flock of scaup and ring-necks. You'll need
the photo ID to convince the cops, FBI, Homeland Security, and
the flashlight-toting security guard that you're not a terrorist or

escaped convict." Drew frequently checks the Southern Poverty
Law Center's hate-group map and the Equal Justice Initiative's
"Lynching in America" map and overlays them. The blank spaces
are those he might travel to.

I never thought to lay out the data like that until the day I went
to Abrams Creek.

Three weeks into my residency, I made an early-afternoon visit
to the national park archives. I needed to know what information
they had on Black people. I left with one sheet of paper—a slave
schedule that listed the age, sex, and race ("black" or "mulatto")
of bodies held in captivity. There were no names. There were no
pictures. I remember chiding myself for believing there might be.

Emotionally wrought and with a couple of hours of sunlight
ahead of me, I decided to go for a drive to clear my mind. I came
to the Smokies with dreams of writing about the natural world. I
wanted to talk about the enigmatic Walker sisters, the park's brook
trout restoration efforts, and the groundbreaking agreement that
the National Park Service reached with the Eastern Band of Cherokee Indians about their right to sustainably harvest the edible
sochan plant on their ancestral lands. My Blackness, and curiosity
about the Black people living in this region, was not at the front
of my mind. I naively figured I would learn about them in the
historical panels of the visitor center, along with the former white
inhabitants and the Cherokee. I thought there would be a book or
a guide about them.

There was nothing.

Vacations are meant to be methods of escapism. Believing this
idyllic wilderness to be free of struggle, of complicated emotions,
allows visitors to enjoy their day hikes. Many tourists to Great
Smoky Mountains National Park see what they believe it has always
been: rainbow-emitting waterfalls, cathedrals of green, carpets of
yellow trilliums in the spring. The majority never venture more
than a couple of miles off the main road. They haven't trained
their eyes to look for the overgrown homesites of the park's former inhabitants through the thick underbrush. Using the park as
a side trip from the popular tourist destinations like Dollywood
and Ripley's Believe It or Not!, they aren't hiking the trails that
pass by cemeteries where entire communities of white, enslaved,
and emancipated people lived, loved, worked, died, and were buried, some without ever being paid a living wage. Slavery here was

arguably more intimate. An owner had four slaves, not four hundred. But it happened.

There is a revisionist fantasy that Americans cling to about the people in this region of North Carolina and Tennessee: that they were dirt-poor, struggled to survive, and wrestled the mountains into submission with their own brute strength. In reality, many families hired their sharecropping neighbors, along with Black convicts on chain gangs, to do the hard labor for them.

These corrections of history aren't conversations most people are interested in having.

After a fruitless stop at Fontana Dam, the site of a former African American settlement where I find precious little to see, I try to navigate back to where I'm staying. Cell service is spotty. My phone's GPS takes me on a new route along the edge of the park, through Happy Valley, which you can assume from the moniker is less than happy.

Early spring in the mountains is not as beautiful as you might believe. The trees are bare, and you can see the Confederate and Gadsden flags, the latter with their coiled rattlesnakes, flapping in the wind, so they do not take you by surprise. At home after home, I see flag after flag. The banners tell me that down in this valley I am on my own, as do the corpses of Jonathan A. Ferrell and Renisha McBride, Black people who knocked on the doors of white homeowners asking for help and were shot in response.

In the middle of this drive back to the part of the park where I belong, I round a corner to see a man burning a big pile of lumber, the flames taller than my car.

I am convinced that pyrophobia is embedded in my genes. The Ku Klux Klan was notorious for cross burnings and a willingness to torch homes. The fire over my shoulder is large enough to burn up any evidence that I ever existed. There is a man standing in his yard wearing a baseball cap and holding a drink, watching me as my white rental car creeps by. I want to ask him how to get out of here. I think of my mama's frantic phone calls going straight to voice mail. I stay in the car.

Farther down the road, another man is burning a big pile of lumber. I know it's just coincidence, that these bundles of timber were stacked before I set off down this path, but the symbolism unnerves me.

I round a bend and a familiar sign appears—a national park

placard with the words ABRAMS CREEK CAMPGROUND RANGER STATION in white letters. Believing some fresh air might settle my stomach and strengthen my nerves, I decide to enter that section of the park. The road I drive is the border between someone's property and the park. Uneven, it forces me to go slowly.

The dog is at my car before I recognize what is happening. It materializes as a strawberry-blond streak bumping up against my driver-side door. Tall enough to reach my face, it is gnashing at my side mirror, trying to bite my reflection.

I'm not scared of dogs, but this one, with its explicit hostility, gives me pause.

Before emancipation, dogs hunted runaway slaves by scent, often maiming the quarry to keep them in place until their owner could arrive. During the civil rights movement, dogs were weaponized by police. In the modern era, use of K-9 units to intimidate and attack is so common that police have referred to Black people as "dog biscuits."

I force myself to keep driving.

When I reach the ranger station, the building is dark: closed for the season. I see a trail inviting me to walk between two shortleaf pines, but I decline. There is something in me that is more wound up than it has a right to be. No one knows my whereabouts. Despite making up 13 percent of the population, more than 30 percent of all missing persons in the US in 2019 were Black. A significant portion of these cases are never covered by the news. The chances of me disappearing without a mention are higher than I'd like.

There are three cars in the little gravel parking lot. A pair of men, both bigger than me, are illegally flying drones around the clearing, and there is palpable apprehension around my presence. They don't acknowledge me, and I can't think of what I'm supposed to say to convince them I'm not a threat. I have no idea who the third car belongs to—they are somewhere in my periphery, real and not real, an ancillary portion of my calculation.

I take photos of the clearing, including the cars, just in case I don't make it out. It is the only thing I know to do.

I run my odds. No one in an official capacity to enforce the rules, no cell service to call for help, little knowledge of the area. I leave. Later, my residency mentor gently suggests that maybe I don't visit that section of the park alone anymore.

*

I promise that there are parts of this park, and by extension the outdoors as a whole, that make visiting worth it. Time in nature is integral to my physical, spiritual, and mental health. I chase the radiant moments, because as a person who struggles with chronic depression, the times I am enthusiastically happy are few and far between. Most of them happen outside.

I relish the moments right before sunrise up at Purchase Knob in the North Carolina section of the Smokies. The world is quiet, my mind is still, and the birds, chattering to one another, do not mind my presence. I believe this is what Eden must have been like. I still live for the nights where I sink into my sleeping pad while I cowboy-camp, with nothing in or above my head except the stars. I believe in the healing power of hiking, the days when I am strong, capable, at home in my body.

The fear, on some level, will always exist. I say this to myself all the time: *I know you're scared. Do it anyway.*

Toward the end of my writing residency, the road to Clingmans Dome opens. At 6,643 feet, Clingmans is the highest point in Tennessee and in the park. About two days before I'm scheduled to leave, I go to see what this peak holds for me.

There is a paved trail leading to the observatory at the summit. It isn't long, just steep. Maybe it's the elevation; I have to do the hike 20 steps at a time, putting one foot in front of the other until I get to 20, then starting over again. I catch my breath in ragged clips, and there are moments when I can feel my heartbeat throbbing in my fingertips. I'd planned to be at the top for sunset, but I realize the sun might be gone when I get there. I continue anyhow. I'm slow but stubborn.

If there's anything I appreciate about the crucible we're living in, it's the role of social media in creating a place for us when others won't. We're no longer waiting for outdoor companies to find the budget for diversity, equity, and inclusion initiatives. With the creation of a hashtag, a social media movement, suddenly we are hyper-visible, proud, and unyielding.

As I make my way up the ramp toward its intersection with the Appalachian Trail, I think about Will Robinson (@akunahikes on Instagram), the first documented African American man to complete the triple crown of hiking: the Appalachian, Pacific Crest, and Continental Divide Trails. I understand that I'm following in

Robinson's footsteps, and those of other Black explorers like writer Rahawa Haile (@rahawahaile) and long-haul hiker Daniel White (@theblackalachian)—people who passed this way while completing their AT through-hikes and whom I now call friends, thanks to the internet. I smile and think of them as the trail meets the pavement, and stop for a moment. We have all seen this junction.

Their stories, videos, and photographs tell me what they know of the world I'm still learning to navigate. They are the adventurers I've been rooting for since the very beginning, and now I know they're also rooting for me.

It's our turn to wish for good things for you.

When I get to the summit the world is tinged in blue, and with minimal cloud cover I can see the borders of seven states. There is nothing around me now but heaven. I'm grateful I didn't quit.

My daddy had a saying that I hated as a child: "The man on top of the mountain didn't fall there." It's a quote by NFL coach Vince Lombardi, who during the '50s and '60s refused to give in to the racial pressures of the time and segregate his Green Bay Packers. It took me decades to understand what those two were trying to tell me, but standing at the top of Clingmans Dome, I get it. The trick is that there is no trick. You learn to eat fire by eating fire.

But none of us has to do it alone.

America is a vast place, and we often feel isolated because of its geography. But there are organizations around the country that have our backs: Black Outside, Inc., Color Outside, WeGotNext, Outdoor Afro, Black Folks Camp Too, Blackpackers, Melanin Base Camp, and others.

The honest discussions must happen now. I acknowledge that I am the descendant of enslaved people—folks who someone else kidnapped from their homeland and held captive in this one.

We were more than bodies then.

We are more than bodies now.

We have survived fierce things.

My ancestors survived genocide, the centuries-long hostage situation they were born into, and the tortures that followed when they called for freedom and equality. They witnessed murder. They endured as their wages and dreams were taken from them by systemic policies and physical force. And yet, because of their drive to survive, I am here.

I stand in the stream of a legacy started by my ancestors and

populated by present-day Black trailblazers like outdoor journalist James Edward Mills, environmental-justice activist Teresa Baker,
and conservationists Audrey and Frank Peterman. Remembering
them—their struggles and triumphs—allows me to center myself
in this scenery, as part of this landscape, and claim it as my history.
This might be the closest thing to reparations that this country,
founded on lofty ideals from morally bankrupt slaveholders, will
ever give me.

I promised you at the beginning that I would be candid about
the violence and even-keeled about the hope. I still have hope—I
consider it essential for navigating these spaces, for being critical
of America. I wouldn't be this way if I didn't know there was a better day coming for this country.

Even when hope doesn't reside within me—those days happen,
too—I know that it is safely in the hands of fellow Black adventurers to hold until I am ready to reclaim my share of it. I pray almost
unceasingly for your ability to understand how powerful you are.
If you weren't, they wouldn't be trying to keep you out, to make
sure they keep the beauty and understanding of this vast world to
themselves. If we weren't rewriting the story about who belongs in
these places, they wouldn't be so focused on silencing us with their
physical intimidation and calls for murder.

The more we see, the more we document, the more we share,
the better we can empower those who come after us. I've learned
during all my years of historical research that even when white
guilt, complacency, and intentional neglect try to erase our presence, there is always a trace. Now there are hundreds of us, if not
thousands, intent on blazing a trail.

It is true: I cannot protect you. But there is one thing I can
continue to do: let you know that you are not alone in doing this
big, monumental thing. You deserve a life of adventure, of joy,
of enlightenment. The outdoors are part of our inheritance. So I
will keep writing, posting photos, and doing my own signaling. For
every new place I visit, and the old ones I return to, my message to
you is that you belong here, too.

ELIZABETH MILLER

The Losing Coast

FROM *The Statesider*

WE TOOK THE boat out farther than it was built to go. The field notes later tersely reported, "Should have come inside earlier. Significant chop." On the spine-compressing ride back toward the dock, the boat galloped from one swell to the next in the kind of open water it wasn't really meant to ride. I kept my seat by holding on to it with both hands while seawater splashed over the sides. The trolling motor smashed against the bow and broke.

We'd launched onto a quiet bayou an hour's drive south of New Orleans, then cruised through calm waterways, raising binoculars after herons and egrets. We were aiming for a man-made island that marks what used to be Louisiana's southern edge and looking for evidence of the efforts to reconstruct a vanishing coastline along the way. At one point on our southbound trip, Healthy Gulf community science director Scott Eustis showed me his GPS. The screen indicated we should be in a channel. Instead, open water surrounded us.

Every map you look at of Louisiana is a lie. They simply can't keep up. A relatively current print edition will show a chunk missing from between the highways that run alongside the farmland, fishing docks, and oil-and-gas processing stations to the southern fringes of the state. In satellite images of the coast, pond names hover over expanses of blue. The broad fans of the Mississippi River's delta have washed away into thin strips. That river poured the landscape into place over millennia, but it's taken just a century to unravel it.

I live in the Southwest, where climate change seems to creep closer while your gaze is elsewhere. You turn back and think, *Doesn't that seem closer than it was the last time I looked?* We perceive absences—less rain, fewer cold days—belatedly. When it shifted is tough to say; we won't know the last hard winter until it's long gone. So when an ecologist from the Gulf Coast offered to show me places where you could see the changes unfolding now, I set a date to head southeast. I came, as well, to draw my own map of a place before that place is erased.

My boat trip south with Eustis meandered through placid bayous to widening bays, along the bleached skeletons of ghost forests. Rising salt water has poisoned hardwoods and sea pines, leaving empty twigs reaching for the sky. Drowning grasses swayed in salt water. We slowed down where houses bracket the waterway like it's main street through downtown. People waved from some front porches. On others, rooftops have chipped away, opening their contents to the weather. Too-long-docked boats have buckled.

Louisiana's is a working coast, and we caught it at work. We passed through corridors lined with poles that signal oyster beds and the metal pipes and platforms for oil wells. Oystermen returning from fishing overnight sped in the opposite direction while shrimping boats, their season just starting, waited with their nets up like raised wings. The long-term forecasts suggest that none of this will last. Not the ground, not the houses, not the way of shuttling out here in small boats to oyster beds laid into place on top of generations of other oysters' shells, or, as we watched one fisherman do, standing on a dock, throwing a small net into the tide, and pulling it back writhing with sea life.

When Eustis suggested finishing a tour of the bayous by seeing a rebuilt barrier island, it meant venturing far beyond the mellow backwaters that our boat captain, Chad, frequents with customers fishing for speckled trout and redfish. We looked at a sky piling up with dark blue and purple storm clouds and decided to make a run for it. Almost as soon as we set off, lightning cracked the horizon. We picked up speed, and so did the waves. Repeatedly, Chad shouted over the wind and engine noise, "How far to the island?"

Eustis checked his GPS and urged him onward until we reached the place where dredged and heaped sand from the Gulf of Mexico brought the surface of the island back above the water. Now it's an emerald band, its gray beach promptly swallowed by dense, tall grasses and then the thick foliage of trees.

"Even if the island goes underwater, it's still protection, because it's 10, not 15, feet of water in the storm surge," Eustis said. "In 2012, it was worth it. In 2022 . . . ?"

We watched a line of pelicans undulating on the wind and dolphins shadowing a shrimp boat, leaping in arcs through its wake. Then, Chad declared it time to turn back.

Eustis stood at the wheel beside Chad, steady as we hurried to the dock. A Louisiana native in his mid-30s, with a boyish face and short hair he anxiously combs with his fingers, Eustis was in a graduate program in Georgia when Hurricane Katrina hit in 2005. He came home to help rebuild his family's house, which is now done, and the rest of the coast, work that may outlast his lifetime.

Humans are rebuilding islands and marshes to thwart, or at least stall, their loss to rising seas, sinking soils, and worsening storms. But Louisiana's $50 billion plan, their latest figure as of 2017, won't buy back as much land as has been lost or preserve every coastal community. Some measures could displace people, and some deliberately relocate them. Others may deplete fisheries. Many of the communities the state says it can't afford to save are rural, poor, and African American or Native American communities on Louisiana's coastal plain. They are scrambling on a shifting landscape, determining whether to adapt or move. This place is changing faster than people can forget what it was like before. What I'll see here are the impossible choices that change demands, and the many sacrifices layered in so much compromise.

In his work with Healthy Gulf, Eustis both champions restoration efforts and watchdogs how they balance or provide for the matrix of people, habitats, and wildlife affected. The state has said it'll monitor how river diversion projects affect marine life, including oyster beds and shrimp fisheries and the people who make their living from them, as well as wildlife like dolphins, who could be pushed out if, as the state plans, a diversion reroutes fresh water into these brackish channels.

"I don't think they want to forgo an approach to building land just because there are some sick dolphins or some oyster beds," Eustis said. "If that's the decision you're going to make, then you need to compensate people. And I don't know how you compensate dolphins."

Despite one of the largest efforts to reshape their own landmass underway in the world, research suggests that efforts to rebuild these wetlands can't keep pace with the speed at which they're lost. Still, if they do nothing, the sea will swallow all the barrier islands now lining the Gulf of Mexico and the most determined stands of grass, blurring it all into one large body of water. In the next half century, another 2,250 square miles of land is likely to disappear. Today's maps won't just look a little off. They'll look like the product of myths.

At the LSU Center for River Studies in Baton Rouge, a group of 70- and 80-year-olds peered down from the second-floor balcony onto a scale model of 14,000 square miles of river delta. It's the size of two basketball courts. While images of reedy wetlands and maps of future scenarios projected across the model's white, molded-foam surface, a man seated on a collapsible stool, his elbows propped against his cane, asked Chuck Perrodin, the Coastal Protection and Restoration Authority public information director, "What's happening in Atchafalaya basin? Is that covered?"

"No," Perrodin replied, "there's only so much money in the world, and we're glad we got the money to do this."

The man remembered when gates were installed across the Atchafalaya River and the color of its water changed. This landscape has shifted within human memories—their memories. They recall a very different bayou from their youth.

The Center for River Studies, part of a growing cluster of buildings for the partnered operations of Louisiana's Coastal Protection and Restoration Authority and Louisiana State University, is part museum, part laboratory, and part campaign effort. Its centerpiece is the model, which uses running water and black plastic pellets that mimic sediment to allow researchers to test cumulative and lasting effects of the state coastal restoration efforts. In an hour, they can mirror a year's worth of change. The computers that run it sit beside stairs that ascend to its surface and a cluster of white sandals used for walking atop it. I caught it at the semester's end, after water had been flushed over the surface to reset it. Some still pooled over the grid marking New Orleans.

As the senior group headed back toward their bus, Perrodin guided me back to the museum-like portion of the center, with its floor-to-ceiling map of tributaries as far away as the Canadian border, and an airboat and fronds of plastic grass stationed in front of a painted screen of wetlands. In a small auditorium, he sped through the presentation they give to visitors, explaining how the delta was built, how the levees have deprived it, how the state has a plan to save the place and its people, and what's at stake for the rest of the country if they don't.

As ice sheets melted and mountains eroded from tributaries covering almost half the United States, the Mississippi River poured that sand, silt, and clay into the Gulf of Mexico. Over 7,000 years, the river drew its delta out into the sea. Routinely flooded wetlands built up like a layer cake of mud. The river's webbed course so confounded early explorers that it took three centuries to determine where, exactly, it ended. That was the beginning of its end. The 1900s saw the river dredged to make a shipping channel, dammed, and leveed after a flood covered 26,000 square miles and killed 200 people in 1927. Scientists warned that the levees would devastate the ecosystem. The Army Corps of Engineers built them anyway.

Wetlands naturally compress over time, but that's accelerated now by oil extraction, which left subterranean gaps that soil sinks down to fill and was facilitated by thousands of miles of canals dug to access those wells, each working like an invitation for water, as well as rising ocean levels. Add to that increasingly frequent and severe storms. The result: almost 2,000 square miles of wetlands have disappeared from Louisiana over the last century, according to the US Geological Survey, a loss unprecedented in the last thousand years.

Water swallows the land from the roots up. The trees die first. Then, they're followed by the dense thickets where birds hide. Grasses survive for a while, essentially up to their necks in water, before they, too, die. When their grip on the earth releases, the sea has easy work eroding the soil.

The delta's destruction will make it harder for Americans to gas up their cars, buy bread, and find oysters on the half shell or a shrimp cocktail. The delta supports 30 percent of the United States' commercial fishing catch, protects five shipping ports that move 500 million tons of cargo each year including 60 percent of the nation's grain, and sees roughly 20 percent of the nation's oil and gas transported through it. The state estimates the value of the ecological systems in the Mississippi delta at somewhere between $237 billion and $4.7 trillion. There is, in other words, an economic case to be made for saving these areas. Which is good, because it also comes with an enormous price tag.

The Louisiana Coastal Protection and Restoration Authority's plan to preserve wetlands and barrier islands calls for some of the most expensive and large-scale ecological restoration projects in the country. They're building barrier islands, stabilizing banks, dredging or piping sediment in to create marshes, constructing levees, heaping barrier reefs of oyster shells, and pouring muddy freshwater into increasingly saline bays. The plan's 2017 draft listed 120 projects affecting more than 800 square miles, including $18 billion in marsh creation and $5 billion in sediment diversions. Much of the money will come from oil-and-gas-industry royalties, compelling state leaders to push for more fossil fuel extraction even as burning that fuel warms the atmosphere, melts the ice caps, and brings the ocean a little closer to their front doors.

It's also a plan that leaves some people out. The dock Eustis and I sped back to in Jean Lafitte and everything south of it are outside the lines of any levee, left to be overtaken by water surging inland with the next hurricane. There's "angst," Perrodin said, "about not having the resources to save everybody and everything . . . How do you tell Jean Lafitte, 'Sorry, can't do it'?"

But they can't. Even what they've already done won't last. Piped-in or poured sediment can rebuild wetlands. Seedlings take root and, for a while, the ground is firm enough to walk on. But the soil immediately begins compacting. Plants sink, then drown. And these projects work on a smaller scale, a pocket-size solution to an ocean-size problem.

"We've done hundreds of thousands of acres," Perrodin said. "But we don't need thousands of acres. We need thousands of square miles."

So the state has proposed to slice the levee walls open. Up to 50,000 cubic feet per second of the muddy Mississippi would rush into blue-green saline water, streaking it beige. The remnants of Appalachian mountains, Iowan farms, and Nebraskan prairie dust would settle atop the twiggy muck of decaying vegetation. Layers of new soil would smooth over the mass of rot. If you were to take a soil core years later, the line between the two could be visible to the naked eye. Eventually, it would make marshes appear in open water.

"What we're trying to do here, in a controlled way, is mimic what the river used to naturally do," Perrodin said. "It's not going to make a visible difference in what's left of my lifetime, but in the long run, the sediment diversion will build more sustainably . . . Some people want us to keep piping and dredging, and not diverting. We have to do it all."

For best effectiveness, those solutions should have been deployed decades ago. Perrodin has a well-trodden metaphor for this work: the best time to plant a tree is 30 years ago, but the second-best time is now.

Success is not assured. Recent research out of Tulane University found diversions rebuild land slower than these wetlands are disappearing. The study's own sites will likely soon be submerged.

"Even with the best restoration strategies, it's not possible to build land at the rates we've been losing it," said study coauthor Elizabeth Chamberlain. "The language 'restore the coast' gets used, and the reality of what we're finding is that it's pretty unlikely that the coast can be restored to what it looked like one hundred years ago, before we lost all this land. Really, our best hope is to build something sustainable or a sustainable delta, which will be different than what we're looking at right now or what people remember when they were kids."

Perrodin scrolled through maps of projections for Louisiana's coastline in 2050. In the worst-case scenario, the one in which they do nothing, the only land that remains is what asphalt highways hold in place.

"The future without action," he said, "is, *everything goes away.*"

After Hurricane Katrina, a forest of cranes clustered to construct miles of levees, floodwalls, gates, and pumps to defend New Orleans. Projects consumed more than $20 billion in federal, state, and local government aid. Some surge barriers are 26 feet high and almost 2 miles long, but even that may not be enough to save the city. Those levees work best with a buffer of wetlands, but it was their construction, not wetlands restoration, that was expedited. The levees may worsen conditions for the communities outside their walls if they block tidal surges that accompany storms and that water stalls out amid these towns. In some places, the coastal restoration plan largely comes down to making sure highways stay clear so people can drive away from their flooding homes.

I drove those highways south, heading out of the city of New Orleans for as far as they go. I passed over or through earthen berms and cement walls and between steel floodgates. A well-groomed four lanes led into Plaquemines Parish, passing citrus orchards, cattle pastures, and yards full of crab traps, as well as pipelines, storage tanks, and oil-and-gas processing and shipping infrastructure. When I reached the sign marking the southernmost point of the state, I was hours south of protective measures other than good pavement.

About 20 miles from that southern terminus, a sign pointed toward the Grand Bayou Road, a Native American village—primarily Atakapa-Ishak/Chawasha—that I'd seen by boat with Eustis. The shell-gravel road started with a steep climb over a levee. The air smelled brackish. The road led to a dock because the place is still, as it has always been, accessed only by water. As we passed through Grand Bayou Indian Village's rows of houses, Eustis told me, "This is one of the places where they look, like Buras, at hurricanes in 2067, and say, 'Maybe we can't keep people here.' [But] like a lot of places in Plaquemines Parish, people want to stay as long as they can."

Pickup trucks and boat trailers were parked among heaps of oyster shells by a dock lined with several motorboats topped with shade awnings and shrimp boats with their gray and green nets carefully draped away. An abandoned boat slumped against the wooden platform. It was left so quickly that curtains still fluttered against shattered windows and fishing gear rusted in a jumble covering its decks.

As colonists moved into Louisiana in the 1700s, they fixed some once semi-migratory Native American tribes into these coastal areas. Most of the members of the Houma Nation, the largest tribe in Louisiana, live between the Atchafalaya and Mississippi Rivers, a homeland that overlaps with some of the fastest land loss in the world.

Some have decided the only solution is to move. Already, the Biloxi-Chitimacha-Choctaw community Isle de Jean Charles has begun the process of moving from an island that was once 24 square miles and is now just half a mile long and a quarter mile wide. High tide regularly reaches front yards and swamps their road, and salt water has wiped out their fruit trees and farms. The federal government is spending millions to relocate these first climate change refugees to a former sugarcane farm. Monique Verdin, a Houma Nation member, documentary filmmaker, and activist, pointed out that the move plants them among two impaired water bodies and oil-and-gas facilities.

"Is that really better?" she asks. "Are we upping our quality of life here? Or should we remain and develop a way to adapt?"

Verdin lives on land her grandparents settled when that scrap of marsh at the southeastern tip of Louisiana was all Native Americans were allowed to own. Her house is ringed by cypresses, bottomland hardwood forest, and two major oil refineries. Fifteen minutes down the road, the woods give way to fishing docks. After Hurricane Katrina submerged the area, three-quarters of its population moved away. Some residents have returned, but not as many as there were.

"Especially after Katrina, people are like, 'Oh, people shouldn't live here,'" Verdin told me. "Actually, our people have lived here for a really long time. You just have to know how to and respect the water in a way we have not respected it for a really long time, especially the Mississippi River."

On my drive south, I stopped for the night in Buras, taking a room in a hotel where I was the only occupant. My room looked over a swimming pool hosting a flotilla of leaves. The receptionist summarized the town: "At one time, there was a Dairy Queen and a bowling alley, but guess what? It wasn't long before they both closed . . . Ain't nothing down here. Nothing for kids to do. But I've been here my whole life and I guess I'm all right."

It was true, there was little to do. A few roadside stands served food—I searched for dinner options and landed only a take-out shrimp po'boy. One gas station advertised itself, with its bowl of bananas beside the cash register, as a "grocery store." In the morning, I bought coffee, a banana, and a prepackaged muffin there and continued driving. So much land has eroded that the road was lined with parked vehicles and people fishing out of their trunks. Oystercatchers strolled through roadside puddles. Where the pavement stopped, water pooled over the highway.

The Breton and Chandeleur Islands curve against the ocean like a drawn bow. The two form part of the nation's second-oldest wildlife refuge, designated by President Theodore Roosevelt to protect the pelicans that live and nest there. In addition to critical habitat, these barrier islands and others like them offer the first line of defense against storms for the mainland. But, like coastal wetlands, they're also disappearing. When Louisiana started its restoration effort, it began by pouring islands back into place, like the one I visited with Eustis. Those islands drew back onto the map the line for where the state used to reach, marking the space restoration efforts aimed to reclaim from the sea.

But barrier islands are not made to last. The hydrology that builds them also breaks them down. They migrate on prevailing currents west toward Texas from where they emerge near Florida. Storms wear them down, shuffle their sediment through the system, and then settle it elsewhere. Islands have always vanished. But they used to reappear. Dams and levees on the Mississippi River that deprived wetlands of sediment similarly starved these islands. Now islands disappear, sometimes in a single storm, and never re-emerge.

Researchers found Breton and Chandeleur are losing land faster than any other islands in the Gulf of Mexico. Adding sand to the islands' flanks would build marshes, dunes, and sandy shorelines where birds and sea turtles can lay their eggs, the researchers concluded, but only for a while. They could not be saved. In the next two decades, Breton Island is expected to become a recurrent sandbar, useless to the nesting seabirds it was supposed to help save.

I had hoped to see it, but at a full two hours by boat from the coast, even refuge staff rarely visit. So I drove into Mississippi instead, where the closest islands of the 160-mile-long Gulf Islands National Seashore are visible from the beach. It was my best chance to see hints at what's happening far offshore, and another ecologist with a boat had offered to show me. His recurrent contracts with federal agencies prompted him to ask me not to use his name. It's a tough time for a government hire who wants to talk about climate change.

He steered the boat past an island where a curl of smoke wafted off a wildfire and a state-funded project had dumped tons of sand in hopes of shielding casinos onshore from future storms. Those casinos were just pastel blips on a murky horizon when we reached West Ship Island, 10 miles off the coast. Beachgoers unloaded from a ferry and traipsed by an old military fort. The fort was built at the island's edge during the Civil War, but the island has shifted around it, and the fort now sits near its center. Waves had reached its redbrick walls by 2010. The National Park Service, which manages the national seashore, doesn't intervene in natural processes, even when it means watching islands they're overseeing deteriorate. But this wasn't an altogether natural process. Dredging a nearby shipping channel was accelerating erosion, park service staff decided, so they stepped in. Sand was added to the beach to push back the water, and now it seeps in some of the ground-level windows. Stepping onto the dunes to peer in at a sun-filled interior courtyard, I came immediately under assault of sand fleas stinging their way up my ankles. I scrambled back onto the boardwalks that traverse the island.

Their path passes ponds where red-winged blackbirds called from cattails and rattlebox bushes offered seedpods for shaking. On the island's Gulf-facing side, umbrellas and chairs lined the beach just past the changing rooms and snack bar. The buildings' lower walls have been so routinely flooded that they're now built with plastic siding instead of drywall. Those boardwalks have been torn up by storms and reconstructed so many times that this iteration has been nailed together instead of screwed. In the next storm, water and wind can lift the planks out of place and leave the struts in place, reducing the costs to rebuild. This is yet another place people are trying to learn how best to adapt, how to rebuild, and what to let go.

At one time, trees shaded these islands. They housed indigenous villages, then small military outposts. As these islands erode, layers of those historic inhabitants surface: belt buckles and buttons from early colonists, and arrow points and even human remains from those who lived and died here centuries ago.

If National Oceanic and Atmospheric Administration forecasts of three feet of sea level rise over the next half century bear out, that will swallow half of the islands in the Gulf Islands National Seashore. By some forecasts, sea levels could rise as much as six feet. At that point, almost nothing would remain. There's every reason to expect that we will outlive this geography.

"There's a lot of pieces in motion—rising sea levels, storms, human impact—like cogs in a breaking machine," my guide told me. He takes his teenage sons to these islands as much as he can, certain that they won't still exist by the time his boys are his age.

"This is not a unique story. Anywhere in the world we have barrier islands, this is occurring," he said. "It's all going to change. We just don't know how."

He'd said he'd show me climate change in action, and he did, pointing out edges broken by erosion, ghost forests, and places water had already claimed. As we visited other islands, these without docks, I jumped off the boat into warm, thigh-deep shallows. My sunscreen washed off and my calves burned as we walked one island's edges after another. These sandy beaches provide habitat for endangered sea turtle nests, and a trail of clawed footprints on either side of the line of a dragged tail suggested one was also home to an alligator. Osprey and eagle nests added knotted tops to spindly, dead trees.

With a peak elevation of about four feet, in an area where an afternoon thunderstorm's worth of wind can override the tide and carry water inland, these islands are living on borrowed time. In one such washover, standing salt water had broiled in the sun so long that it was almost too hot to walk through. The water marked a weak point where a storm could rip the island in two. I wanted a map not to see where we are going, but to show where we have been. I wanted a map as a record of everything we used to have.

At certain corners of barrier islands, where the current curls around one edge and merges with those washing off the opposite face, the waves seem to stand still. They're just a subtle gesture moving over the earth and catching the light. Standing shin-deep in that water, all that moves is the sand sinking away underfoot.

To the Doctor of Bujumbura's Quarantine Hotel

FROM *Off Assignment*

I SEE YOU UP close. You stand in front of me twice a day, and if we social-distanced, you couldn't do your job, and I would never get out of here.

In the mornings, the omelet men knock, waking me. I slip my mask over my head and slide my feet halfway into my sneakers. Sleep still stuck in my eyes, I adjust my pajamas and hurry down the dark hallway. I like to reach the buffet table first, before the other 19 "guests" on my floor, before anyone can breathe on the plates. I collect eggs, white toast, and a teacup's worth of coffee. I carry them back to my room, where I eat, and wait for you.

You're eating, too, of course. You sleep in a room identical to mine, a few doors down the hall. You never start your shift until we've had the chance to finish our breakfast, unhurriedly, like we might at home. I like to think this is premeditated kindness, but I also know you're not in a hurry, either. *We* are your job, and none of us in this old hotel—built, after the Belgians left, with all the optimism of independence, now worn of glory—is going anywhere.

Eventually you knock, and brandish a little white gun. You are mouth-masked, only eyes, so close they are legible. *"Mwaramutse,"* I say. Good morning, in your Kirundi. Those eyes say that you like the sound of your consonants lilting oddly in my mouth. I hear you make the same word but I can't see your lips. Do you get a new mask each morning, or does yours also smell like a full week's worth of human breath? Are those lake-blue scrubs like my paja-

mas—same as yesterday, same tomorrow? Or did you come prepared, with spares?

I step forward slightly, toeing the seam between the dirty beige
carpet of my room and the dirty red carpet of the hallway, the
great outdoors. I bow my head. You raise your gun to my forehead
and pull the trigger. Its laser reads my body temperature but not
my fear. The gun speaks Celsius, in a female voice. *"Trente-quatre
trois."* I am 34.3, around 93 degrees Fahrenheit, accused of being
so cold I'm nearly dead.

Not yet, I want to say, but I'm humbled. She might one day
be just as wrong, but in the other direction, igniting emergency.
There hasn't yet been a fever in the quarantine, and when I ask
what would happen if there was, no one answers me.

I keep quiet and fold forward. We shoot me again. I feel like I'm
waiting for a judge's score on my performance. If I fall short, will
there be mercy? I wonder where I'd be taken, if they would ask me
who they should call.

Thirty-six point five. You write it down.

How often do you think about the fact that we're stuck here
because, scientifically speaking, it's possible that I could kill you?

I'm a "traveler coming from or through the United States," one
day too late. While I was in an airplane, maybe somewhere over
Algeria, the government here in Burundi decided I might be a
bomb, virus-wired, time-delayed. They want me detonated carefully.

They are wise—wiser, I think, than the men who run my dis-
ease-ridden native USA, where almost no one knows this place. If
they do, they know newspaper Burundi—sickly, poverty-stricken,
violent. That's how it works, that kind of knowing. Newsmen pilfer
"objectivity" from science, chain stereotypes together like nucleo-
tides, and code what and how and who is seen.

The genome map of news is not sophisticated enough to see
you in close-up, as I do here, and no one would believe me if I
told them this place is paradise—this country, this quarantine. I'm
locked in, yes, but five floors up, with a scalene balcony higher
than even the oldest mango trees. When I lean on the railing, my
gaze rolls across the treetops, loops the minarets of downtown Bu-
jumbura, skips across Lake Tanganyika, and lands in the foothills
of the mountains, over there in Congo.

On the lake, rain chases pirogues across an invisible water bor-

der, and lightning flees upward and back down again. When I'm
early to rise, I inhale the quiet before traffic, and when I wait for
lunch, I wait in the company of the muezzin, who cannot be dis-
suaded, even now, of the greatness of God. On Sundays, the air
exhales church choirs and deep staccato drumbeats, and on the
course next door, sportsmen take it out on golf balls with hollow
pops.

What I cannot see or hear is the world I used to live in—gardens and barbecues, hippos who graze along the lakeshore when
the sun sets, civilians and soldiers who sweat side by side on long
Saturday jogs, and the red-tarped fruit stand on the east side of the
road that goes south, where I can always find Sara, who always has
the best mangoes.

This miniature world of the hotel, the one where I am held because my body threatens others, is only us: you, me, and the men
who give us the same omelet every morning, who know by now
that I like my coffee black but who do not know my name. Downstairs, next to the yellow postbox that has seen fresh paint more
recently than it has held a letter, sits Claude, the receptionist. He
speaks to me like I am a vacationer, not a patient-in-waiting—as
if I have arrived with holiday outfits, sightseeing checklists, and
pockets of money for the pool bar. Sometimes, in the lobby, I also
find Honoré, the handyman, who takes a chance and speaks to
every new arrival in German, which he's missed in these 20 years
since he came back from engineering school, just before the war.

I like these men, who transport me from this reality by offering
up the one they usually preside over. But with my fellow ensnared
passengers, I feel estranged. They are mostly Burundian, and they
mostly speak French, though I find a Congolese, a couple of Ken-
yans, and occasionally, I see an Asian man stash his empty plate on
the floor before the elevator doors. In the first days, I asked questions, but replies were stunted and dull, so I stopped. Quarantine
is a vacuum; no answer can withstand the pressure of this caesura,
holding us all back from our real lives, out there, where we might
even have enjoyed meeting one another. In here, we have nothing
in common except having had other plans.

The quarantine hotel is full, but talking to others makes me
feel lonely. I realize I will only make it through these two weeks
if I protect my wonder and keep my questions to myself. Why do
those two Burundian teenagers speak such good English? Whose

little girl traverses the lobby, demanding a look at any cell phone she sees? What kind of traveler is that man jogging in the parking lot, who carried a black warm-up suit with neon-colored triangles in his luggage?

I don't ask. I wish people "bon appétit" in the hallway, or offer a hearty hello on the days I circle the parking lot like a lame bird. I say nothing more; I look away. Pretending we aren't there feels like the nicest thing we can do for each other. *It's okay. Don't see me.*

But you, I have to see. Every day, twice a day, for two weeks. You're the only prescription there is for coronavirus. And so far, you're working. As I sit here in late March, Burundi, nearly alone in Africa, still has no cases. I know already it must be lurking, as it is everywhere. This probably won't work forever. But someone should notice that it is working now. Someone should see you.

You knock. It's time for the evening reading. I'm at the end of the hall, the end of your rounds. From my room you'll go back to yours. You'll sleep. You'll wake. You'll knock again. If you didn't, one of us could explode out there, risking everything you and I know and love and assume will last—family and neighbors and Saturday jogging and Sunday church choir and Sara and her mangoes.

Instead, we keep the bomb between us, hoping that, if it goes off, our bodies can contain the blast.

A Change in Perspective

FROM *Travel + Leisure*

I USED TO LIVE in Cornwall. It's a sad sentence. People's faces drop, as if I'd said, "I used to be happy." *What happened?* they ask. *Why did you leave?*

Cornwall is a county on England's narrow southwestern peninsula, once known for seafaring, smuggling, and fishing. The region was mined for slate, tin, and silver from the Bronze Age to the twentieth century, though now Cornwall's main business is tourism. The flora and fauna are different from what's found elsewhere in England. The Cornish language is Celtic, similar to Welsh or Breton. There's a Cornish nationalist movement, and in some ways it feels like another country.

I used to live in a whitewashed seventeenth-century cottage with camellia trees at the gate, and the trees used to flower all winter. I used to stand on the toilet lid while I brushed my teeth, so I could put my head out the window and see past the grand Georgian town houses to the sea. I used to walk my kids to school along the South West Coast Path, a long-distance hiking trail following every indent of the jagged peninsula, and in winter we used to see the sun rise over the water. I used to take photos when I went to the bank, or to buy milk, because the beauty of the Fal Estuary—the bobbing sailboats and the green headland with its ancient castle —never stopped surprising me.

Now I live in a 1920s semidetached house in suburban Coventry, a small city in the West Midlands that was once a center of manufacturing and is as far from the sea as you can be in England. My area is nice enough. Coventry tries hard, but England's beautiful landscapes are far away. It was badly bombed in World War II, the postwar rebuilding was hastily done, and the industries that had sustained the city for decades withered and died in the 1980s. I feel vaguely protective of the place. It's a young, diverse city with a proud tradition of welcoming refugees who bring energy, expertise, and interesting food. People are friendly and the drivers unusually polite. The cycling infrastructure is excellent because there used to be bike factories. But let's just say tourists don't often come here.

We left Cornwall for sensible reasons, mostly related to work and schools. Cornwall is spectacular, but, as the locals say, you can't eat the view. Most jobs are low-paid, seasonal, and casual. At the local high school there were stories of hair set on fire and knife fights on the playground. Still, I mourned when we arrived in the West Midlands. The bluebells at the roadsides here reminded me of the bluebell woods stretching down to the sea there. I would cycle out onto the country lanes and make the best of bramble hedges and birdsong, but there were always industrial parks behind the woods and the noise of traffic in the air. Still, I don't want to live in discontent. I am too young—everyone is too young—for constant nostalgia. I didn't need to love the West Midlands, but we'd be here for 10 years and I needed to learn to enjoy the place for itself rather than picking out what reminded me most of where I wasn't.

I started by changing the scale, which is one of the exercises I often use in writing workshops. Go outside, I tell my students, and find something you don't mind picking up. Anything at all: a leaf if you're somewhere with leaves, a stone (gravel will do), a blade of grass. The more advanced version could include a discarded bus ticket or an empty bottle—whatever the world has brought to your feet. Touch it, look at it, think about how it grew or was created, where it began, and what carried it to you. If you have a magnifying glass, use it. If the object is man-made, consider who made it, where, and why. What was the weather like there, how did the air smell, what did people eat for lunch?

The point is the specificity of your encounter with this object, the coincidence of your stories. It's more obvious to change the scale the other way, to look at the moon or the sunset, but in the middle distance I started to notice the shapes of particular trees on my bike rides and runs, to enjoy murmurations of starlings and the overhead passages of migrating geese. After all, spring comes everywhere.

The next stage was the city itself. Coventry was once a medieval city famous for its many spires, its monastic buildings and ancient streets. On the night of November 14, 1940, German aerial bombardment left nothing but rubble and flames. Firefighters on the roof were unable to save the fourteenth-century cathedral, and most of those who had stayed in the city that night died. In the 1950s, Coventry was planned and rebuilt for a new generation, careful attention given to the needs and comfort of its battered population.

There's little provision for cars in the center, but ready access for pedestrians and cyclists. Covered arcades were intended to allow shoppers to stroll in comfort whatever the weather, wide walkways accommodated strollers, and the streets were oriented around the library, a new public sports center, a new indoor market, and the new cathedral. The ideas and design were generous, but the task of rebuilding Britain was huge and the resources were limited.

It's easy to admire the new cathedral, a stunning answer to the question asked across Europe in those days about what to do with sites of trauma. European towns and villages have always been built around churches, so what do communities do after the church is bombed or burned out or has become the site of an atrocity? If left as a memorial, there's a wound at the town's heart, a constant reminder of what was lost when you're only trying to buy potatoes. If rebuilt entirely, as in the city of Dresden, the trauma is denied, repression planted.

In Coventry, the old cathedral stands roofless, its sandstone stumps rain-sculpted, the traceries of stained glass holding only sky. But at an angle to the ruin, pushed out of the correct east-west alignment by it, stands Basil Spence's new cathedral, a hymn to the new materials of concrete and plate glass. I love it because it's the creation of war, made by craftspeople haunted by their experiences but ready to bring the technologies of military hardware to a new and better purpose. The West Screen, standing between new and old cathedrals, between hope and anguish, swirls with raucous angels who look skeletal, enraged, triumphant.

The rest of the city is harder to befriend, but the more I learned, the more I admired. The trick is the same as my writing exercise:

ask who built it like that. Why? What were their hopes and inspirations? How was the world, the country, the city, the street in those days? Which hands shaped it, which feet have known it, which dreams and fears ghost its windows and doors? To who might this building have seemed beautiful, and why?

For now, most of us have to stay local. If we are to see anything new, it will be the familiar made strange. I won't pretend that a new way of looking is any permanent substitute for new places to see, but maybe we can learn to see better while we wait.

LIGAYA MISHAN

Thousand Fields of Grain

FROM *T: The New York Times Style Magazine*

IN THE VAST departure hall of Shanghai's decade-old Hongqiao Railway Station, an epic writ in 80,000 tons of steel, everything looks new and tired at once, tinged with gray—even the October sunshine that filters down from skylights so high it can't quite reach the floor. This is architecture meant to set the soul asoar, but I am conscious only of how far I am below, in the horde at the gates. Down the stairs, the bullet train waits, sleek-nosed and sealed in on itself, like a missile. A stoic janitor steers a Zamboni-like machine down the platform, buffing it to a gleam. When the train sets off, it feels like nothing: the slight give of a door unlatched. If I don't look out the window, I can imagine myself absolutely still.

The Chinese government started laying intercity high-speed track in 2005, and today, its network is the longest and most heavily relied upon of any nation's. Six hours are enough to devour the over 900 miles from Shanghai to Xi'an, the landlocked capital of Shaanxi Province in China's central northwest, standing on the bones of the imperial city of Chang'an. In the seventh and eighth centuries CE, this was the center of not only China but the globe —the eastern origin of the trade routes we call the Silk Road and the nexus of a cross-cultural traffic in ideas, technology, art, and food that altered the course of history as decisively as the Columbian Exchange eight centuries later. A million people lived within Chang'an's pounded-earth walls, including travelers and traders from Central, Southeast, South, and Northeast Asia and followers of Buddhism, Taoism, Zoroastrianism, Nestorian Christianity, and Manichaeism. All the while, Shanghai was a mere fishing village, the jittery megapolis of the future not yet a ripple on the face of time.

When the train docks, I emerge from the metal cocoon into another hangar, swooping and skylit. Outside, Xi'an is at once grander and more prosaic than its distant ancestor, a grid of choked streets traversed by a population verging on 10 million. It takes an hour to drive 10 miles into the oldest part of the city, a rectangle marked off by a moat and defensive walls 40 feet tall and 45 feet wide, which today are popular as an exercise circuit. (Facebook's CEO Mark Zuckerberg once posted photographs of himself jogging along the cobbled ramparts.) When the taxi driver can't find the right alley, I continue on foot to my hotel, a converted house equipped with chic furniture and questionable plumbing, where a few days later the electricity will fail and the young staff, who have been busy icing cookies for Halloween—a holiday with roots among the Celts of Ireland two millennia ago, as foreign to this country as Christmas—will scrounge up tiny Mickey Mouse–shaped candles for guests to light the way.

At night, I walk alone, down pitch-dark lanes that yield to pedestrian malls and broad boulevards, tracking the icon of myself on my phone's maps app, one of the few unhindered by China's formidable firewalls. It works everywhere, even underground, in the sea of life churning through the circular underpass below the fourteenth-century Bell Tower—a former military alert system turned tourist attraction, lit up in red and green LEDs. Skyscrapers are restricted in this part of town, but there are KFC franchises and fake Apple stores that look like the real thing: minimalist white boxes with products posed like relics on maple altars. (The products at least are genuine, as I discover to my relief when I have to buy an emergency power cord.)

The more we chase the past, the further it recedes.

I have come to Xi'an, like many before me, to eat yangrou paomo in the old town's Muslim Quarter, a warren of aged alleys measuring roughly a square mile. It has been home to generations of the city's Hui, members of one of China's 56 officially recognized ethnic groups and the largest of the country's 10 Muslim minority communities. (As of China's last census, in 2010, there were 10.5 million Hui nationwide.) "Hui" is an inexact label for a people that comprises many sects, scattered across the country, with no language of their own. What they share is an ancestry often traced back to the first Muslim Arabs and Persians to enter China during the Tang dynasty, as merchants and, in the northwest, as mercenary warriors sent by the Abbasid caliphate (750–1258 CE) to help quash the An Lushan Rebellion. In the early years of Islam, Muslim traders mostly bypassed the Silk Road in favor of crossing the Indian Ocean to the ports of southeastern China, where they were designated *fan ke*—"foreign guests"—a foreignness that persisted even for their children by Chinese wives: *tusheng fan ke,* "native-born foreign guests." As the British Sinologist Michael Dillon has chronicled, Islam didn't truly take root in the country until five centuries later, when the Mongol leader Genghis Khan and his successors conquered almost a quarter of the globe and forcibly marched as many as 3 million Muslim soldiers, along with untold numbers of Muslim artisans, scientists, and scholars, from Central Asia to China. Under the rule of his grandson Kublai Khan, their descendants intermarried with the locals and were accepted as Chinese, becoming known as the Hui.

At Lao Liu Jia Paomo, a clattering, no-nonsense canteen, the meal begins with an empty bowl and a pale round of flatbread, steamed and crisped until it's hard on the outside but still spongy within. All customers are enlisted as prep cooks: before we can eat, we must tear the bread into a hundred tiny pieces to fill that bowl. The ideal size for each piece, I'm told, is that of a soybean—otherwise "they judge you," says Hu Ruixi, who with her American-born husband, Brian Bergey, runs the Xi'an-based food-tour company Lost Plate. She sits across from me, wrists flicking in practiced gestures as she reduces the bread to rubble. The same task takes me longer, my fingers fumbling as I try to get the pieces small enough, twisting and pinching, and I imagine the chefs sneering at my scraps.

I end up with a coarse confetti that looks like popcorn dregs, which I return to the kitchen with a paper ticket dropped on top so the servers can remember whom it came from. Soon the bowl is thunked back down on the table, the bread now submerged— *mo* meaning "bread" and *pao* "soak"—in a fennel-laced broth of lamb bones simmered for half a day, with fatty cuts of *yangrou* (lamb) on top. There's a side saucer of pickled garlic cloves, sharply sweet, to suck on as a respite from the lushness. The painstaking demolition makes sense: the smaller the nubs of bread, the better they absorb the soup. The drenched crumbs suggest a proto-noodle, as if knots of raw dough had been dropped directly into the broth to boil and set. It's life-affirming; I can feel a plush new layer forming under my skin, protecting me from winter.

Yangrou paomo belongs wholly to China's north. Lamb is a legacy of nomadic herding on the Eurasian Steppe that reaches from Mongolia to Hungary; Hu admits she isn't fond of the meat, having grown up in the south, in neighboring Sichuan Province. The presence of bread, too, attests to a geographical rift, marked by the Qinling Mountains just outside of Xi'an, which run through the heart of the country from east to west, separating the cool north from the warm and humid south, the wheat fields from the rice paddies. It's a division that endures to this day, in both eating habits and character, between the collaborative rice farmers of the south, who had to rely on irrigation systems that bound them to their neighbors' fates, and the more independence-minded wheat farmers of the north, who tilled their fields alone.

While rice is native to China—and so essential to Chinese culture that the word for cooked rice also signifies food—wheat was once foreign. It thrives on dry summers and winter rain, the opposite of the climate in northern China, and its migration here in the third millennium BCE from the Fertile Crescent, a sweep of land from the Mediterranean Sea to the Persian Gulf, was an early example of ingredients crossing borders, as the archaeobotanist Robert N. Spengler III notes in *Fruit from the Sands: The Silk Road Origins of the Foods We Eat* (2019). For centuries, the Chinese ate wheat only out of necessity, and then only simply steamed, like millet, which did little to endear it to them. Wheat noodles appeared during the Han dynasty (206 BCE–220 CE), but making them was laborious enough that they were reserved for the rich; milling technology, imported from Central Asia, did not become widely available until the Tang dynasty (618–907 CE), when Persian merchants sold sesame seed–studded cakes on the street corners of Chang'an. Today, wheat is unequivocally Chinese: the government devotes more land to its cultivation than any other nation, and the grain is the foundation of entire genres of dishes, from noodles and dumplings to bread steamed, baked, or fried.

"We think of globalization as a uniquely modern phenomenon, yet 2,000 years ago too, it was a fact of life," the British historian

Peter Frankopan writes in *The Silk Roads: A New History of the World* (2015). But arguably, globalization—the passage of goods, beliefs, and peoples from one part of the world to another—began here, in this valley fed by the Wei River, in the lost splendor of Chang'an.

There was no China, only a collection of squabbling states, before the short-lived but powerful Qin dynasty (221–206 BCE) brought terror and unity to the land. The Qin were the first to stake their capital here, on the Wei River, but the country's Han majority—now the world's biggest ethnic group, more than a billion strong, representing nearly one out of every six people on earth—take their name from the Qin's successor, the Han dynasty, which raised a new capital nearby, Chang'an, in 202–200 BCE Not long after, the emperor Wudi sent an envoy to the West: the dawn of China's engagement with civilizations beyond its frontiers. Where the landing of Europeans in the Americas in the fifteenth century was sudden and calamitous, the Eurasian cultural exchange happened slowly, over centuries, between nations meeting as relative equals.

The trade routes—strengthened and expanded under the Tang dynasty in the seventh century—were never known as the Silk Road to the people who walked them. The German geographer Ferdinand Freiherr von Richthofen wielded the term in 1877, in support of nineteenth-century Western colonialism; the name tells us only what the West took from the East. Certainly the Roman Empire spent a fortune in its lust for Chinese silk, a scandalous cloth that some critics believed left women as good as naked and that was all the more desirable for being difficult to procure. But the Chinese had wants, too: horses from Central Asia for their armies. And as the Romans fantasized about a land beyond their horizons, the Chinese exalted the otherness of the countries to their west. In *The Golden Peaches of Samarkand: A Study of T'ang Exotics* (1963), the American Sinologist Edward H. Schafer writes of Chinese aristocrats enthralled by the customs of erstwhile "barbarians"; one moony prince set up a Turkish camp on palace grounds and sat there dressed like a khan, slicing boiled mutton with his sword. Soon, Western influence had become so pervasive that the early-ninth-century poet Yuan Zhen warned about the risk of losing Chinese customs in the quest for crass novelties:

Ever since the Western horsemen began raising smut and dust,
Fur and fleece, rank and rancid, have filled Hsien [Chang'an] . . .
Women make themselves Western matrons by the study of Western
makeup;
Entertainers present Western tunes, in their devotion to Western
music.

Nostalgia for the Silk Road was, until the past decade, a Western
indulgence. But in 2013, President Xi Jinping explicitly invoked
the Silk Road as the inspiration for a multibillion-dollar, transcon-
tinental investment in infrastructure, domestic and abroad, over
land and sea—encompassing roads, railways, pipelines, and ports
—to tighten the connections between East and Central Asia, Europe, and Africa, expanding China's sphere of influence. Key to
this new global dominion is boosting the laggard economies of
western China, which have missed out on the boom of coastal cities like Shanghai. Xi'an's Muslim Quarter, "once dilapidated and
little mentioned in any local brochure," as the Chinese anthropologist Jing Wang has written, is now being promoted as "one of
the living testimonies to the cosmopolitan spirit" of the Silk Road.

On a bright and chilly Sunday morning, the main street of the
quarter is thronged by tourists, mostly Chinese, clutching skewers
like neutered swords. Every other storefront seems to sell them,
meat of all kinds (except pork) impaled and charred, even whole
baby squid, which Hu, my guide, warns against: "Are we anywhere
near the ocean?" Instead, we head for narrower alleys. In one
shop, a young man yanks belts of dough back and forth, snapping
them down on the steel counter with a *biang biang,* a sound so singular that the convoluted Chinese character for it—which doubles
as the name of the resulting noodles, heaped with garlic and chile,
and then glossed with hot oil and vinegar—doesn't even appear
in modern dictionaries. It's a swirl of sub-characters, among them
those for "moon," "heart," "speak," "cave," and "horse," requiring
more than 50 strokes; cruel teachers have been known to assign
the writing of it as a punishment for tardy students.

Down another lane, Jia Wu Youhuxian is mobbed, but by locals. Jia Yu Sheng, the 73-year-old owner, has been making the
house specialty since he was 16: thick pancakes with shining layers
as translucent as vellum, brimming with beef and spring onions.
Now he keeps vigil over his sons, Jia Yun Feng and Jia Yun Bo, as

they pull the dough into kerchief-thin panels that stretch but do not break. Half of each panel is heaped with meat and gilded with sauce, then rolled into a rough ball, while the other half is left long and stretched further still, into a rippling ribbon, and then it, too, is furled and the ball is pressed flat and fried into a great gold coin. The layers multiply, flaking, perfumed with fennel and its faint smack of menthol, another gift of the Silk Road.

At Lao Liu Kaorou, Liu Xin Xian and his wife, Li Sai Xian, now in their 60s, have been selling beef skewers since 1987, out of what is essentially their living room. (They sleep upstairs.) The meat is dusted with salt, cumin, and pulverized chile, but the secret, as with all barbecue, lies in the sauce, about which they will reveal nothing. Outdoor charcoal grills were recently banned as part of a government effort to ease pollution, and Liu feared that going electric would ruin the flavor of the meat; fortunately, the skewers, turned over a long trough of glowing red bars that resemble a xylophone, still come out blackened and smoky, and, as his wife points out, "it's better for the environment." With retirement looming, they can only hope that their son—who borrowed their recipe for his own barbecue spot, which he runs with a friend a few blocks away—will keep the tradition alive.

As we walk, we pass a man in a white skullcap standing on a ladder, daubing paint on a restaurant sign. I begin to notice other signs with little scars: a swath of paint or tape or otherwise improvised appliqué to hide the Arabic script and symbols that vouch for the cooking as halal—coverings mandated by the government as part of a crackdown on Islamic expression. The main targets of this campaign have been the Turkic-speaking Uighurs, who are concentrated on China's northwestern frontier in Xinjiang, a late and reluctant annexation to the Chinese Empire in the eighteenth century. Since the 1950s, the state has encouraged Han migration to the region, diluting the Uighur majority and overriding their culture. Unrest has been met with ever-increasing police controls and surveillance, and in the past few years, more than a million Uighurs have been detained in hundreds of reeducation camps, which officials have characterized as correction facilities and job training centers. While news analysts have framed the conflict as primarily ethnic rather than religious—as well as geopolitical, intensified by the collapse of the Soviet Union and the rise of Turkic Muslim republics bordering Xinjiang—in 2015, President Xi Jinping openly called for the "Sinicization" of Islam throughout the country, extending beyond the Uighurs to the Hui. In Xi'an, the hijab, *gaitou* in Mandarin, was banned at Shaanxi Normal University, and a Hui protest against the sale of alcohol in the Muslim Quarter—along with a nationwide call by the Hui for proper regulation of halal (*qingzhen*) food—was exploited on social media to provoke fears over the rise of Shariah, the legal code of Islam (*jiaofa*), as a threat to secular Chinese culture.

For centuries, the Hui have lived, for the most part, quietly alongside the Han, although the relationship has never been easy. The American anthropologist Dru C. Gladney has observed that the Hui often experience a degree of "physical and linguistic invisibility" alongside their Han neighbors and are sometimes identified dismissively as "Han who do not eat pork." Still, that dietary distinction reveals a deeper schism: pork is considered essential to China's culinary heritage—Mao declared it a "national treasure," and the character for *jia*, meaning "family" or "home," depicts a pig under a roof, honoring the animal that over millennia kept many Chinese alive in times of scarcity, surviving off scraps and requiring little land—and rejection of the meat can be read as rejection of China itself.

Little acknowledgment is given to Muslim contributions to Chinese civilization. After the decline of Chang'an and the Tang dynasty, when Baghdad, the seat of the Islamic empire, became the new cultural center of the world, Muslim scholars and artisans brought China advances in medicine, mathematics, astronomy, and the arts, from metalwork and glassware to the cobalt pigments that would become the signature of Chinese porcelain. Under the Mongols, the Hui were privileged over the Han and revered as masters of finance, responsible for a new prosperity. But this holds no sway in more recent historical memory; as the American anthropologist Maris Boyd Gillette has written, Chinese officials tend to portray the Hui as "feudal" and "backward," with "a racial predisposition to violence," harking back to a Hui uprising in the northwest in the last half of the nineteenth century that was suppressed so savagely, it was reported that out of Shaanxi's 700,000 Hui, no more than 60,000 survived.

Even as China is embracing internationalism, proposing partnerships with more than 60 countries as part of its New Silk Road initiative—which would effectively mean touching the lives of two-thirds of the world's population, a neo-imperialist reach greater than even Genghis Khan's—it still seeks to promote conformity within its borders, both ideologically and, increasingly, in the definition of what it means to be Chinese. Gladney has argued, controversially, that the elevation of the Han as the standard-bearers for Chinese culture is a relatively new construct, with roots in late-nineteenth-century Japanese nationalistic ideology. It's a rigid conception that, he believes, has displaced "more indigenous Chinese notions of identity"—ones that accepted and honored difference, rather than tried to subsume it.

Kublai Khan consolidated power in 1279 as the self-declared Yuan emperor, head of the first non-Han dynasty to rule all of China. It lasted barely a century and is remembered for its brutality. But Yuan feasts, as documented in *Proper and Essential Things for the Emperor's Food and Drink,* a dietary manual codified for the Chinese court in the fourteenth century, offer a more complicated picture of the tension between conquest and assimilation. The Mongol influence was clear, especially in dishes involving lamb, every part used, as described by the Chinese biochemist Hsiang Ju Lin in *Slippery Noodles: A Culinary History of China* (2015): deep-fried tendons, air-dried intestines, raw liver, ears, tongue, and whole head garlanded with kidneys, stomach, and lungs. A number of ingredients, such as red currants and smartweed, were not cultivated but foraged from the wild, following the folk wisdom of the steppes. At the same time, imperial menus also reflected "a collective culinary heritage," the American scholars Paul D. Buell and Eugene N. Anderson note in *A Soup for the Qan* (2010), and included Turkic noodles, Tibetan tsampa (roasted barley flour), and dishes from as far away as Baghdad and Kashmir. This was "a deliberate attempt to represent the Mongolian world order in visible, tangible, edible form"—the empire made manifest on the table, in a show of might.

The breadth of Chinese cuisine today is still testament to those disparate origins. Historically, scholars divided Chinese cooking into four major regional styles, a pantheon expanded to eight in the early twentieth century, but both classifications left out much of the country, betraying a bias toward the eastern coastal provinces and the south. Chinese foodways are manifold, both hyper-regional and micro-regional; a recipe beloved in one part of the country may be unknown in another, or so altered to suit the local palate, it no longer counts as the same dish. Partisans will insist that the best Sichuan food—from a region in the country's southwest famed for its juxtaposition of *huajiao* (Sichuan peppercorns), at once floral and numbing, and brazen chile—belongs to Chongqing, wholly committed to flame, while others champion Chengdu, ever so slightly gentler and sweeter; the cities lie less than 200 miles apart. Within Xi'an, Hui and Han alike eat roujiamo, the Chinese hamburger: meat tucked into flatbread that's been crisped on the grill until it shows tiger skin on one side—shades of orange and black—and a chrysanthemum whorl on the other. The Han make it with long-braised pork, doused with a spoonful of its own broth, and the Hui with beef or lamb, stewed, then salted and dried.

But the triumphal Mongol table, stocked with delicacies from far-flung, hard-won territories, is long gone. For much of the twentieth century, Chinese historians treated the Mongols as an aberration, a so-called alien dynasty that was inevitably doomed to collapse because they stayed mired in their "barbarian" ways and failed to adopt Han customs. Only in recent decades has the Communist Party begun to extol China's status as a multiethnic state, not out of a desire to promote diversity but to underscore the idea that minority groups have always been part of China and thus owe their primary allegiance to the Chinese nation, legitimizing the government's control over potentially restive populations. The cultural heritage of minorities can be tolerated and even celebrated, like the food in Xi'an's Muslim Quarter, so long as the deeper rituals behind it remain hidden. One folktale collected in the 1994 anthology *Mythology and Folklore of the Hui, a Muslim Chinese People* tells of Hui men who journey to Chang'an during the Tang dynasty and are permitted to take Han wives. When the wives' parents ask what the Hui are like, the women confess that they can't understand what their husbands are saying—but that "their food is good." The concluding moral is almost flip: "Eat Hui food; there is no need to listen to Hui words."

I think of this as I walk the knotted streets of the Muslim Quarter, trying to listen. Then, on my last day, I dutifully head northeast of the city to see what every tourist in Xi'an comes to see: the tomb of the first Qin emperor. He died while traveling in the east, reportedly in search of life-prolonging herbs, and his corpse was brought home in a convoy of carts loaded with salted fish, to disguise the stench and keep the news from the public until royal counselors had settled on a malleable successor. His subterranean necropolis, larger than the Great Pyramid of Giza in Egypt, is reportedly contoured with man-made rivers of liquid mercury —it has yet to be excavated—and houses the bodies of the craftsmen who built it, who were sealed in at the last moment so they would never reveal its secrets. Eight thousand terra-cotta statues of soldiers were posted at its gates to guard the emperor in death, only to be shattered by a vengeful warlord and lost to history until 1974, when shards were discovered by local farmers digging a well.

This is the past, forgotten, recovered, and revised for each generation. Restorations here are still under way, although enough statues have been put back together to draw daily throngs, a living legion to face off with the dead. I steel myself for a nationalistic display of raw power, an overwhelming assembly poised to conquer. Instead, I feel a strange lightness, hemmed in by the crowd, gazing down into the great ashen pit. History belongs to the powerful, not those who serve them, but here the emperor is absent. How individual the soldiers are, six feet tall and dressed forever for battle, hair braided and wrapped in a tight bun tilted to the right or flattened beneath a cap or plated crown. I didn't know we'd be so close that I could look them in the eye. Only from a distance are they an army; this near, each has a face entirely his own. Some seem caught midstride, cast down in thought, with a trace of a smile. Others brood and glower, or lie in parts on wheeled steel tables, as if in a makeshift hospital. They are beautiful, these broken sentinels, still half-animated by the flesh-and-blood warriors who were their models, and by the invisible artisans who carved each knuckle, each puckered sleeve. Unmoored from their mission, they wait. Among them stand conscripts from minority peoples who were vanquished and swallowed up by empire. Their eyes and cheekbones are evidence: We, too, were here.

PAUL THEROUX

A Fear-Filled Lockdown

FROM *The New York Times*

IN THIS SEASON of infection, the stock market little more than a twitching corpse, in an atmosphere of alarm and despondency, I am reminded of the enlightenments of the strict curfew Uganda endured in 1966. It was, for all its miseries, an episode of life lessons, as well as monotonous moralizing (because most crises enliven bores and provoke sententiousness). I would not have missed it for anything.

That curfew evoked—like today—the world turned upside down. This peculiarity that we are now experiencing, the nearest thing to a world war, is the key theme in many of Shakespeare's plays and Jacobean dramas, of old ballads, apocalyptic paintings, and morality tales. It is the essence of tragedy and an occasion for license or retribution. As Hamlet says to his father's ghost, "Time is out of joint."

In Uganda, the palace of the king of Buganda, the Kabaka, Mutesa II—also known as King Freddie—had been attacked by government troops on the orders of the prime minister, Milton Obote. From my office window at Makerere University, where I was a lecturer in English in the extra-mural department, I heard the volleys of heavy artillery and saw smoke rising from the royal enclosure on Mengo Hill. The assault, led by General Idi Amin, resulted in many deaths. But the king eluded capture; he escaped the country in disguise and fled to Britain. The period that followed was one of oppression and confusion, marked by the enforced isolation of a dusk-to-dawn curfew. But, given the disorder and uncertainty, most people seldom dared to leave home at all.

The curfew was a period of fear, bad advice, arbitrary searches, intimidation, and the nastiness common in most civil unrest, people taking advantage of chaos to settle scores. Uganda had a sizable Indian population, and Indian people were casually mugged, their shops ransacked, and other minorities victimized or sidelined. It was also an interlude of hoarding, and of drunkenness, lawlessness, and licentiousness, born of boredom and anarchy.

"Kifugo!" I heard again and again of the curfew—a Swahili word, because it was the lingua franca there. Imprisonment! Yes, it was enforced confinement, but I also felt privileged to be a witness: I had never seen anything like it. I experienced the stages of the coup, the suspension of the constitution, the panic buying, and the effects of the emergency. My clearest memory is of the retailing of rumors—outrageous, frightening, seemingly improbable —but who could dispute them? Our saying then was, "Don't believe anything you hear until the government officially denies it."

Speaking for myself, as a traveler, any great crisis—war, famine, natural disaster, or outrage—ought to be an occasion to bear witness, even if it means leaving the safety of home. The fact that it was the manipulative monster Chairman Mao who said, "All genuine knowledge originates in direct experience," does not make the apothegm less true. It is or should be the subtext for all travelers' chronicles.

The curfew—three years into my time in Africa—was my initiation into the misuse of power, of greed, cowardice, and selfishness; as well as, also, their opposites—compassion, bravery, mutual aid, and generosity. Even at the time, 24 years old and fairly callow, I felt I was lucky in some way to be witnessing this convulsion. It was not just that it helped me to understand Africa better; it offered me insights into crowds and power and civil unrest generally, allowing me to observe in extreme conditions the nuances of human nature.

I kept a journal. In times of crisis we should all be diarists and documentarians. We're bound to wail and complain, but it's also useful to record the particularities of our plight. We know the progress of England's Great Plague of 1665 because Samuel Pepys anatomized it in his diary. On April 30 he wrote: "Great fears of the sickness here in the City it being said that two or three houses are already shut up. God preserve us all!" Later, on June 25: "The plague increases mightily." And by July 26: "The Sicknesse is got into our parish this week; and is endeed everywhere."

A month later he notes the contraction of business: "To the Exchange, which I have not been a great while. But Lord how sad a sight it is to see the streets empty of people, and very few upon the Change, jealous of every door that one sees shut up lest it should be the plague—and about us, two shops in three, if not more, generally shut up."

In that outbreak of bubonic plague, spread by rat fleas, a quarter of London's population died.

My diary these days sounds a lot like Pepys's, though without the womanizing, snobbery, or name-dropping. The progress of the COVID-19 pandemic is remarkably similar to that of the plague year, the same upside-down-ness and the dizziness it produces, the muddle of daily life, the collapse of commerce, the darkness at noon, a haunting paranoia in the sudden proximity to death. And so much of what concerned me as important in the earlier pages of my diary now seems mawkish, trivial, or beneath notice. This virus has halted the routine of the day-to-day and impelled us, in a rare reflex from our usual hustling, to seek purification.

Still writing gives order to the day and helps inform history. In my journal of the Ugandan curfew I made lists of the rumors and tried to estimate the rate at which they traveled; I noted the instances of panic and distraction—there were many more car crashes than usual, as drivers' minds were on other things. Ordinary life was suspended, so we had more excuses to do as we pleased.

My parents' habits were formed during the Great Depression, which this present crisis much resembles. They were—ever after —frugal, cautious, and scornful of wasters: my father developed a habit of saving string, paper bags, nails, and screws that he pried out of old boards. The Depression made them distrustful of the stock market, regarding it as a casino. They were believers in education, yet their enduring memory was of highly educated people rendered destitute—"college graduates selling apples on street corners in Boston!" My mother became a recycler and a mender, patching clothes, socking money away. This pandemic will likely make us a nation of habitual hand-washers and doorknob avoiders.

In the Great Depression, Americans like my parents saw the country fail—and though it rose and became vibrant once more, they fully expected to witness another bust in their lifetime. Generally speaking, we have known prosperity in the United States since the end of World War II. But the same cannot be said for other countries, and this, of course, is something many travelers know, because travel often allows us glimpses of upheaval or political strife, epidemics or revolution. Uganda evolved after the curfew into a dictatorship, and then Idi Amin took over and governed sadistically.

But I'd lived in the dictatorship and thuggery of the Malawi of Dr. Hastings Banda ("Ngwazi"—the Conqueror), so Uganda's oppression was not a shock. And these experiences in Africa helped me deconstruct the gaudy dictatorship of Saparmurat Niyazov, who styled himself "Tukmenbashi"—Great Head of the Turks —when, years later, I traveled through Turkmenistan; the Mongolia of Jambyn Batmönkh, the Syria of Hafiz Assad, the muddy dispirited China of Mao's chosen successor, Hua Guo Feng. As for plague, there have been recent outbreaks of bubonic plague in Madagascar, Congo, Mongolia, and China, producing national moods of blame-shifting and paranoia not much different from that of Albert Camus's *The Plague.*

We're told not to travel right now, and it's probably good advice, though there are people who say that this ban on travel limits our freedom. But in fact, travel produces its own peculiar sorts of confinement.

The freedom that most travelers feel is often a delusion, for there is as much confinement in travel as liberation. This is not the case in the United States, where I have felt nothing but fresh air on road trips. It is possible to travel in the United States without making onward plans. But I can't think of any other country where you can get into a car and be certain at the end of the day of finding a place to sleep (though it might be scruffy) or something to eat (and it might be junk food). For my last book, I managed a road trip in Mexico—but with hiccups (bowel-shattering meals, extortionate police, bedbugs). But the improvisational journey is very difficult elsewhere, even in Europe, and is next to impossible in Africa. It is only by careful planning that a traveler experiences a degree of freedom, but he or she will have to stick to the itinerary, nagged by instructions, which is a sort of confinement.

In fact, most travel is a reminder of boundaries and limits. For example, millions of travelers go to Bangkok or Los Cabos, but of them, a great number head for a posh hotel and rarely leave: the hotel is the destination, not the city. The same can be said for many other places, where the guest in the resort or spa—essentially a gated and guarded palace—luxuriates in splendid isolation.

The most enlightening trips I've taken have been the riskiest, the most crisis-ridden, in countries gripped by turmoil, enlarging my vision, offering glimpses of the future elsewhere. We are living in just such a moment of risk, and it is global. This crisis makes me want to light out for the territory ahead of the rest. It would be a great shame if it were not somehow witnessed and documented.

Wanderlust

FROM *The New Yorker*

LAST YEAR, I took more than a hundred flights, traveling to 23 countries on four continents. From my home, in an old town on the English coast, I went east to Switzerland and Greece, and south to Mexico, El Salvador, Venezuela, Bolivia, and Chile. There were trips into the Kenyan bush, across Siberia, and to remote settlements in the Brazilian Amazon. I wasn't home for more than a few weeks at a time—my habit since I started working as a foreign correspondent, almost 40 years ago.

During the quarantine, I've spent five long months at home. My office here is festooned with mementos of reporting trips: a rug from one of Saddam's palaces, a gilded leather box that belonged to Muammar Qaddafi, a piece of a Bosnian tombstone. On a wall are two nudes, painted in oil by one of Che Guevara's guerrillas; on another is a silk heraldic flag used at the coronation of King Faisal I.

In one of my early jobs, a bureau chief at *Time* encouraged me to be a "fire-eater"—to go where other reporters wouldn't. I didn't need any encouragement to get myself in trouble. Among the artifacts in my office are a pile of journals, which I began keeping in my early teens. One of them contains the record of a formative trip that I took in 1978, when I was 21. That summer, I traveled to Alaska to make my fortune from musk-ox wool.

I hadn't planned on it, exactly. I was staying at my aunt Doris and uncle Warren's house in Woodside, a village tucked into live oaks and redwoods, about an hour south of San Francisco. For two months, Doris had been teaching me how to cook. I wasn't hoping to become a chef; she had assured me that if I acquired some basic kitchen skills I might be hired to join a US Geological Survey expedition to the Alaskan wilderness.

Warren, my mother's older brother, was a geologist who had worked for years in remote places: Alaska, the Mojave Desert, Liberia. He was now posted at the USGS office in Menlo Park, but he spent summers mapping the Alaskan backcountry with a team of geologists. Like Warren, most of them were hardy, deeply tanned men of few words. I met a colleague of his at a USGS picnic one weekend: a young woman with prosthetic arms, to replace the ones she'd lost when a bear mauled her. Warren noted laconically that she was lucky to be alive.

Warren had grown up, with my mother, on a ranch in the San Gabriel Mountains, roaming the countryside and hunting in the woods. My mother told me that he had kept bobcats as pets, and at 12 survived a winter alone in a cabin in the High Sierra, tending traplines for food. During the Second World War, he had spent two years on a desert island in the South Pacific, manning a radio outpost for the navy. Family photographs show him stark naked in a lagoon, hunting fish with a spear.

As a child, I dreamed of having a life like Warren's, and my parents did their best to mollify me. My mother, who wrote children's books, plied me and my siblings with stories about the wild world. On my bookshelf, Thor Heyerdahl's *Kon-Tiki* sat not far from *Birds of the Gambia*. My father was an official in the US Foreign Service, and we moved often, from Korea to Colombia to Taiwan. My family arranged wilderness excursions, and patiently accommodated a succession of feral pets: an alligator, an owl, a parrot, two mongooses, a civet cat, a pangolin.

For my eighth-grade year, my parents sent me to Liberia to live with Warren and Doris. The highlight of my time there was a three-week trip around East Africa, hosted by family friends—Foreign Service types who were meant to keep an eye on me. Instead, I went off the grid for nearly two months. I hunted elephants in Uganda, climbed Kilimanjaro, camped alone in the Serengeti, and traveled to the ancient Ethiopian city of Harar. I had never been happier. My family worried, but when I finally reappeared they forgave me, mostly out of relief that I hadn't died.

My teenage years were largely defined by outward momentum. I worked as a *machetero* in Honduras, learning Spanish but also nearly losing a leg to blood poisoning; I spent six months living on a wharf in Las Palmas, Spain. I went to college for a year, then dropped out to take a job with the Oceanics, a New York–based alternative school that operated out of a tall ship at sea. For seven months, I guided scientists and students through the rainforests, deserts, and mountains of South America.

Afterward, I was uncertain about returning to college; most of all, I wanted to journey deeper into the Amazon. But Aunt Doris suggested Alaska, and it seemed as good a destination as any. Uncle Warren had gone there with a buddy after the war, and built a log cabin in a place called Girdwood. I'd grown up hearing my cousins' stories about their Alaskan adventures, and had read and reread *White Fang* and *The Call of the Wild*. And so I went to Woodside to train in Doris's kitchen.

After a month of baking bread and cooking omelets, I was deemed ready. But, when I applied to the USGS to work as a summer cook, a local got the job instead. Resolved to get to Alaska, I made a list of other employment possibilities: "Kodiak Fish Canneries, laborer; Alaska Fish & Game, fish counter; Alaska Forestry Service, firefighter." Leaving nothing to chance, I'd also written to the National Geographic Institute, asking for funding to search the Honduran jungle for the ancient lost city of Ciudad Blanca. I wrote in my journal, "Can't wait for the reply!" It didn't come.

My dilemma was unexpectedly resolved when I met Mick Hoare, the son of a friend of Uncle Warren's. Mick was a few years older than I was—a rangy guy, with black hair and startlingly blue eyes, who had served in the Special Forces and was studying geophysics at Stanford. He was planning to drive to Anchorage for the summer. Did I want to come along, in exchange for chipping in gas money?

On June 21, we left Woodside in Mick's Datsun pickup truck. Two days later, at a campsite in McLeese Lake, British Columbia, I wrote in my journal, "A frontier air—miles of forest—undulating seas of it. Many lakes and meadows that look like good moose haunts. Our journey began on the Solstice, so it seems full of portents. Good ones, I hope. Maybe I'll make my fortune in Alaska."

The Alaskan economy was booming, but the commodity was oil, not fur; the Trans-Alaska Pipeline had been finished the year before. When we reached Anchorage, after a week on the road, it looked like any other small American city: drab modern buildings that clashed with the wild surroundings, and ticky-tacky suburbs spreading to accommodate newcomers. "The town is raw," I wrote. "Go-go girls and furriers. Gold plated prospecting pans and gold nugget jewelry." A statewide fund had been established to use oil revenues to benefit locals—a kind of payoff for the environmental destruction—but it didn't stop them from resenting the oilmen and the culture they had brought. A bumper sticker on cars around town read HAPPINESS IS A TEXAN LEAVING WITH AN OKIE ON HIS BACK.

Even so, wages were exceptionally high in Alaska; construction was thriving, and that was what had attracted Mick, who was looking to earn money to pay for college. He also had a place to stay, a wooden shack that his older brother owned in Girdwood, a township 40 miles south of Anchorage, at the edge of the Kenai Peninsula.

Girdwood was more like it: a few dozen log cabins in a forested valley, with a general store, a gas station, and an old-fashioned bar that turned into a rowdy disco on weekends. Glacier-covered mountains ringed the valley, and, from the road into town, ghost-white beluga whales could be seen frolicking in the water; Dall sheep stood on rocky outcroppings on the other side.

Mick, a skilled carpenter, quickly got a job framing houses on an Anchorage construction site. Unlike Mick, I had no skills to speak of, but I rode into town with him most days to find a job for myself. On July 1, I summed up my progress: "I called and went by some of the caterers—no dice. No dice with the railroads & so on, either."

My heart wasn't in any of these jobs; the point was to earn enough to finance an adventure. I'd sketched an itinerary for one "reasonable plan": traveling by canoe down the Arctic Red River to Tuktoyaktuk, on the Arctic Ocean. "Some navigation might be necessary as the river course is thru swamp," I wrote. "The idea would be then to live with Eskimos in their villages along Arctic Sea and winter with them, in an attempt to learn all can about hunting, living and travelling on ice." After my father wrote to say that he had accepted a job in Sumatra, I concocted another plan, to meet him there. For the first stage of the journey, I decided, I'd build an outrigger canoe and paddle along the Aleutian Islands to

Japan. Finally, I gave it up as impractical. "Ach, just another idea," I wrote. "I am always agitating, planning, never settling."

It was Mick who told me about musk-ox wool. His father had done some geology work on Nunivak Island, in the Bering Sea, where musk oxen roam wild. In warm weather, they shed their winter coats, called qiviut—the finest wool in the world, eight times warmer than lamb's wool and softer than cashmere. Not long after Mick mentioned this, I visited an Alaska Native cooperative in Anchorage, which sold qiviut garments for vertiginous prices. Diana Vreeland, the editor of *Vogue,* had pronounced musk-ox wool "the ultimate in luxury." Because of its scarcity, it was said to be literally worth its weight in gold.

There is little in the appearance of musk oxen that suggests luxury. They have survived largely unchanged from the last Ice Age—huge beasts that resemble bison, with ponderous heads and swooping horns, but have a bone structure more closely related to that of goats. They can grow to 900 pounds, gorging on nearly any edible vegetation that survives on the tundra. In the winter, they use their hooves to kick through the snow to expose plants trapped underneath. Often led by females, the herds defend against predators by forming a defensive circle—a tactic that works well against wolves but poorly against men with rifles. Musk oxen once ranged across the far north, but by the early twentieth century the Alaskan herd had been hunted to extinction. The cooperative obtained its qiviut from an experimental breeding farm in Unalakleet, in western Alaska. But there were many more living wild on Nunivak, the descendants of captive animals brought from Greenland in the early '30s.

I got the rest of my information from a slim book, *Oomingmak*—the word that Nunivak's Cup'ig Eskimo people use for musk ox, which translates literally as "bearded one." It was by Peter Matthiessen, the explorer and author, who had joined a University of Alaska expedition to Nunivak in 1964 aimed at capturing some of its musk oxen and transporting them to the mainland for breeding. On the cover was a photograph showing two oxen, squared off like tanks in a defensive posture, and another showing an expedition member with his feet dangling rakishly from an open-sided helicopter. I was enthralled. Matthiessen had something in common with the explorers and naturalists I admired as a boy, but unlike them he left no damage behind. His sentences had the sound of someone who loved words, though not as much as he loved experience.

The book had grown out of an article, "Ovibos Moschatus," that Matthiessen wrote for *The New Yorker* in 1966. (*Ovibos moschatus,* I learned, is the Latin name for musk ox, meaning "musky sheep-cow.") The opening was tantalizing: "At Nunivak Island, lost in the cold ocean mists of the Bering Sea, wind and rain give way rapidly to each other. The sun rarely penetrates the mists, and soon retreats before the rush of sea fog, as if uncertain of its authority in this melancholy place." A few pages in, Matthiessen described the bounty available on the island: "Compared to the goat, which supplies but three ounces of wool annually, the musk ox is prodigal in its shedding, and about six pounds per animal, each summer, is scattered on the winds of the northern barrens." By the following day, I had begun sketching out a new plan: "Have decided definitely to go to Nunivak, Bering Sea."

I had finally found paying work, laying cinder blocks for an irascible Czech named Ivan, who was building a cabin in Girdwood. He promised me $8 an hour, which was good money; canning fish paid only five. With 10 days of hard work, I could just about pay for my expedition. Making a very rough estimate of the quantity of qiviut produced by the musk oxen of Nunivak, I concluded that I could quickly collect a hundred thousand dollars' worth—a figure that stayed vividly in my mind. Hearing my calculations, Mick decided to invest in the expedition. He didn't expect anything back, he said; he just wanted to be involved. He procured a map of the musk oxen's migratory patterns, showing where they went to breed and where they shed their qiviut.

The greatest expense was a ticket on the bush airline that flew to Mekoryuk, the Cup'ig settlement on Nunivak. Mick paid for my ticket—$215—and gave me two hundred to outfit myself. With this windfall, I could afford a portable stove, a parka and boots, some food, and other odds and ends, including a handheld scale for weighing qiviut, a compass, vitamins, fishing lures, and a flashlight. Mick lent me binoculars, a mess kit, and a tent. "What a trusting, considerate guy," I wrote. "I shall do my best on Nunivak to come out wi/something."

A few days later, Mick drove me into Anchorage to finish gathering equipment. We arrived early and waited in his pickup for the

army-navy surplus stores to open up on Fourth Avenue. Known
as Eskimo Strip, it was a few blocks dotted with rough bars, peep
shows, pawnshops, and liquor stores. As the sun rose, we saw
shapes stir in a vacant lot: people waking up after a drunken sleep.
We watched a tiny woman walk into a bar that was already open.
A moment later, she was shoved back outside and stood there, be-
seechingly, as a big white man in cowboy boots waved her away. It
was a depressing spectacle. "Sleazeville Alaskan style," I wrote.

At midnight on July 22, with the plane scheduled to leave in six
hours, I took stock. "I am finally packing everything to go," I wrote.
"Got my food, a pair of boots, a Pflueger fishing rod 'n' reel with/
lures, line, sinkers, leaders, hooks. Decided to forgo gun, pants
and parka. Treated a coat of M's with a can of Scotchgard. Hopefully should work out ok." I had also included 10 "qiviut bags,"
which Mick had stitched out of an old canvas tent that neighbors
had given us. We were a bit hazy on how to go about marketing
the qiviut once I had it, but Mick promised to look into it while I
was away.

The first airplane took me as far as Bethel, a frontier town on the
southwestern hump of Alaska. At the airport—a building that
could have been mistaken for a Greyhound station—I learned that
my fishing rod had somehow been left behind by handlers in Anchorage. I was told that it would be sent along on the next flight,
three days later. "Oh well," I wrote. "It'll have to be dried reindeer
meat and seal jerky." Looking through my backpack, I discovered
that my flashlight and compass were gone, too.

From the airplane, Nunivak looked wild and forlorn, a rumpled,
brown, treeless mass sheared off from the continent by a forbid-
ding ocean channel. The island's center was invisible—shrouded
in mist, just as Matthiessen had found it. The only other passengers
were residents returning from a wedding on the mainland. When
we landed, they offered me a lift into Mekoryuk, so I climbed into
the back of their pickup truck and rode on a dirt track into town.

Mekoryuk consisted of a few dozen buildings, mostly weather-
beaten clapboard houses and a few Quonset huts, surrounded by
the detritus of the hunting and fishing life—tin boats, snowmobiles, reindeer antlers tacked to the sides of houses. There was
a school, a general store, a post office, and a makeshift jail. The
most imposing structure was a wooden church, as big and red as a

barn. A few hundred feet out of town, I found a spot on the banks
of the river to pitch my tent—Camp One, I called it.

Uncle Warren had warned that I might "have trouble gain-
ing the sympathy of the natives," but, I wrote in my journal, "everyone's pretty friendly." As I set up camp, some boys came by
in a fishing launch and invited me aboard: the salmon were running, they said, just a few minutes upriver. After a short ride, we
pulled in at a wide bend where the current frayed over a line of
rocks. A few dozen men lined the banks, casting and firing guns
at fish as they splashed and humped through the water. One of
the men handed me a .22 rifle and told me to try my luck. Everyone watched appraisingly as I took aim. A minute later, a big pink
salmon—a "humpy," they called it—poked its bulging back and
head from the water, and I pulled the trigger. The fish thrashed
and then turned dead on its side. When I pulled it from the water,
I saw that my lucky shot had hit it cleanly in the head.

At Camp One that night, I fried the salmon and put it atop a
pot of rehydrated ramen—my first wild meal on the island. The
coffee that I made to go with it was less successful. My camp was
only a few hundred yards from the river mouth, and the water was
as salty as the sea.

The photographer Edward S. Curtis visited Nunivak in 1927, as
part of a project to document Native American cultures, and he
found the island's Cup'ig undisturbed by Christian missionaries.
In pictures, his subjects wear furs that would have cost a fortune
on the mainland, and, often, welcoming smiles. Curtis described
them as "a happy-looking lot," and left hoping that the local traditions would endure. "Should any misguided missionary start for
this island I trust the sea will do its duty," he wrote. Within a decade, though, the missionaries did come.

Matthiessen arrived in 1964, and described the island as one of
the last Alaska Native settlements where aboriginal culture resisted
the "iron hand" of missionaries. There were still walrus skulls
mounted on rooftops and sled dogs tied up on the beach. But,
even then, things were changing. "The kayaks are fast being replaced by outboard skiffs, and the dog teams by the snow sled," he
wrote. "Mekoryuk's young men go away now to the mainland, pro-
testing the mission ban on dancing, drink and smoking." When I
arrived, there were no kayaks left, and hardly a dogsled in sight.

One night in Mekoryuk, a young man invited me to his house, which he shared with his elderly mother. On a side table, she had set up a portrait of Jesus, surrounded by candles and potted plants. Her son nudged me to look closely at the plants. They were marijuana. He didn't think she knew what marijuana was, he told me — but he was sure that if he kept the plants there she'd water them.

My host said that his mother's generation had been converted by Christian missionaries in the years before the Second World War. That was when the Cup'ig's traditional rituals, their songs and dances, had been abandoned, and many of their artifacts destroyed, because the missionaries had insisted that they were sinful. It was only now, he said, that younger Cup'ig were trying to revive some of the old customs, before they were lost forever.

I hung around Mekoryuk for a few days, trying to figure out how to proceed. I would walk back and forth from Camp One to visit the store and to check in with the local flight agent, a woman named Marvella Shavings, to see if my fishing rod had arrived. (It never did.) I found a community pump where I could fill my canteen, but the water came out a queasy yellow. When I asked the locals if it was safe to drink, they laughed and said, "Yes, except if you're pregnant." Most people fetched their drinking water from upriver by boat.

I spent a lot of time at the post office, sitting on its wooden steps composing letters to people back home. It was there that I met a man named Jobe Weston, who invited me to his house, which he said was a better place to write postcards. "I never wrote," I noted in my journal. "Instead we talked, drank coffee, and smoked." Jobe, a Cup'ig man in his 30s with intelligent eyes and a thoughtful presence, had worked for six years as an instructor for Head Start, going to Cup'ig villages and training local teachers. His family stayed in Anchorage while he traveled, and things soured between him and his wife: he described coming home and finding that she'd taken cash he'd saved and gone down to the strip, staying drunk for days. He left her in Anchorage, and took his two kids back to Mekoryuk. He was now drawing unemployment, $110 a week, to provide for his kids, his parents, and a younger brother.

Jobe pointed to a dogsled that lay bleaching in the sun outside the house. It had belonged to his father, who he said was the last man on Nunivak to use a sled with a team of dogs. Everyone had been giving them up in favor of snowmobiles, except for those who lashed their old sleds to snowmobiles to haul supplies. On one of his father's last trips, he'd gone out on the ice beyond the seashore, and the ice pack had separated from the land. Realizing that he couldn't make it back with his dogs, he cut them loose, dived into the freezing water, and swam for shore. Much later, when I had children of my own, I realized that Jobe was offering me a gentle warning about the danger of roaming around Nunivak alone. He also lent me his rifle, "a Luger 10-shot automatic .22."

Jobe told me that the town council had agreed to allow hunters from "outside" to shoot some of the island's musk oxen. It had set up a lottery system, and the winners were allowed to shoot one apiece, for a fee. Jobe mostly hunted walruses, but he had guided eight hunting trips for outsiders looking for musk oxen, earning as much as a thousand dollars per expedition.

Marvella Shavings's husband, Edward, was also a guide, and when he heard about my plan he invited me over to talk about musk oxen. The walls of their house were decorated with photos of him with hunters he'd guided, posing with staunch expressions next to enormous beasts crumpled at the shoulder. For the past three years, Edward explained, the hunters had been allowed to come in March and September, and the community permitted 40 musk oxen to be killed each season. I was shocked: the island's entire population of musk oxen was about 400.

I'd intended to start collecting qiviut at Nash Harbor, an un-inhabited site on the northwest coast where the musk oxen traditionally grazed, and where Matthiessen had set his base camp. But Edward said that the oxen, made skittish by the hunting, had abandoned their usual grazing patterns. Nobody was sure where they were these days. I made a new plan: an overnight hike, for reconnaissance, to an inland summit that the locals called Musk Ox Hill. From there, I was told, I'd be able to see for miles in every direction.

Before leaving Anchorage, I'd bought a USGS topographical map of the island, from the Fish and Wildlife Service, and had it laminated against the weather. The map depicted an arrowhead-shaped mass of volcanic rock, 47 miles wide and 66 long, dotted with ancient cinder cones and dormant volcanoes that ranged as high as 1,700 feet. The coastline was notched in places with lagoons, where rivers from the interior flowed into the sea. Elsewhere, the land ended abruptly in cliffs, where the winds could blow a man over the edge.

The map showed the interior as an expanse of undulating tundra, riddled with hundreds of blue spots that indicated water. The larger dots were crater lakes; the smaller ones, speckled across the island, were muskeg, or Arctic bog. Jackie Williams, an old Cup'ig man in Mekoryuk, had warned me about muskeg. The water was frigid, he said, and the surfaces were thick with algae, making them indistinguishable from the surrounding tundra. If I fell in wearing a backpack, I might not get back out.

Undaunted, I packed a few days' provisions and made my way inland. Jackie hadn't misled me. The island was covered in mosquito-infested bogs, and hiking through them felt like wading through drifts of snow. Dry land was not much less treacherous: tussocks of tall grass made for unstable footing, where it was easy to turn an ankle or break a leg. The weather was raw and cool during the day, freezing at night. Still, I was finally in the Alaskan wilderness, and it was exhilarating. "Totally alone on the tundra," I wrote, from a spot that I named Reconnaissance Camp 1. "Jet streams occasionally, but that's all." I followed reindeer tracks upriver, passing lichens and flowers that covered the terrain in outlandish colors. Gulls and kites wheeled overhead. I slept out in the open that night, with my sleeping bag spread on a waterproof pad. Along the river, I had shot two more humpies with Jobe Weston's rifle, and I cooked one for dinner. I had brought the James Clavell novel *Shōgun*, and I read to keep myself company as I gnawed on salmon.

The next morning, I found myself stalled by two blue dots on the map: a small lake and a stretch of muskeg. I skirted the lake, and cut up a tussocky ridge. As I came over the top, I spied large, dark shapes among the hummocks, about a mile away. With my binoculars, I saw that they were musk oxen—a group of them, resting.

As I made my way toward them, one of the musk oxen, a hulking bull, appeared in my path. He was clearly scouting for trouble, and though he couldn't see me or smell me, he'd heard me, and he was taking off fast back toward the others. I moved cautiously, hopping from tussock to tussock, keeping myself downwind of the bull. By the time I was 60 feet from the group, I was close enough to see their sunstruck hair, the qiviut sweeping off their massive shoulders and into the wind. I waited, hoping that they'd move, so that I could check their resting spot. To rouse them, I attempted some birdcalls: one that I hoped would sound like a kookaburra, and one like an owl. The oxen lay there, oblivious. A stork on a nearby slope strutted about scornfully.

At last, the bull got up, turned, and stared straight at me. His horns were sharply pointed, the size of a man's forearms. A bony plate between them made his head look covered in armor. Male musk oxen in rut are known to butt heads for eight hours at a time, with a speed and a force that no other animal can match. The only advice I had heard about being charged by a musk ox was "run." I braced for an attack, but the bull just stood there, munching grass. Three others got up, too, clustering together with horns radiating out as a calf clambered to the middle of the group. They were, I realized, getting into a ring to protect themselves from me.

When I popped my head over the ridge, they all startled, then loped away, as quick and graceful as gazelles. On the flanks of a nearby hill, they returned to their grazing and seemed to forget about me. I crept up to the spot where they had been resting, bag at the ready for qiviut. There was nothing but grass. *"Nada!"* I wrote in my journal. "I wonder if I'll find *any*."

To reach the summit of Musk Ox Hill was a climb of only a few hundred feet. "Windy at top," I wrote. "Bleak, bleak, bleak." A geodetic marker, dated 1951, sat next to a reindeer skull. To the south, I could see the island's highest peak, Roberts Mountain, and to the east, across the Etolin Strait—the 30-mile stretch between Nunivak and the mainland—I could see the outlines of Nelson Island, its shoulders streaming ice. I'd heard harrowing stories about these waters from Jobe, who hunted there. One June, he told me, he and a friend took a boat onto the strait to look for seals. They stayed out for a few hours, lingering to catch smelt roe and shoot geese. By the time they turned back, a fog had rolled in, and they drifted blindly as the current carried them far north of town and the ice closed around them.

For two days they were caught in this limbo of fog and ice. Finally, they decided to leave the boat and set out on foot. At that time of year, the ice was treacherous—thin and unpredictable. To be as lightweight as possible, they left everything behind in the boat. Eventually, picking their way step by step, they made it back to land. Later, when the fog lifted, they hiked back out to retrieve the boat, but the ice was gone, and so was the boat. "No doubt someone in the Kamchatka Peninsula is happy," Jobe had told me, wistfully.

Scanning in all directions from the summit, I could see no great herds of musk oxen. Below me, the small group that I'd seen earlier had gathered on the shore of a lake. They seemed to be playing a game: the cow was running back and forth, the calf hustling to keep up, the bull giving chase but never catching them.

Back in Mekoryuk, a young man named Tom Nortuk introduced himself. He was about my age, a friendly kid with wide cheekbones, straight black hair, and a ruddy complexion. He'd heard I was trying to get to Nash Harbor, and he and some friends happened to be planning a sealing trip there by boat. I was welcome to come, he said, if I helped pay for gas.

With just one day to get ready, I made a to-do list: "Sharpen knives, put second snowseal on my boots, get water, see Jobe Weston, take a spitbath, write postcards." I bought shells for the rifle and provisions for myself—curry powder, soy sauce, Spam, cigarettes—but decided to leave most of my belongings in storage at the post office, taking along only the qiviut bags. We set off early on August 1 and spent all day tracing the island's north coast, as Tom and his friends shot at seals in the water and the seals dodged every bullet—though there were, I noted in my journal, "some almosts."

At Nash Harbor, we unloaded our gear from the boat and into a reindeer herder's hut. It was all that remained of a once thriving Cup'ig settlement. A census of Nunivak in 1880 had found nine settlements on the island, with a population of 702. Twenty years later, a flu-and-measles epidemic had killed most of them, eradicating the community at Nash Harbor. Now there was only Mekoryuk, a town of fewer than 200 people. On a bluff near our cabin, I discovered some rubble from the old settlement, partly obscured beneath a thatch of bulrushes. Using an old caribou antler, I started digging through loose soil. "I found some cutting edges, and two bone wood-splitting chisels, and a walrus forehead," I wrote. "All ancient!" Along the cliffs, seals and birds were competing for fish. When the seals surfaced with their prey, the birds would dive-bomb them and try to pry it away. The seals seemed to be teasing them: I saw one creep up on a swimming gull, then suddenly flip over, slapping its tail and scaring the bird away.

Musk oxen traditionally shed qiviut in the bushes that grow along cliff edges, and even though their behavior had changed since the hunting began, it seemed worth a look. I had not gone far before I found a clump of hair, which looked at first like a dead rabbit. "Just some of the white outer hairs (not sure if it's as valuable as the darker, which I believe is the real qiviut) but it was an exciting moment. Then, later, skirting under a slanting cliff-face, I was climbing up and stopped dead. There was a huge bundle of it!" Once I had collected everything I could see, I put it on the scale that I carried with me. There wasn't enough of it even to pull down the bar. Still, I estimated that I might have as much as a quarter pound—which meant that, if qiviut was worth its weight in gold, I was holding about $800 worth of matted, pungent fur. I allowed myself a celebration: I crossed the tundra to the river that came out at Nash Harbor and plunged in for a bath, my first since leaving Girdwood.

At nine that night, Tom and the boys took me out on the boat for a shooting trip along the cliff face. It was still dusk on Nunivak, and in the pallid light the birds wheeled above us: ducks, puffins, auklets, terns. The boys spun with them and fired their guns. It was more of a massacre than a sport; we killed 25 birds and left several floating in the water. I shot two myself, a guillemot and an arctic tern. Tom's friend John said they were no good for eating, but he offered to trade me an edible bird for them, because his uncle made masks from the feathers, to sell to tourists on the mainland. (Missionaries had banned such spirit masks in the early twentieth century, but they were retrieved by explorers and traders, and became prized by art collectors in New York and Europe. André Breton was said to have been entranced by them.)

At the hut, the boys built a fire to roast birds, stoking the flames with goose feathers. Over dinner, John confided to me that he made his living as a bootlegger. Many of Alaska's local governments had banned drinking. In Mekoryuk, I'd met the town's two policemen, who seemed primarily engaged with keeping the island dry, holding local drunks in their jail. But people still managed to smuggle alcohol to the island by boat, or on the mail plane. John boasted that he made $1,800 a month smuggling booze into Native communities, where whiskey could sell for $40 a bottle. At the end of the month, he never knew where the money had gone.

With their haul of birds, the boys decided to head back home. Tom told me that if I wanted to stay to collect qiviut I might be able to hitch a boat ride back with his uncle, who spent a month every year at a place called the Dahloongamiut Lagoon, on the southern coast, catching and drying fish. His uncle's time there was almost at an end, he said, but if I hurried I might just catch him.

The next morning, I helped the boys load the boat, giving them some of my gear to lighten my pack: the qiviut, the scale, the artifacts I had collected. At the hut, I cooked two ducks I had shot, which would be my protein for the coming days. Tom had left me a plastic squeeze bottle filled with seal oil, advising me to eat it to stay warm. I planned to hike upriver and then strike out over the hills toward Dahloongamiut. "It'll be a long day, but sunset isn't until 10 pm," I wrote in my journal, adding, "Lonely here. Must have a little more to eat, roast my birds, and be on my way."

I didn't make it far. After a few hours, a fog rolled in and I couldn't see more than 20 feet in any direction. For most of the morning, the southwest wind blew on my right cheek; in the afternoon, it was suddenly on my left, and I became frightened that I was walking in the wrong direction. (As with my fishing rod, I'd never recovered the compass after it vanished on the plane ride over.) It would be reckless to risk getting lost, and so I found a tussock, set up my pack to shield me from the wind, and put on all my warm clothes. I began kicking the grass, trying to make a flat spot where I could pitch my tent, and also to get warm. "I kicked and kicked," I wrote. "My feet were numb, no feeling." When I finally got the tent up, I found a can of V8 juice in my bag; that was dinner.

I awoke to blue sky showing through the heavy bank of cloud. As I walked, though, the mist came in again, dimming everything. I wrote in frustration, "To really hike around the isle, at the rate I'm going, would take three weeks."

Late that afternoon, along the western edge of the river, I startled a flock of Canada geese, which flew off and settled on the other side of a low ridge. I had been subsisting on Bisquick and Spam; goose would be better. As I swung my rifle into position and crept forward, my eyes caught something on the ground: the ravaged carcass of a musk ox. There was qiviut everywhere, in unruly clumps. After an hour stuffing my bag, I tried to separate the ox's skull from the spine but found that there was "still too much flesh and maggots on it to be comfortable." I used a rock to break off the horns and kept those instead.

The hunters who came to the island for musk oxen appalled me, but I understood the impulse to borrow what I could from the natural world. When I was 11, living in Washington, DC, I took a taxidermy class at the Smithsonian, led by Dr. Charles Handley, a bat expert who served as the head mammal curator. A kind man, he arranged for me to work as a summer volunteer in the basement of the museum, stuffing pangolins and flying foxes alongside the scientists.

That fall, my father moved the family to Indonesia, and Handley encouraged me to collect specimens for the Smithsonian. I began to fantasize about expeditions into the jungle. The year in the States had been traumatizing, with the assassinations of Martin Luther King Jr. and Robert Kennedy. Their deaths had been deeply felt in my family, and I could not understand the killers' hatred. The United States seemed like a violent and evil place, and I was happy to leave, especially to explore one of the last great tropical wildernesses.

Our stay lasted only six months; a bout of dysentery nearly killed me and my younger sister, and we were evacuated to Singapore. Then my brother fell ill, too, and my father quit his post and moved us back to Washington. When our flight stopped for a layover in California, I ran away. I set off from the Bay Area with the intention of hiking into the Sierra and living off the land, as Uncle Warren had once done. State troopers stopped me at the edge of national park land, sternly informed me that I was the subject of an all-points bulletin, and drove me back to my furious parents.

I was deeply disappointed to be back in the United States. Not only was it an unhappy and divided society but its natural environment was being rapidly subdued. In the US, with its freeways and subdivisions and shopping centers, nature had been made frivolous, turned into roadside scenery. My parents took me to talks about the end of the wild, the end of the indigenous peoples and their ways of life. I felt that if I didn't hurry up I would miss knowing the natural world altogether.

I was fascinated by men like Geronimo, Richard Francis Bur-

ton, and Shackleton. They were dead, but there was always Warren, who was said to be able to catch trout with his fingers, "like
an Indian." Being "like an Indian," to my childhood understanding, meant casting off the demeaning absurdities of American life,
finding ways to encounter nature without fear.

At camp that night, I thought about Tom's uncle, a trusted
elder, living on his own in nature—not unlike Uncle Warren, in
a way. For weeks, he stayed on the beach in complete isolation,
netting salmon from the ocean and drying them in the sun on
wooden racks. I worried that he might resent my intrusion, so I
mulled how to present myself. What could I say to demonstrate
respect?

The next morning, energized by my haul of qiviut, I followed
the river, skirting its bends to save time. An hour into the hike, I
paused to scan the horizon and noticed a shape against the green
tundra in the distance. Through my binoculars, I could see that it
was an animal, on its side, its belly distended, two legs in the air. It
wasn't a musk ox, but it was big.

I took off my backpack, propped up my rifle as a signpost, and
walked closer. The animal was a reindeer doe. She was in labor,
and she looked terrified, legs swaying, eyes bloodshot and gro-
tesquely wide, ears twitching. I retreated to about 50 feet away and
sat for half an hour, trying to soothe her. I told her that everything
was okay, that I wasn't going to hurt her, and that she was beautiful. I sang the first song that came to mind: "Barnacle Bill the
Sailor," a sea chantey that I'd learned from my grandfather as a
boy. ("It's only me, from over the sea!") But there was nothing I
could do to help her, and I worried that my presence would only
make her more upset. Finally, as I wrote in my journal, "I left her
to her natural fate." Walking on toward the southern coast, I felt
that I was abandoning an intimate. It was the closest thing I'd had
to a conversation since leaving Nash Harbor, three days earlier.

After a few more ridges, I reached Dahloongamiut, a treeless
stretch of lichen-covered rock at the edge of the open sea. On the
beach was a sod hut, dug halfway into the earth—Tom's uncle's
shelter. But there were no racks of drying fish outside, no boat
pulled up on the shore. Inside the hut, it was dank and deserted.
I had come too late.

Overwhelmed with loneliness, I pitched my tent on the beach.

Better to be outside than to be sheltered in a place that reminded me of other human beings. Looking south across the water, I knew that there was no one between me and the Aleutian Islands, 400 miles away. Beyond that lay the entire Pacific Ocean.

There was no qiviut at Dahloongamiut—there was nothing there at all. I resolved to make it back to Mekoryuk as fast as I could, a 47-mile hike across the heart of the island. I had no written accounts to guide me. Matthiessen had tracked his musk oxen by helicopter, or in boat landings on the coasts. The Cup'ig did not often venture into the interior, either. The seals and walruses they hunted were on the coast, or out at sea; the salmon could be caught near the mouths of the rivers.

Hiking to Musk Ox Hill, I'd spent hours navigating around bogs. Now they were unavoidable; the terrain was almost all muskeg. By the afternoon, I was plagued by mosquitoes; at one point, I hurled down my pack and began cursing at them, only to realize, in shocked embarrassment, that I was yelling at *insects*. The water in the bogs was nearly freezing. Once, I stumbled in up to my knees, and, with a fright, recalled Jackie Williams's warnings about the risk of drowning. After that, I started carrying my pack over my head. Later, I saw musk oxen far in the distance, and spent an hour approaching them, but when I got to the spot there was no qiviut to be found.

Toward sundown on the second night, I could see the northern coast, the valley lakes to the east giving off eerie mist. By then, I was hungry and cold enough to try Tom Nortuk's seal oil. When I took the cap off the bottle and sniffed, I nearly gagged—it gave off a stench like vomit. But I squirted it on a piece of dried fish, and ate it holding my nose. Before long, my body felt warmer, just as Tom had said it would.

On the third day, exhausted but determined to make it back to Mekoryuk, I hiked 18 miles under a threatening gray sky. I arrived in darkness. "A killer, an absolute killer of a day," I wrote in my journal. "I was within sight of the northern coast all day, crossing swampy tundra and over two hills then tundra and then tundra again to reach the goddamn airstrip." But I'd been lucky, too. The grasslands were covered with wildflowers and will-o'-the-wisps, and I had picked wild celery and small, sweet nagoonberries. And I'd found a few more swatches of qiviut: the most I'd encountered since the cliff tops at Nash Harbor. By then I must have collected two or three pounds.

In quiet moments, something had been nagging at me. Before leaving the mainland, I'd received a telegram from the director of the Oceanics school, my old employer, asking me to get in touch with her. As I slogged through miles of frigid bog water on Nunivak, I found myself seized by the idea of returning to Peru. In my journal, I recorded a vivid fantasy of a seaside table, laden with "ceviche, stuffed avocados, shrimp and beer." Back in Mekoryuk, I went to the post office to call the director. She had an offer: if I could get to Lima, she'd hire me to guide an American teenager into the backcountry. I was free to go into the jungle, but I should keep him, and myself, out of trouble. I told her I would be there in a few days. "Is it my wisest move? I dunno. It's certainly the most appealing," I wrote. "Always dying to see the landmark, the destination, beyond the next tussock, river, or hill."

I booked a seat on the next mail plane, then ran around saying goodbyes and thanking people for their help. I returned Jobe Weston's rifle, along with some extra ammo, and retrieved my qiviut and my Cup'ig artifacts from Tom Nortuk. Back in Girdwood, I left the qiviut and the horns with Mick. If there were to be any financial rewards, they lay in his hands. I was already sketching out an itinerary: south from Lima via Nazca, then across the desert by burro and over the Andes toward the Madre de Dios.

My time in Peru was eventful, if not quite as I'd planned it. We climbed the peak above Machu Picchu, a kind of pilgrimage site for me. (On my previous trip, I had traveled with a titi monkey, who liked to curl up inside my shirt as we walked. She had died on the journey, and I buried her near the peak.) We made it to the Madre de Dios, and camped near an indigenous Amarakaeri community, but couldn't enter: they had closed themselves off to outsiders because of a flu outbreak. Downriver, prospectors had set up pumps and sluices along the banks, the pioneers of a gold boom that would ravage the area in the coming years.

In the jungle, I forgot about the qiviut and my dreams of riches. But, this spring, as I was held in place by quarantine, it occurred to me to wonder what had happened. I tracked down Mick, whom

I'd lost touch with decades before. It turned out that he'd stayed in Alaska, and had a rough-and-tumble life. For a while, we told stories and caught up. When I asked about the qiviut I'd left with him, he said that he'd given it to a friend in Girdwood. Had the friend got rich? Built himself a wilderness compound? No, Mick said: he had knitted himself a hat. "A hat?" I said. "That's all it came to?" "Well," he replied, "it was only one small bag."

Contributors' Notes
Notable Travel Writing of 2020

Contributors' Notes

Jon Lee Anderson began traveling early in his life and has never really stopped. After spending his boyhood in South Korea, Taiwan, Indonesia, El Salvador, Honduras, Colombia, England, Spain, and Liberia, he began working as a journalist in Peru in 1979. Over the years since then, he has reported from dozens of countries and continues to feel drawn to the exploring life. He was born in California but lives in Dorset, England, and has been a staff writer for *The New Yorker* since 1998.

Carrie Battan is a writer living in New York City. She has been a staff writer at *The New Yorker* since 2018 and has contributed to *GQ, Outside,* the *New York Times, Elle, Bloomberg Businessweek,* and more.

Jim Benning is the editor in chief of *AAA Explorer* and the travel editor of *Westways.* Over the years, he has served as a reporter at the *Los Angeles Times,* deputy travel editor at BBC.com, and a contributor to *Outside, National Geographic Adventure,* and the *Washington Post,* among many other publications. He also cofounded and coedited *World Hum,* where he published many stories later featured in *The Best American Travel Writing.* He lives in Southern California, where he's working on a novel about travel, love, and survival along the US-Mexico border.

Meg Bernhard is a writer from California's Inland Empire who spent several years living in Spain and Belgium. She's written for the *Los Angeles Times,* the *Virginia Quarterly Review, The New Yorker,* the *Washington Post, Hazlitt, Guernica,* and *Pipette.* She also edits for the London-based *Point.51* magazine. Prior to writing full-time, she worked on small family vineyards in Spain.

Jackie Bryant is a freelance cannabis, travel, and culture journalist living in San Diego, California. Originally from New York, she writes the cannabis culture newsletter *Cannabitch* (cannabitch.substack.com) and hosts a podcast by the same name. Her cannabis and travel writing has been published in *Forbes, AFAR, Harper's Bazaar, Sierra,* the *San Diego Union-Tribune,* SFGate, *New York, San Diego Magazine, High Times, San Diego CityBeat, Roads & Kingdoms, American Way, Eater,* and many other places. She is working on a book about cannabis culture.

Bill Buford is the author of *Dirt, Heat,* and *Among the Thugs.* He was the founding editor of the British literary magazine *Granta,* the literary and fiction editor of *The New Yorker,* a staff writer there, and a regular contributor. In 2008, he moved to Lyon, France, where the BBC made two one-hour films of his time in the kitchens there called *Fat Man in a White Hat.* He now lives in New York City with his wife, the wine educator and writer Jessica Green, and their twin sons.

Doug Bock Clark is a *GQ* correspondent whose work has also appeared in the *New York Times Magazine, The New Yorker,* and many other national publications. His first book, *The Last Whalers,* was named one of the *New York Times'* 100 Notable Books of 2019 and won the Lowell Thomas Travel Book Award Silver Medal. He has received numerous honors, including the Arthur L. Carter Journalism Institute's Reporting Award and being named a finalist for the Livingston Award in International Reporting, a Mirror Award, and an Excellence-in-Features Award from the Society for Features Journalists (twice).

Meghan Daum is the author of six books, most recently *The Problem with Everything: My Journey Through the New Culture Wars.* Her book of original essays, *The Unspeakable: And Other Subjects of Discussion,* won the 2015 PEN Center USA Award for Creative Nonfiction. She has written for *The New Yorker, The Atlantic,* the *New York Times Magazine,* and *Vogue,* among other publications. She is the creator and host of *The Unspeakable Podcast.*

Bathsheba Demuth is the author of *Floating Coast: An Environmental History of the Bering Strait,* which was named a best book of 2019 by *Nature* and NPR, among other outlets. She is an assistant professor of history and environment and society at Brown University, and lives in Rhode Island when not in the Arctic. She is currently writing a book about the Yukon River.

Amanda Fortini has written for the *New York Times, The New Yorker, T: The New York Times Style Magazine, The Believer,* the *California Sunday Magazine,*

Vanity Fair, New York, Rolling Stone, the *New Republic, Elle, Slate,* and the *Los Angeles Review of Books,* among other publications. She was a recipient of the Rabkin Prize for arts journalism and is currently the Beverly Rogers Fellow at the Black Mountain Institute at the University of Nevada, Las Vegas. She divides her time between Livingston, Montana, and Las Vegas, Nevada.

Noah Galuten is a chef, author, and the cohost of *Don't Panic Pantry.* He was nominated for a James Beard Award for coauthoring the acclaimed cookbook *On Vegetables* with Jeremy Fox and has two more upcoming cookbooks: *The Bludso Family Cookbook* with Kevin Bludso and his own cookbook, *The Don't Panic Pantry Cookbook.* Noah has opened, run, and consulted for restaurants both locally and abroad, including the popular Bludso's Bar & Que, Prime Pizza, and Cofax Coffee in Los Angeles.

Latria Graham is a journalist and fifth-generation South Carolina farmer. She is a graduate of Dartmouth College and later earned her MFA in creative nonfiction from the New School in New York City. In 2019, she was awarded a position in the Great Smoky Mountains Association's Steve Kemp Writers Residency program, and for two years she has been in and out of conservation spaces, intent on unearthing long-forgotten Black history that she finds crucial to the narrative we tell about the American South. She holds contributing editor positions at *Garden & Gun* and *Outdoor Retailer.* Her essays, profiles, and reviews have appeared in *The Guardian,* the *New York Times,* the *Los Angeles Times,* espnW, *Southern Living, Bicycling,* and *Backpacker.* You can find more of her work at latriagraham.com.

Meghan Gunn is a Missourian writer based in New York. Her work centers on gender, power, and rugged terrain.

Leslie Jamison is the *New York Times* best-selling author of *The Recovering; Make It Scream, Make It Burn; The Empathy Exams;* and *The Gin Closet.* She is a contributing writer for the *New York Times Magazine* and teaches at Columbia University.

Sarah Khan is a freelance travel and food journalist who has reported from six continents for the *New York Times,* the *Wall Street Journal, Condé Nast Traveler, Food & Wine, Travel + Leisure,* and others. She's based in New York City, though she's lived in five countries on three continents and holds 2.5 passports.

Glynnis MacNicol is a writer and the author of *No One Tells You This: A Memoir.* Her work has appeared in print and online for the *New York Times,*

The Guardian, The Cut, the *New York Daily News, W, Town & Country,* the *Globe and Mail,* The Daily Beast, *GEN,* and *ELLE,* among others. She lives in New York City.

Kiese Makeba Laymon is a Black southern writer from Jackson, Mississippi. He is the author of three books, including *Heavy: An American Memoir.*

Elizabeth Miller is an independent journalist who has written for *Backpacker, Outside, Undark,* and *Atlas Obscura.* Her work has won awards from the Society of Professional Journalists and the Association of Alternative Newsmedia and been supported by the National Press Foundation and the National Geographic Society. The story selected for this anthology was written during an environmental reportage residency at the Banff Centre for Arts and Creativity.

Ligaya Mishan writes for the *New York Times* and *T: The New York Times Style Magazine* and was a finalist for a National Magazine Award and a James Beard Award in 2020. Her criticism has appeared in the *New York Review of Books* and *The New Yorker,* and her essays have been selected for *The Best American Magazine Writing* and *The Best American Food Writing.* The daughter of a Filipino mother and a British father, she grew up in Honolulu, Hawai'i.

Jina Moore is the editor in chief of *Guernica,* a global magazine of art and politics, and a member of the board that supports *Adi Magazine,* an American literary magazine that is devoted to rehumanizing policy and is written, edited, and published by women of color. Her work has also been published in *The New Yorker, Lapham's Quarterly, The Atlantic, Boston Review,* the *Columbia Journalism Review,* and many other publications. She has been the East Africa bureau chief of the *New York Times,* the inaugural global women's rights reporter for BuzzFeed News, and a roving Africa correspondent for the *Christian Science Monitor.* A 2009 Ochberg Fellow of the Dart Center for Journalism and Trauma at Columbia University, she is a leading voice on bringing a trauma-informed approach to reporting and writing on violence, conflict, and tragedy. She's on Twitter @itsjina and on the web at jinamoore.com.

Sarah Moss is a novelist and travel writer, the author of eight books, including *Ghost Wall* and *Summerwater.* Born in Glasgow, she has lived around the UK and in Iceland. Sarah has now left Coventry and settled in Ireland, where she teaches English literature and creative writing at University College Dublin.

Intan Paramaditha is a writer and an academic. Her novel *The Wandering*, translated from the Indonesian language by Stephen J. Epstein, was nominated for the Stella Prize in Australia and won the Tempo Best Literary Fiction award in Indonesia, the English PEN Translates Award, and a PEN/Heim Translation Fund Grant from PEN America. She is the author of the short story collection *Apple and Knife* and the editor of *Deviant Disciples: Indonesian Women Poets,* part of the Translating Feminisms series. She holds a PhD from New York University and teaches media and film studies at Macquarie University, Sydney.

As a quintessential third culture kid born in New York City and raised in Tunisia, Morocco, Argentina, England, and the United Arab Emirates, **Natalie Stoclet** might not know where she's from, but a life on the move has left her seeking the hidden marks that make a place unique. Having traveled to more than 50 countries and counting, she offers unconventional takes on the idea of travel itself, from exploring roads less traveled to asking larger questions. Natalie's work has been published in *Playboy, Condé Nast Traveler, Suitcase,* and other publications.

Ben Taub joined *The New Yorker* as a staff writer in 2017. He has written for the magazine about jihadism, crime, conflict, climate change, exploration, and human rights, on four continents and at sea. In 2020, he won the Pulitzer Prize for Feature Writing for his work on the lasting effects of American abuses on former detainees and guards in Guantánamo Bay. He has also received a National Magazine Award, two consecutive George Polk Awards, a Livingston Award, a Robert F. Kennedy Award, an Overseas Press Club Award, and other honors.

Paul Theroux has published more than 50 works of fiction and nonfiction, including a dozen travel books, his latest *On the Plain of Snakes: A Mexican Journey.* His novel *Under the Wave at Waimea* (HMH) appeared earlier this year.

Notable Travel Writing of 2020

SELECTED BY JASON WILSON

LISA ABEND
  Meet the Artisans Keeping Tuscany's Bookmaking Culture Alive. *AFAR*,
    November 30.

SIVANI BABU
  When the World Is Withdrawn. *Hidden Compass*, Spring.
FRANK BURES
  Exploring the Polar Bear Capital of the World. *Artful Living*, September 24.

JAED COFFIN
  Port in a Storm. *Down East*, October.
MILAGROS COSTABEL
  My Sense of America. *The Statesider*, July 3.

GEOFF DYER
  Home Alone Together. *The New Yorker*, April 13.
CERIDWEN DOVEY
  The Great Koala Rescue Operation. *Smithsonian*, June.

ROXANE GAY
  The World, Opened Up. *ZORA*, July 2.
CAITLIN GIDDINGS
  I Rode Across the Country Five Times and All I Got Was Whining and Grief.
    Outside, January/February.
ADAM ROY GORDON
  We Returned to Normal. *The Atlantic*, July 4.

HARRISON HILL
  Rapture. *Chicago Quarterly Review*, December.

CARSON VAUGHN
    An Anniversary Canoe Trip Down "Divorce River." *Outside,* January 27.

CRAIG WELCH
    The Road to 2070. *National Geographic,* April.
ALISON WELLFORD
    To the Taxi Driver Who Never Arrived. *Off Assignment,* December 9.

THE BEST AMERICAN SERIES®

FIRST, BEST, AND BEST-SELLING

The Best American Essays

The Best American Food Writing

The Best American Mystery and Suspense

The Best American Science and Nature Writing

The Best American Science Fiction and Fantasy

The Best American Short Stories

The Best American Travel Writing

Available in print and e-book wherever books are sold.

Visit our website: MarinerBooks.com/BestAmerican